W £9.30

THOREAU
and the American
Indians

THOREAU
and the American Indians

Robert F. Sayre

PRINCETON UNIVERSITY PRESS

PRINCETON, NEW JERSEY

Frontispiece:

Joseph Aitteon, who guided Thoreau in Maine in 1853.
This photograph, recently found in the
Fannie Hardy Eckstorm Collection at the Fogler Library,
University of Maine at Orono, was described
by Mrs. Eckstorm as "copied from the only known
likeness extant, a tintype taken . . . most likely in 1862
when he was selected [tribal] governor for the first time
. . . aged 32 years." Later elected governor six more times,
he died July 4, 1870, during a log drive on the
West Branch of the Penobscot River (see Marion Whitney
Smith, Thoreau's West Branch Guides, 1971).

TO

Hyemeyohsts,

FOR THE PEOPLE

Contents

Preface
ix

Acknowledgements
xvii

References
xix

CHAPTER I. Savagism
3

CHAPTER II. "As Long as Grass Grows
and Water Runs"
28

CHAPTER III. The Vision Quest—*Walden*
59

CHAPTER IV. A Book about Indians?
101

CHAPTER V. Beyond Savagism
123

CHAPTER VI. Maine—The Lessons of the Forest
155

CHAPTER VII. On the Sky-Tinted River
194

APPENDIX. On the Name and Number of the
"Indian Books"
217

Notes
221

Index
233

Preface

TODAY, in our time of ecological crisis, people turn to the writings of Henry Thoreau and the speeches and prophecies of great Indian chiefs as if they give a common spiritual support. The words of Thoreau and the warnings of Black Elk, Chief Joseph, or Chief Seattle—showing up on fundraising leaflets, on posters, and in luxurious picture books—seem almost interchangeable. And despite repetition and inappropriate surroundings, the words move us. They seem to come from Nature and an unviolated Past, speaking for the Land and the Animals and those generations which modern man forgets, those Ahead. Thoreau, that most thoroughly naturalized American, is at one with the great chiefs. Together, he and they are our modern admonitors.

This book is a study of some of the reasons why this similarity exists—not simply in a few phrases or slogans but in the center of Thoreau's major works. It traces his own fascination with Indian life, his attempts to learn about it and imitate it, and also some of the differences between Indians as he read and wrote about them and as they were. Thoreau was indeed the most Indian-like of classic American authors, a truth which is easily documented, even if it has also been too frequently ignored.

During his lifetime many of his friends, like Emerson, Hawthorne, and William Ellery Channing, compared him to "the Indian" and exclaimed at his uncanny gifts for conversing with animals or finding arrowheads and former campsites. "These, and every circumstance touching the Indian, were important in his eyes," said Emerson.[1] Thoreau was Concord's leading Indian expert and defender. Shortly after his death, his biographer-to-be, Franklin Sanborn, wrote that Thoreau had intended to write a book about the "history and qualities of the American Indian," a theory that was passed along in his *Life of Henry David Thoreau* and in another early biography by Henry S. Salt.[2] In the

1920s the literary scholar Albert Keiser announced the rediscovery in the Pierpont Morgan Library of eleven manuscript notebooks, totaling 2,800 pages, which Thoreau had
made of information on the subject. Keiser presumed that
these collections of reading notes and quotations were to
have been the basis of Thoreau's book. Later he included a
chapter, "Thoreau—Friend of the Native," in his book, *The
Indian in American Literature.*[3]

Since then, a number of other scholars have speculated
about what Thoreau's unwritten masterpiece might have
contained and what were his Indian interests.[4] In his observations of Nature, Thoreau recognized Indians as people
who had spent their lives in Nature and developed a knowledge of it that was superior to white men's. Red men were
teachers. They were also custodians of the American past,
and Thoreau, in common with others of his time, was eager
to uncover their little-known history. Seeking also a fusion
of classical and native traditions, he endeavored to be a
synthesis of savage and civilized man himself. In the fullest
sense he was a literary Leatherstocking, a poetic pioneer.

But the true character and significance of Thoreau's interest in Indians are more complex than these generalizations suggest. To a great extent, Thoreau was prejudiced, favorably and unfavorably, by the white stereotypes of Indian
life. He did not study Indians, in all their variety and social
relationships; he studied "the Indian," the ideal solitary
figure that was the white Americans' symbol of the wilderness and history. This symbol had been created by Euro-
pean-Americans as a part of "savagism," their universal
myth of the condition of uncivilized people. "Savagism,"
which Noah Webster defined as *the state of rude uncivilized men,* must actually be understood as what the
"civilized" men of Noah Webster's time *thought* was "the
state of" American Indians. Savagism was the anti- and pro-
Indian racism of the nineteenth century. It was ethnocentric
and wrong in so many important particulars that the word
is better used now to name the white men's ideology, mythology, and theory. For, as Roy Harvey Pearce showed

over twenty years ago, savagism was at once a political and historical ideology, a literary and cultural mythology, and a scientific theory.[5] It was so widely held in Thoreau's time that when he began seeking facts about Indian life, it was the conception from which he started and the description often confirmed by what he read. Indians, to the savagist, might be noble or base, but they were always simple hunters who were not Christian and not civilized.

The extent of Thoreau's savagism must be realized. As I try to show in the opening chapter, it pervaded his early reflections on Indians and his idealization of them as solitary, self-reliant hunters, albeit doomed ones who could not hold back Anglo-Saxon farmers. It also provided an organizing theme for his first book, *A Week on the Concord and Merrimack Rivers*, whose seven chapters contained the history, in abbreviated visionary form, of savage-civilized relations in America. When this visionary history is followed, the *Week* reads much more coherently, and a great many of its digressions on religion, war, friendship, and literature fit into place. Moreover, in the *Week* Thoreau tried to make a kind of native American aesthetic out of the phrase, "as long as grass grows and water runs," which appears in treaties. Great literature, he thought, was written while grass grew and water ran and would endure by the same standard. So, as was fitting in a book about rivers and camping, he listened to the sounds and silence of grass and water and made them part of his poetry.

In *Walden* Thoreau not only made his primitivist attack on civilization, but also portrayed his own example of a pure savage life. Yet in *Walden* we must distinguish between his ideal of the noble Indian life and some of the realities which he was simultaneously probing in his travels and reading. The book both suffers and profits from being a white man's imitation, and we must at times compare Thoreau to the people whose image he adopted in order to lead a higher life himself. He enacted the white fantasy of living like an Indian, and the fantasy—or fantasies—are still strong enough to need criticism. At other times, intentionally and unintentionally, he did repeat the experience of the people whose spirits he pursued.

One trouble with the notion that Thoreau planned a book on the "history and qualities of the American Indian" is that it silently takes these savagist myths about "the Indian" as correct. Sanborn and the others who have perpetuated the notion have, I think, accepted the myths themselves. And "the Indian" of savagism, though extremely interesting as a cultural and literary invention, is a simple figure, by definition anticultural, childlike, and naive. To speak of Thoreau, or any learned and subtle writer, as having a literary debt to such a source is ridiculous. Thus I firmly agree with earlier scholars who have shown that Thoreau's real literary and intellectual heritage was the classics, East Indian philosophy, the great prose stylists of the seventeenth century, travel literature, and the English romantic poets.[6] "The Indian" of savagism served Thoreau in other ways. But having written about the savage and used him as a primitive ideal in *A Week* and *Walden*, Thoreau had exhausted him.

This helps explain both Thoreau's enormous "Indian [Commonplace- or Fact-] Books," which were filled mainly in the 1850s, and his second and third trips to Maine in 1853 and 1857. He needed refreshment. If he did for a time wish to write a book about Indians, he realized that he had to know much more about them and know them personally. These are some of my conclusions from study of the "Indian Books," as he called them (not "notebooks"). He began by reading about the tribes of Massachusetts and New England, then gradually extended his study to the people of the South, New York, and the West, meanwhile taking comparative notes on Aztecs, Incas, and peoples of other continents. The books are extremely interesting. The material itself is informative; its now mostly forgotten source-authors sometimes reveal starkly the prejudices and misconceptions from which they wrote; and Thoreau's thoughts and reflections reveal much about him. He was a very painstaking researcher. He was skeptical of exaggerations and imitations; he sought the most authoritative, firsthand information available, often reading it in French, German, and other languages. But his problems in organizing such immense, heterogeneous material were severe. The "Indian Books" resemble, in some ways, Charles Olson's "Bibliography on America" and *Letters to Origin*, except that Olson had a small audience for his insights, anger, and discovery, while Thoreau mostly was his own audience. He collected his facts with the private pleasure with which he collected arrowheads and plant specimens, so that even after he had clearly rejected any plans to write a book based mainly on the information, he continued growing wild gathering it. Gathering the wild whether berries or spearheads or original history was a way of growing and being wild.

The "Indian Books" and the trips to Maine also took him, to some degree, beyond savagism. *The Maine Woods* has been set aside too long as mere nature writing, or has been examined only in trivial debates about whether Thoreau ever reached the top of Katahdin. It is his intense downeast version of the then popular travel books about the West. In those accounts, as written by Washington Irving, Francis Parkman, Margaret Fuller, and others, description of Indians was always a major theme. But Thoreau's accounts of his three Maine trips cover a much longer period of initiation. They record his progress in breaking through many of the prejudices of savagism to a point where he could present his guides Joe Aitteon and Joe Polis as both Indians and complex, interesting individuals. In the 1850s this was an extraordinary achievement. In recognizing his guides' humanity, he also found a part of his own. The book is a masterpiece of his form of accurate, sequential travel narrative.

His trip to Minnesota in 1861, which seems to have been made both for his health and to see some of the West and its native people, provides an opportunity for a final assessment. His rough field notes of the trip show his perceptive comments on the process of American agricultural and commercial expansion. At moments he saw the farmers of the Middle West as burrowing mice—a comparison which would have made striking sense to E. W. Howe or Hamlin Garland and later writers who described the defeat of the American agrarian dream. But where the literary naturalists saw the farmers as diminished by the power of banks and railroads, Thoreau saw them as rodentlike in their numbers and in the power of their own gnawing and burrowing and acquisitiveness. His trip to the Sioux agency, on the Minnesota or Sky-Tinted River, was short and made in the company of officials and sightseers. He had no knowledge of the bitter conflicts at the agency and among the Sioux themselves that would result in a war just a year later. Nevertheless, the fact that he did make the rather strenuous effort, considering his health, to attend a meeting between the Sioux and the government officials shows how concerned he then was with all phases of the life of American Indians. If he could go no further beyond savagism, there were few other "civilized" Americans who had come so far.

This book traces this progress from savagist prejudice to clearer knowledge. My explications of *A Week, Walden,* and *The Maine Woods* show what Thoreau wrote about Indians; the chapters on his "Indian Books" show what he studied and how he refracted his studies in his *Journal.* I have not dealt with *Cape Cod, An Excursion to Canada,* or his other essays on travel and natural history. They do not involve Indians to so great a degree. But more could be written, both about them and the works I have treated. The wider issues here—of savagism; of how nineteenth-century Americans, red and white, synthesized their cultures; the contexts of war, greed, and idealism in which this occurred; and the consequences in our time—also need deeper, new investigation. Pearce's *Savagism and Civilization,* Richard Slotkin's *Regeneration Through Violence,* Michael Rogin's brilliant psychological study of President Jackson, *Fathers and Children,* and Richard Drinnon's fascinating work on John Dunn Hunter have made a fine beginning. I hope that *Thoreau and the American Indians* will add to it.

From Tahattawan and the Musketaquid to Wachusett,

Agiocochook, Ktaadn, Chesuncook, and the musquash, Thoreau knew his shrines and sacred figures by their original names. The seasons, the seeds, the directions, Earth, and water were sacred also. I may at times have overemphasized the differences between Thoreau and the original people and overstated the difficulties he had with his cultural illusions about them. Even so, both he and they must be more wisely known.

Oxford, Iowa
June 30, 1976

Acknowledgements

MANY people have aided me at various points in the research and writing of this book, and I am glad for this opportunity to repeat my thanks.

In 1972, after struggling for over a year with microfilms and Xerox prints of Thoreau's "Indian Books," I learned through Herbert Cahoon about Mary K. Dobbie of Columbia University. As literary executor for the late Professor Arthur Christy, Mrs. Dobbie generously gave me access to the typed transcripts of the "Indian Books" which Professor Christy's students had made in the 1930s. These seven women—Martha Nowlin, Marion A. Wells, Josephine M. Eppig, Alberta Torrence Tate, Geraldyn Ann Delaney, Louisa Pearson, and Cornelia MacEwan Gorel—who transcribed about 450 pages each of Thoreau's difficult handwriting (with varying accuracy, it must be said) have made it possible for me to read the "Indian Books" critically and not just puzzle over them. By checking their readings against the Xeroxes (and, in some cases, the prior sources), I have, I hope, made my quotations accurate. In recognizing the importance of the "Indian Books," Professor Christy showed great foresight.

I also want to thank my own graduate research assistants, Lee Paradise, Carol Krob, Bill Seaton, José Garza, and Bill Palik.

John Aubrey, director of the Ayer Collection at the Newberry Library in Chicago, and Keith Rageth, Wayne Rawley, and Francis J. Paluka of the University of Iowa Library were extremely patient and obliging in locating some of the rare editions Thoreau copied. They and O. M. Brack, Jr., my former colleague, have given me practical lessons in Early American bibliography.

John Gerber, recent head of the English Department, and Alex Kern, recent director of the American Civilization program at the University of Iowa, have encouraged my efforts to do research and teaching in Indian literature.

For financial assistance I want to thank the American Council of Learned Societies, the University of Iowa Graduate College, and the John Simon Guggenheim Memorial Foundation.

Herbert Cahoon of the Pierpont Morgan Library has given me permission to quote from Thoreau's "Indian Books," and has guided me in his quiet, magical way. William Henry Harrison, Director of the Fruitlands Museums at Harvard, Massachusetts, was very kind in allowing me to examine Thoreau's fabulous collection of arrowheads and artifacts.

The photograph of Joe Aitteon was provided by Eric S. Flower, Special Collections Librarian at the Raymond H. Fogler Library, University of Maine at Orono. Aiding in my search for pictures of Aitteon and Polis were John Salter, Roger Ray at the Maine Historical Society, and Susan Wight at the Bangor Historical Society.

For various other kinds of aid and direction, I thank James Axtell, Sally Baldus, Dorothy Corder, Con Merker, Richard Thomas, John Salter, Austin Warren, Alfonso Ortiz, and Don Wanatee.

John Grant, Sherman Paul, Fred Misurella, Wayne Franklin, and Lyn Angstedt have been the most patient of friends and colleagues—ones to read early drafts and help an author to say what he means. It was also Sherman Paul, who, from his own work on Thoreau, loaned me the microfilms of the "Indian Books."

Finally, my thanks go to William Howarth and Thomas Blanding, Robert Brown, Carol Orr and Herbert Bailey of the Walden Pond society at Princeton. When Mrs. Thomas McGrath of the Thoreau Lyceum in Concord introduced me to Bill Howarth and Tom Blanding in the summer of 1972, I knew I had found my Thoreau experts. Professor Howarth's invitation to work at Princeton University in 1973-74, as a Visiting Fellow, then brought me in touch with the Thoreau Edition's accumulating discoveries. His continued support has been invaluable.

References

THROUGHOUT this work, references to Thoreau's *Journal* are made by date rather than by the volume and page numbers in the Torrey and Allen edition (1906), which will soon be replaced by the MLA-CEAA edition in the process of being published by Princeton University Press. The date is given in parentheses after each quotation or in the accompanying text, except for *Journal* material that Torrey and Allen called undated. With it, volume and page numbers are given.

Quotations from Thoreau's "Indian Books" are identified in the text by an arabic number for the book number—in the proper sequence, as explained in the appendix—followed by the page number in that book, e.g. (10/295).

I have tried to keep footnotes minimal, while using them for explanation and comment as well as identification.

R.F.S.

THOREAU
and the American
Indians

CHAPTER I

Savagism

ANY study of Thoreau and American Indians must begin with a description of savagism, the nineteenth-century white men's idea of Indian life. With its intricate and influential relationships to other American ideas of civilization and manifest destiny, Christianity and the purpose of Europeans in the New World, savagism was the complex of theories about Indians held by nearly all Americans of Thoreau's time. His use of it, his testing of it in various ways, and his eventual liberation from it are the story of this book.

In his widely approved *American Dictionary*, Noah Webster defined *savagism* as "the state of rude uncivilized men; the state of men in their native wildness and rudeness." The definition was broad enough from the European-American point of view to cover everyone from children to rustics, or anyone in the "uncivilized" parts of the world. But primarily, it referred to the condition of American Indians, who, in turn, were thought to be like children and rustics in many respects. All were "savage" in some ways, and Webster defined *the* savage as "a human being in his native state of rudeness, one who is untaught, uncivilized or without cultivation of mind or manners." Giving an illustration, he wrote, "The *savages* of America, when uncorrupted by the vices of civilized men, are remarkable for their hospitality to strangers, and for their truth, fidelity and gratitude to their friends, but implacably cruel and revengeful toward their enemies."

Thus Webster and his contemporaries did not think of savagism as an idea. To them it was an actual, verifiable condition, the way "the *savages* of America" lived. I am insisting on calling it an idea for several reasons, however. All states or conditions of life may, from an epistemological

3

point of view, be ideas rather than, or as well as, realities. But savagism, as we will soon see, was not a very accurate description of reality. It was not based on how the natives of America described themselves but on how the white conquerors and missionaries and travellers described them. These descriptions, moreover, had been written and repeated so many times that they developed a history and existence of their own, shaping later men's judgements and perceptions.

In *Savagism and Civilization: A Study of the Indian and the American Mind*, Roy Harvey Pearce has written the intellectual history of the idea of savagism from 1609 to 1851. He shows how the European-American ideas of the Indian combined European preconceptions and American experience and were constantly associated with European-American self-images. It is an informative book. Yet by the nature of its contents, it is, unavoidably, a rather repetitious one. The missionaries, explorers, and Indian agents who supplied the direct observations were almost monotonous in their reports on the deficiencies of savage life and its differences from civilization. The more detached philosophical speculators on the subject, writing from their libraries in eastern cities or in England, Scotland, and France, were equally repetitious. The differences among them were in the emphases which they gave to "savage" vices or virtues, weakness, and strength. They also supplied sometimes ingenious reasons for the Indians' being as they were. But they all agreed that savage life was rude and unrefined, natural, and uncivilized.

The contents of savagism thus can be summarized very briefly. The Indian is a hunter. He has the virtues of the hunter, like fortitude and self-reliance, but also the vices, like cruelty and cunning. After his success in hunting, he is generous and hospitable to strangers, but when he is destitute, he is untrustworthy. He has not learned the farmer's skills of planting and saving for the morrow. Nor does he have a sense of private property and ownership of land. The Indian no more owns the land he hurries over in his hunts than do the animals he chases. He has not improved it.

4

This lack of improvements must stem from laziness and lack of mental curiosity. Such basic arts as the Indian possesses—in weaponry, dress, and ways of building the wigwam—are ingenious and show that he may be capable of improvement, but his failure to adopt the higher arts of civilization is a melancholy proof of his noble adherence to his traditions. He and his people are also much under the spell of their chiefs and sachems and their necromancers (called powwows), who are powerful orators. He holds the Hebrew and pagan laws of an eye for an eye, and of helping friends and harming enemies; he finds it hard to comprehend Christian revelation and the abstractions of civil law. Lost in the darkness of the forest, the Indian goes his accustomed way.

This simple and childlike life is admirable in some ways. It is hardy, and the savage hunter is a brave warrior. But this life has not withstood the inroads of civilization. It has melted like dew before the morning sun, and the simple inhabitants of the forest have fled like deer into the protecting shadows. Or they have acquired the vices of civilization —rum, deceit, and greed—and destroyed themselves. Unfortunately, they have been more attracted to the white man's vices than to his virtues of thrift, industry, and mechanic skill. They usually come in contact with only the lower sort of representatives of civilization—trappers, unscrupulous agents, and other riffraff of the frontier who spread corruption and disease. Europeans have been dishonest and unfair with these children, but there is really little that can be done. The history of mankind is one of progress from hunting to the agricultural estate. The land which will barely support one family of hunters in filth and miserable subsistence will support forty families of farmers in comfort and decency, and thence smiths and tradesmen. The Indian has not learned this. Having it shown him, he has rejected it. In God's providence he is doomed, and in a few more generations he will be extinct.

I have composed this summary and imitation of savagism in order to compress its major ideas into a manageable space and to suggest the tone and favorite metaphors of its believers. The major stereotypes in savagism were that Indians were (1) solitary hunters, rather than farmers; (2) tradition-bound and not susceptible to improvement; (3) childlike innocents who were corrupted by civilization; (4) superstitious pagans who would not accept the highest offerings of civilization like Christianity; and, therefore, (5) doomed to extinction. The dominant attitudes, as Pearce has said, were pity and censure. The white American pitied Indians, Pearce wrote, "because in his yearning for a simpler life, he could identify with them. He censured them, because he was ashamed to be tempted and he refused to deny his higher nature."[1] But pity and censure are also very close to the classical tragic emotions of pity and terror, and "the Indian" was the most popular tragic figure in early nineteenth-century America.[2] He was, according to these stereotypes, solitary and ancient, simple and heroic, and doomed by a fate he could but rarely see. Pity responded to these qualities, acknowledging the Indian's childlike simplicity and heroic virtues; censure was a balancing attitude which condemned the Indian for his childish recalcitrance, his brutality in warfare, and his refusal to be like white men. Pity was a concession to the Indian's loss of his land, his ancient customs, and his former grandeur. Censure was an expression of civilized superiority over this dying race. Provided with such a picture of the Indian and with these attitudes about it, "civilized Americans" could honor him as a noble predecessor and at the same time justify their conquest and usurpation of his land.

Savagism contained, therefore, a great deal of vain interpretation of truth and error combined. The native Americans, who called themselves simply "the people," were not merely hunters. They grew corn, beans, melons, squashes, tobacco, and many other crops. They had, in fact, domesticated a larger number of plants and foods than had the Europeans.[3] In most communities, to be sure, the farming was done by the women, the hunting by the men. But there is also ample evidence that both men and woman were frequently quick to adopt European farm implements (as well as guns and knives) and that, when they did, their productivity exceeded the Europeans'. Even with stone and wooden tools they had repeatedly had sufficient surpluses to supply the hungry first immigrants. They were hunters *and* farmers, as the immigrants learned to be also. Thus the notion that they were tradition-bound does not square with reports that we have now of Iroquois-country farms—destroyed in Sullivan's Expedition during the Revolution—which had log cabins, barns, abundant orchards, and fields with better crops than those of the soldiers who burned them.[4] The reports were in the soldiers' own diaries, which were not published until years later. But even in the 1820s and 1830s, during the controversy over the removal of the Cherokees, white Americans could read of the large numbers of wagons, cattle, hogs, plows, and mills which were owned by these supposed simple hunters.[5]

The same reports on the Cherokee people mentioned schoolhouses and churches, nor were these unusual. Earlier, in all parts of eastern North America, many people had been converted to Christianity. Yet these "praying Indians" were the most likely to be killed by diseases like smallpox and cholera. They, and other "friendlies," were also the most likely to be shot by mobs, like the Paxton Boys of Pennsylvania in 1763, or hanged by courts, because they *did* submit to European laws. They were "children" only in the sense that they accepted the benefits of civilization and trusted the missionaries and treaty commissioners with whom they bargained. They had a sense of honor, even though it was "corrupted"—in the Europeans' interest—by European trade and alcohol. The savagist philosophers did not speak so loudly about the profits from such corruption. Instead, after a ritualistic reproof of the unprincipled white traders who were the agents of it, they went on to pity and censure the victims. For once an Indian had been corrupted by whiskey and white ways, the savagists believed, he could never be the same. The only real and true Indians, still living in their "natural state," were those beyond the range of civilization. This was the benevolent argument, in fact, for removal of the eastern tribes west of the Mississippi!

Thus the truest element of savagism was not in its descriptions of the Indians but in its prophecies of their extinction. So long as white influence and conquest continued, as all white men assumed would happen, extinction was certain. Yet in another sense this was also the cruelest error. With their superior numbers, weapons, and technology, the European Americans were largely responsible for the Indians' fate. Believing this to be fate, an inevitable destiny ordained by God or some divine principle of progress, was a way of just letting it happen without bearing responsibility. The prophecies of extinction made the wish for white conquest and domination into a cosmic inevitability.

Our understanding of savagism and of Thoreau's relation to it will be increased if we look briefly at some of its principle theorists and popularizers. The derivation of the word *savage*, as Thoreau knew (and told readers in *The Maine Woods*), was the Latin *sylva* "woods." Inhabitants of the woods were *selvaggia*, which in Old French and Middle English became *salvage* and *sauvage* respectively. Etymologically, therefore, the word *savage* simply meant "woodsperson," as *civilized* meant "of cities"; but attached to such etymologies were, of course, all the prejudices and fantasies of city people about the woods. After the European discovery of America, and the discovery of people thought to be "Indians" because they lived in "India," beyond the *Indos* or Indus River, speculations on the nature of these new savages began to occupy European minds. The New World (with its people) was, to Montaigne, one that had known "neither letters, nor weights and measures, nor clothes, nor wheats, nor vines. It was still quite naked at the breast, and lived only on what its nursing mother provided."[6] The debate thus began (or intensified) over what the meaning and values of such a natural life might be, and over whether the savage was a pure and noble unspoiled child of nature or an ignorant and rude beast, a Caliban. There is reason to believe, since Montaigne and later Locke and Rousseau were compiling their portraits of the so-called noble savage from the first relations of the earliest missionaries and explorers, that the Noble Savage was not a myth. The original inhabitants of America apparently were very handsome and intelligent, hospitable and kind.[7] Yet in the context of the debate, this scarcely mattered, since such an ideal was bound to bring to life its opposite, the image of an appalling and degenerate ignoble savage. The images of noble savage and ignoble savage were the European predecessors and later the contemporaries of the American images of the good Indian and the bad Indian.

In European literature, however, the figure of the noble savage was primarily a device for criticism, satire, and imaginary escape from civilization. The noble savages of Rousseau, Diderot, and Chateaubriand were expressions, in one form or another, of a sophistication in which the authors and readers were so secure that they could step back from it and view its injustices and extravagances critically. Nature was an idea cultivated for its freshness or sentiment. Benjamin Franklin, while living in Paris, successfully adopted this primitivist manner in his "Remarks Concerning the Savages of North America." In the 1790s Philip Freneau attempted the same in *Tomo-Cheeki, the Creek Indian in Philadelphia.* But most white Americans, not wanting to promote such fictitious Indians as artful or penetrating critics of their own young civilization, were not so sophisticated. They did not believe that their country was as corrupt as Europe. And they could read criticism of their behavior in the printed speeches of real Indians like Logan and Red Jacket. What they needed from Indian cultures was assistance, not criticism. For even to acquire Indian land they needed Indian help. Once they had the land, they needed and adopted Indian methods of farming, hunting, travel and dress. Then they looked again to the Indians for the traditions and history of the land, for human

9

figures who would personify and represent what otherwise was unknown, a raw wilderness. Savagism was the white idea out of which the figures were born.

We can find a good illustration of this myth-making in an early essay by Washington Irving. In "Traits of Indian Character," published in 1813 in the *Analectic Magazine* (which Irving was then editing), and later in *The Sketch-Book*, Irving began by identifying "the character and habits of the North American savage" and "the scenery over which he is accustomed to range, its vast lakes, boundless forests, majestic rivers, and trackless plains." Both the savage and his scenery were "sublime," Irving thought, and he tried to present Indian character in as positive a way as he could. White writers had wronged Indians. Indians were not properly represented by the "miserable hordes which infest the frontiers . . . corrupted and enfeebled by the vices of society." Wars and broken treaties had been the result of white misunderstanding of the Indian character, which was not stoical and unfeeling but proud and acute.

"How different was their state while yet the undisputed lords of the soil!" Irving exclaims. Then nature supplied all their needs, everyone shared equally in bounty and hardship, and they were generous and compassionate—until deprived of this birthright. "They resembled those wild plants, which thrive best in the shades of the forest, but shrink from the hand of cultivation, and perish beneath the influence of the sun." It is the same, Irving says, with all other traits: courage, rigid adherence to moral law, vengeance, superstition, filial piety, and stratagems in war and the hunt. These all have a basis in the conditions of the Indian's close patriarchal life in the dark and dangerous and yet sublime and bountiful forest. The Indians are to be explained by wild nature.

By an unstated reversal of this formula, Irving also symbolized and ennobled wild nature in the character of the Indian.

> He traverses vast forests, exposed to the hazards of lonely sickness, of lurking enemies, and pining famine. Stormy

10

lakes, those great inland seas, are no obstacles to his wanderings: in his light canoe of bark he sports, like a feather, on their waves, and darts, with the swiftness of an arrow, down the rapids of the rivers. His very subsistence is snatched from the midst of toil and peril. He gains his food by the hardships and dangers of the chase; he wraps himself in the spoils of the bear, the panther, and the buffalo, and sleeps among the thunders of the cataract.[8]

In these rapidly sketched landscapes—the forests, lakes, rivers, and cataract—"the Indian" is the solitary human figure. His dangerous but successful travel through them is what unites them, visually and syntactically. He shows that life among them is possible—and glorious. Thus he not only humanizes this wilderness, he makes its very difficulties and unknown challenges heroic. He is guide and example, an ideal of human life in an open land.

What is further interesting about this passage is that, as in many other parts of the essay, Irving wrote about "Indian Character" in the generic singular. Knowing very little about tribal organization or even about the varieties of Indian societies, Irving imagined this one solitary messenger who stood for all. This, too, is very typical of the literature of savagism, and is a convention which was of great influence on Thoreau's writing, thought, and character. To symbolize nature, one Indian was as good as a hundred—or better, since alone he could unify it, as Irving's did. But we can also see that Americans were much more interested in this solitary ideal Indian than in Indians in numbers. The latter were simply a dirty and backward people standing in the way of progress. Their social variety was not interesting because "civilized" society was assumed to be much more useful and virtuous. Moreover, to study Indian societies too carefully might have forced the recognition that these were societies as refined as those of civilization.

American authors and readers in the early nineteenth century further indicated this preference for "the Indian" in the scores of books on the biographies of great chiefs. The Boston antiquarian Samuel Gardner Drake's *Biography*

and History of the Indians of North America, first published in 1832, had been revised and republished ten times
by 1857. Benjamin Thatcher's *Indian Biography,* also first
published in 1832, went through almost as many editions,
sometimes under the title *Indian Traits.* Thomas McKenney,
a superintendent of Indian Trade, and James Hall, a western lawyer and journalist, attempted to produce the most
impressive of all such collections, their three-volume *History
of the Indian Tribes of North America.* Published in luxurious folios between 1836 and 1844, it contained more biographies of famous chiefs, accompanied by over a hundred
color portraits. The other materials of these books and their
imitators were captivity narratives, speeches, anecdotes, and
histories of white-Indian wars. Their specific historical material on the people alone, before white arrival, was necessarily small, as was the material on tribal government and
structure. They simply rephrased the tragic saga implicit
in the idea of savagism. A tribe, "once a powerful nation"
as these writers liked to say, was met and corrupted by
civilization, its land purchased or lost in war, and though
a heroic leader tried to resist, he failed and the tribe was
now almost extinct. In such cases, the generic singular had
further logic because a chief like Pontiac, Corn Planter, or
Tecumseh did speak for and lead his people. He was "the
Indian" in both the representative and honorific senses. But
the focus was also on him because the tragedy was more
dramatic when embodied in one person.

American painters conformed to these same tastes and
assumptions when they devoted so much of their effort to
the portrait, the visual biography of "the Indian." Enumerat-
ing the results of his eight years of work among "forty-eight
different tribes . . . containing in all 400,000 souls," George
Catlin wrote that he had done "310 portraits in oil" and
"200 other paintings in oil, containing views of their villages—their wigwams—their games and religious ceremonies—their dances—their ball plays—their buffalo hunting, and other amusements."[9] Despite the variety of all these
other activities, Catlin painted, by his own publicized

calculation, three portraits to every two pictures of other kinds. He was out to capture "the Indian," and the history of that figure was to be found in a face, even though Catlin often had to resort to many tricks and persuasions to get his subjects to pose.

In the American transformation of the noble savage into "the Indian," the master was, of course, James Fenimore Cooper. Cooper's treatment of Indians was considered by some Americans to have been so favorable and benign that Francis Parkman called him uninformed,[10] but Parkman and other critics did not fully realize how successful Cooper had been at what they wished to do also. He made a convincing romance of the conquest of the wilderness, justifying it and passing on in a white man the most admirable virtues of "the Indian." To do this, Cooper accepted the white experience that there were good and bad Indians. The dying good Indians aid in the destruction of their bad-Indian enemies, then give way themselves to their initiated white brother Leatherstocking, who in turn, gives way to civilization. Cooper's bad Indians are always many —a great tribe of cruel, superstitious savages, like the Huron in *The Last of the Mohicans*. The good Indians, because they are the last, are few, like Uncas and Chingachgook. In the Leatherstocking novels the noble savage figure is thus broken into several parts. The savage's most immediate and severe criticisms of white behavior are placed in the mouths of the bad Indians, like Hard-Heart or Magua, where they seem petulant, menacing and vindictive, however understandable. The savage's more philosophical utterances are then given to the elegiac, doomed good Indians, who are thoughtful and detached, and to the garrulous, ungrammatical white man, Leatherstocking. Leatherstocking, though he has no Indian blood, no "cross," is the inheritor of Indian skills ("red gifts") and values. He embodies all the better "Traits of Indian Character" listed by Irving, and he is white. He symbolizes American nature, and he too is a solitary figure.

The historical accuracy of this idea of Indian individualism, bred by nature and solitude, seems no more reliable than the myth of "the Indian" to which it was related. Native life in America seems to have been far more communal than individualistic. A chief, at least in the north, was not a king or patriarch. With fields and longhouse dwellings held in common, not even the most successful hunters or warriors could be prominently wealthy or independent of others. Excess wealth was given away. The hunters, serving their families and groups of families, customarily hunted in groups, and an individual who shot prematurely or just for himself was punished vigorously. He endangered the general success and safety. The seasonal gathering of berries, clams, fish, wild rice, and so on were also communal, as was the tending of fields and gardens.[11] Today we see this deference of individual to community and tradition in, of all places, the autobiographies which white editors and authors encouraged people to dictate, even though mostly done in this century. "My friend, I am going to tell you the story of my life, as you wish," the Oglala Sioux holy man Black Elk began, speaking to John G. Neihardt in 1931, "and if it were only the story of my life I think I would not tell it; for what is one man that he should make much of his winters, even when they bend him like a heavy snow?"[12] Other contributors to these personal narratives showed a similar modesty, analogous to the reluctance of people to sit for Catlin's portraits. An individual life is unthinkable outside of or apart from the supporting (and supported) community. A person does not even know when he was born or how he was raised except on other people's testimony; one's upbringing must have been "in the same manner as all babes of the Lakota tribe."[13] Then one was raised to be like admired forebearers, generous and valuable to the community. One was not a solitary hunter.

The Cooperesque image of a solitary white man who acquired Indian skills from his adopted red father or brother was also the historical exception, not the rule. It arose from captivity experiences, like Daniel Boone's and Col. James Smith's, and the most perfect illustration of it is Wawatam's adoption of Alexander Henry, which was very meaningful to Thoreau. But the majority of early white woodsmen learned their "red gifts" from their mistresses and wives. To all levels of frontier society, from government agents like Lewis and Clark to anonymous soldiers and traders, these "daughters of the country" were far more popular and useful to the lonely white males.[14] Accepting this fact, however, would have forced Cooper to alter entirely his racial thinking. He could not have made his half-breeds so hateful and diabolical, symbols of the corruption which supposedly infected all mixing of races. Nor could he have painted the wilderness as a somehow sexless, virgin land, fit only for white-red brothers saving imperiled white damsels. Yet Cooper's notion of racial mixing as sinful was surely the opinion of the later, middle-class settlers, who were as anxious to drive out the "half-breeds" and "squaws" as they were the "bucks." These "squatters" were also obstacles to progress.

But the influence of savagism was not impaired by its inaccuracies. It was a persuasive, universal ideology and mythology, the basis of governmental policy, the material of popular novels and plays, and the assumption of respected historians and antiquarians. The historian Richard Drinnon has recently shown its power in his study *White Savage: The Case of John Dunn Hunter*.[15] Captured at age two or three, Hunter had been raised among the Kansas and Osage Indians west of the Mississippi and lived with them nearly twenty years. When he returned to white society in 1816, he did not dictate the usual captivity narrative containing gruesome descriptions of Indian atrocities. He learned English and wrote his own *Memoirs of a Captivity among the Indians of North America*, published in 1823 and 1824. But Hunter's reports of his people's great intelligence, religious conduct, and communal holding of property were vexations to Lewis Cass, who rose in Indian affairs from territorial governor of Michigan to secretary of War. Cass was regarded as an expert on "the Indian," and he had authoritative allies like Henry Rowe Schoolcraft, who had explored with him the headwaters of the Mississippi and served under him in Michigan. Cass and Schoolcraft and their associates denounced Hunter as an "impostor." Cass was equally anxious to discredit the Moravian missionary John Heckewelder's *History of the Indian Nations . . . ,* which praised the Delaware (Leni-Lenape), with whom he had lived many decades. As a missionary, the most Heckewelder could say against his people was that they were not Christian, and were therefore vengeful rather than merciful. Savagist prejudices were so strong that the truth was hard to accept.[16] The number of literate, persuasive men and women like Heckewelder and Hunter who could give independent accounts of Indian life was so few that the mythologizers and reputed experts drowned them in accusations and pseudolearned disputes.

Still another reason for the dominance of savagism, however, was the appeal of the Indian figure to the white imagination which had largely invented it. Certain savagists were, indeed, outright Indian haters. John Adams and other conservatives were opposed, on principle, to Rousseau's "notions of the purity of Morals in savage Nations."[17] They did not have that faith in nature and natural man. Early frontier writers like Hugh Henry Brackenridge spoke venomously of "the animals, vulgarly called Indians," and sneered at the sentimentalists who in any way defended them.[18]

But both the haters and defenders were savagists, and to most Americans the solitary Indian hunter-warrior was an exciting romantic character. He was a national emblem.

Washington Irving is again a good example of the savagist. In 1832, almost twenty years after "Traits of Indian Character" and some seventeen years in Europe, Irving returned to the United States, suspected by many of his readers of having rejected his native land. But, following months of dinners and celebrations in the East, Irving went West, all the way to what is now Oklahoma. In *A Tour on the Prairies*, a memoir of his happy, boyish excursion (though he was forty-nine years old), Irving described Indians on horseback as in some ways like knights-errant and

16

romantic Arabs. At other points, his party was temporarily exposed to the hazards he had previously imagined of sickness, ambush, and famine. He also readily defended the Indians he encountered against the prejudices of suspicious frontiersmen. *A Tour on the Prairies* is thus a kind of *déjà vu*, an enactment of the fantasies of the much-earlier sketch, on a half-dangerous, half-comic holiday. The author was reviving his youth by participating in the life of the young nation to which he had returned. But instead of darting like an arrow down a roaring rapids,

> [I] found myself . . . afloat, on the skin of a buffalo, in the midst of a wild river, surrounded by wilderness, and towed along by a half savage, whooping and yelling like a devil incarnate . . . I discharged the double-barrelled gun, to the right and left, when in the center of the stream. The report echoed along the woody shores, and was answered by shouts from some of the rangers.[19]

This is typical of Irving's delighted version of experience, as opposed to imagination: being towed across the Arkansas River in an awkward tub-shaped skinboat. But the clumsy travesty of a swift canoe did not hinder his enjoyment in playing savage. It enhanced it, for one of Irving's other surprises was the recognition that Indians were wonderful mimics and comedians themselves. There could be affinity between Irving and Indians in humor as well as romance.

That a man does imitate his enemy and that the pursuer projects himself into the object he pursues were two profound insights of Herman Melville. Ahab's projection of his own proud, vengeful nature into the whale, until his own worn, scarred frame resembles the lines and scars on the whale, is a commentary on the great ironies of the savagist process of thought. In *The Confidence Man*, the story of Colonel Murdock—the "Indian-hater *par excellence*," who becomes indistinguishable from the wilderness and his prey—is a more explicit allegory of the white man's twin-ness to his idea of his enemy. In one way it is the most brilliant indictment of savagism ever written. Melville clear-

17

ly realized that one root of the forked tongue of pity and censure was unrestrained sadistic violence in the cause of conquest. But the "Indian-hater" was not the only kind of American to project his own vices, virtues, and ideals onto "the Indian." Beside the desire for conquest was the desire for the direct relationship with nature and the wild which "the Indian" symbolized. From this might come the traditions and character of the viewer, the American himself. Having divided the world between savage and civilized, the white Americans also had to turn and cross over into the savage half in order to reunite themselves. So while missionaries and official philanthropists were trying to convert the Indians, other Americans—authors, artists, soldiers, and many more—were in various ways converted too, "Indianized." There was no other way, apparently, of having the land, free of the enemy, and becoming a part of the land which still held in it the enemy's ghosts. It was a complex fate, on both sides.

For a long time Thoreau has been called a "Friend of the Native" or "Friend of the Indian."[20] But such a piety is meaningless, because men like President Jackson, Secretary Cass, and Henry Rowe Schoolcraft, all disasters to the native, were sometimes praised in the same words. A similar hollow piety is attached to the theory that Thoreau intended to write a book about Indians, "free of prejudice, rhetoric, and melodrama, depending instead upon poetry, or the exact imitation of real life in the right images."[21] Yet on this subject he was not free of "prejudice, rhetoric, and melodrama." No savagist was, and Thoreau certainly began his literary vocation and his early pursuit of Indian relics and lore under the spell of savagism. That his position was closer to Washington Irving than to Melville's character of Colonel Murdock does not make as much difference as we might think.

That position can be seen clearly in two examples of Thoreau's early writing, which I now want to analyze closely. The first is an unfinished Harvard essay dated June 2, 1837,

18

and the other an undated *Journal* entry which his editors assigned to the period 1837–1847.

The Harvard essay has two titles: One, "The mark or standard by which a nation is judged to be barbarous or civilized," could have been the topic given out by his professor (for dozens of students must have written on it); the other, "Barbarities of civilized States," sounds more like Thoreau's title. He took an occasion for rhetorical praise of civilization and turned it upside down. "The justice of a nation's claim to be regarded as civilized," he began, "seems to depend, mainly, upon the degree in which Art has triumphed over Nature. The culture implied by the term Civilization is the influence of Art, not Nature, on man." This distinction is so standard that it could have come straight from the *American Dictionary*. In his second paragraph, however, Thoreau stopped himself from going ahead to praise art and civilization when he asserted that "the end of life is education." And nature, he said, provides a higher education than art, which cuts man off from nature. "Art paves the earth, lest [the civilized man] may soil the soles of his feet, it builds walls, that he may not see the heavens, year in, year out, the sun rises in vain to him, the rain falls and the wind blows, but they do not reach him." Thoreau then turned to savages, past and present, to show the influence of nature.

> Our rude forefathers took liberal and enlarged views of things, rarely narrow or partial. They surrendered up themselves wholly to Nature—to contemplate her as a part of their daily food. Nature is continually exerting a moral influence over man, she accommodates herself to the soul of man. Hence his conceptions are as gigantic as her mountains. We may see an instance of this if we will but turn our eyes to the strongholds of liberty, Scotland, Switzerland, and Wales. . . .
>
> The savage is far sighted . . . he looks far into futurity, wandering as familiarly through the land of spirits as the *civilized* man through his wood lot or pleasure grounds. His life is practical poetry—a perfect epic; the earth is his

hunting ground—he lives suns and winters—the sun is his time-piece, he journeys to its rising or its setting, to the abode of winter or the land whence the summer comes. He never listens to the thunder but he is reminded of the Great Spirit—it is his voice.

Close to nature, the savage thus develops a deeper religious sense, leading to wisdom.

The savage may be, and often is, a sage. Our Indian is more a man than the inhabitant of a city. He lives as a man— he thinks as a man—he dies as a man. The [civilized man], it is true, is more learned; Learning is Art's creature; but it is not essential to the perfect man—it cannot educate.[22]

Connecting American Indians to "our rude forefathers" and "the strongholds of liberty, Scotland, Switzerland, and Wales" was consistent with late eighteenth-century and early nineteenth-century racial and political theory. In America one of the most influential authorities on the subject was the Scottish historian William Robertson, whose *History of America* (1777) portrayed Indians as being like bold, free, and exuberant Highlanders. There was also a belief that the Indians had migrated to America from Wales. The relationship between the savage and the poet was common in both neoclassical and romantic theories of the epic. Thoreau's premise that civilized man was instructed by art and savage man by nature was the essence of Rousseauism. What Thoreau left out, either intentionally or from lack of time to finish the essay, were the references to progress and refinement by which Americans customarily extricated themselves from concluding that savage life was superior to civilized life. He also avoided laying the usual honorific stress on "civilization" by making "education" a higher value which both savage and civilized societies seek. But he was merely taking sides within the Rousseauistic debate, appraising the savage life as it was described in theory and adding a few images from the American stock of Indian phrases, like "hunting ground," "suns and winters," and "the Great Spirit."

When Thoreau reflected more closely on the Indians in America, he fell into the other line of savagist argument—the deficiencies of hunters and their inevitable extinction. The following paragraphs are from the undated *Journal* material.

For the Indian there is no safety but in the plow. If he would not be pushed into the Pacific, he must seize hold of a plow-tail and let go his bow and arrow, his fish-spear and rifle. This is the only Christianity that will save him.

His fate says sternly to him, "Forsake the hunter's life and enter into the agricultural, the second, state of man. Root yourselves a little deeper in the soil, if you would continue to be the occupants of the country." But I confess I have no little sympathy with the Indians and hunter men. They seem to me a distinct and equally respectable people, born to wander and to hunt, and not to be inoculated with the twilight civilization of the white man.

Father Le Jeune, a French missionary, affirmed "that the Indians were superior in intellect to the French peasantry of that time," and advised "that laborers should be sent from France in order to work for the Indians."

The Indian population within the present boundaries of New Hampshire, Massachusetts, Rhode Island, and Connecticut has been estimated not to have exceeded 40,000 "before the epidemic disease which preceded the landing of the Pilgrims," and it was far more dense here than elsewhere; yet they had no more land than they wanted. The present white population is more than 1,500,000 and two thirds of the land is unimproved.

The Indian, perchance, has not made up his mind to some things which the white man has consented to; he has not, in all respects, stooped so low; and hence, though he too loves food and warmth, he draws his tattered blanket about him and follows his fathers, rather than barter his birthright. He dies, and no doubt his Genius judges well for him. But he is not worsted in the fight; he is not destroyed. He only migrates beyond the Pacific to more spacious and happier hunting-grounds.

A race of hunters can never withstand the inroads of a race of husbandmen. The latter burrow in the night into

21

their country and undermine them; and [even] if the hunter is brave enough to resist, his game is timid and has already fled. The rifle alone would never exterminate it, but the plow is a more fatal weapon; it wins the country inch by inch and holds all it gets.

What detained the Cherokees so long was the 2923 plows which that people possessed; and if they had grasped the handles more firmly, they would never have been driven beyond the Mississippi. No sense of justice will ever restrain the farmer from plowing up the land which is only hunted over by his neighbors. No hunting-field was ever well fenced and surveyed and its bounds accurately marked, unless it were an English park. It is a property not held by the hunter so much as by the game which roams it, and was never well secured by warranty deeds. The farmer in his treaties says only, or means only, "So far will I plow this summer," for he has not seed corn enough to plant more; but every summer the seed is grown which plants a new strip of the forest.

The African will survive, for he is docile, and is patiently learning his trade and dancing at his labor; but the Indian does not often dance, unless it be the war dance. (*J.* I, pp. 444–46)

Here the Indian-as-hunter is the dominant idea, and Thoreau makes the usual further points that hunters do not own land, cannot hold it, and do not use it so effectively. The hunter's life is the first "state of man," the farmer's is the second; and civilization is coming up on the eastern horizon like a morning twilight, while "the Indian" is vanishing in the west like a copper-red sunset. The process is like the turning of the earth, and Thoreau supplies other natural metaphors, like the farmer's taking only what he has seed for and each summer growing more. The Cherokees could hardly have "grasped" their plows "more firmly" than they did, however; Thoreau is mistaken in thinking that being still-better farmers would have saved them. He, like so many other Americans, simply could not imagine that any Indians could be both farmers and hunters. They had one occupation, just as they had only one dance, "the war dance." His stereotypes were as stubborn as they were wrong.

They were all the more stubborn, paradoxically, because he had such idealism about these "Indians and hunter men." The Indian is noble because he has not consented to civilization, "not, in all respects, stooped so low" as the farmer and city dweller. Thus it can even be said, with high-sounding illogic, that "He dies. . . . But he is not worsted in the fight; he is not destroyed." This line of speculation about Indian fate thus leads back to the other speculations about savage poetry and wisdom. The two reinforce one another. Indians are noble because they are dying rather than changing; not changing proves they are noble; and therefore they are dying. It was a vicious circular reasoning, and yet was connected to Thoreau's—and other men's—idealism and concepts of honor. "The Indian" supplied a tragic sense of life.

Just preceding these paragraphs, in fact, were some *memento mori* reflections. "The future reader of history will associate this generation with the red man in his thoughts, and give it credit for some sympathy with that race. Our history will have some copper tints and reflections, at least, and be read as through an Indian-summer haze." As he went on, Thoreau extended the contrast. The Indians are "a race who have exhausted the secrets of nature, tanned with age, while this young and still fair Saxon slip, on whom the sun has not long shone, is but commencing its career." It is the Indians who are dying, not his own young generation. But in such a mood it was impossible to look at Indians except tragically, and, in turn, their sorrowful fate carried the burden of tragedy, renewing the world for "this young and still fair Saxon slip."

In April 1838, when Emerson heard that the Army had been ordered to begin the removal of the Cherokees in May, he wrote a strong letter of protest to President Van Buren. "A crime is projected," he said in this public letter, "that confounds our understandings by its magnitude, a crime that really deprives us as well as the Cherokees of a country, for how could we call the conspiracy that should crush these poor Indians our government, or the land that was

cursed by their parting and dying imprecations our country, any more?" In also noting that injustice to the Cherokees had developed "in a great part of the Northern people
a gloomy diffidence in the *moral* character of the government,"[23] he defined the problem that Thoreau would face
ten years later over slavery and the Mexican war, and to
which he would respond by not paying taxes, his act of
"Resistance to Civil Government." "Under a government
which imprisons any unjustly, the true place for a just man
is also a prison," said Thoreau. "It is there that the fugitive
slave, and the Mexican prisoner on parole, and the Indian
come to plead the wrongs of his race, should find them"[24]
("them" being the "freer and less desponding spirits" of
Massachusetts). Emerson's letter of 1838 shows, too, that
he was well informed about the changes in Cherokee life
and the appeals they had made in Congress, just as every
informed American would have been aware of the two
famous Supreme Court cases, *Worchester* v. *Georgia* and
Georgia v. *Cherokee Nation*, and of Justice Marshall's mo-
mentous decisions.

It is interesting that Thoreau never wrote any letter like
Emerson's or made a public protest over Indian policy similar to his famous protests on slavery and in behalf of John
Brown. The sentence I quoted above is the only reference
to Indians in the essay known as "Civil Disobedience." One
explanation for this might be that in 1838 he was only twen-
ty-one and through the 1840s and 1850s Indian policy was
not so controversial. Slavery and the Mexican war replaced
it as the issues of philanthropists and social critics. But there
is another explanation: his acceptance of these illusions
of savagism. The slave, "docile, and . . . patiently learning
his trade and dancing at his labor," needed help. With help,
he would have a future. The Indian, old and solitary, was
beyond help. His future was extinction. The slave was a
pathetic figure, the Indian a tragic one, a warrior-hunter
who would fight or just wrap himself in his blanket and
depart. Both images, however distorted, provoked strong
responses in Thoreau. In his abolitionism and refusal to pay

his tax, his hiding of escaped slaves and championing of John Brown, he indeed did help slaves. But the near absence of anything in his writing *about* the slaves which he helped reveals how little interest he had in them. Their pathos was a call on his manhood, but they were not his manly equals. Towards Indians he was exactly the opposite. He scarcely did a thing *for* them, but he read, thought, and wrote about them throughout his adult life. Their natural grandeur evoked his envy and admiration. They were examples of manhood rather than calls upon it. Moreover, they were not African, but American, native predecessors essential to his own sense of history. The missionaries' attempt to supply them with Christianity was distasteful to him because it would wipe away what he most valued in them. And since the missionaries were so involved in the Indian philanthropies of his time, the best he could do was side with Indians against them! He could not help or improve Indians; all he could do was praise and imitate them.[25]

This image of the Indian as old and manly usually eclipsed, for Thoreau, the antithetical image of the Indian as a simple child. Government policy treated Indians as wards, independent but "domestic" nations which must be dealt with through treaties and yet also supervised and elevated. In such negotiations American presidents were regularly referred to as the Indians' "white father." The philanthropists and missionaries assumed that their responsibility was like a father's also. The pastoral relationship of shepherd to flock was supplemented by the further responsibility of a more "advanced" race to a more "backward" and "primitive" one.[26] Knowing of Le Jeune's statement that Indians were "superior in intellect to French peasantry," Thoreau would not use that language. But his picture of Indians as old and wise merged with his image of their tragic nobility.

The only further step he might have taken towards the Indians' side—admittedly an improbable one—would have been to join them, live with them, fight beside them against the soldiers, farmers, and missionaries. His advocacy for

John Brown indicates that he might have done as much for the slaves—had he been in good health and had Brown's guerrilla war in the South really gotten under way. But given the predictions of the Indians' imminent doom, this would have been almost suicidal, the act of a fool joining forces with a lost king. Besides, Indians in numbers did not originally interest him as much as "the Indian." In this Thoreau was again more like than unlike his contemporaries. "The Indian" could be sought and joined in more peaceful ways. Finally, though Thoreau was an admirer of Indian-fighters, as we shall see in the next chapter, their attraction was that they fought *like* Indian warriors, not *for* them. We can hardly imagine him so great a turncoat that he would give up his literary ambitions and the advantages of civilization like books and travel. His subversiveness was militant but not military, profound and not merely flamboyant. So the Indian side was, instead, to be taken as a point of view in the philosophic and cultural war against the Christians, the village, and the farmers. This was the true noble-savage role, and savagism had fitted it out and provided it for him. With civilization and savagery as antonyms, the savage was a predestined moral ally against civilization.

Thus savagism, with all its errors, race-stereotypes, and civilized origins, was still a challenge to civilization. Indians, as a people, were largely unknown, unknowable, and doomed. But "the Indian," as an idea, was enormously powerful: the emblem of self-reliance, nature, and wisdom—the daemon of the continent. And Thoreau was peculiarly situated to come under the spell. What D. H. Lawrence said about Cooper is even more applicable to Thoreau:

> A curious thing about the Spirit of Place is the fact that no place exerts its full influence upon a new-comer until the old inhabitant is dead or absorbed. So America. While the Red Indian existed in fairly large numbers, the new colonials were in a great measure immune from the daimon, or demon, of America. The moment the last nuclei of Red life break up in America, then the white men will have to reckon with the full force of the demon of the continent.[27]

26

The "last nuclei of Red life" were thought to be breaking up. As Lewis Henry Morgan, Thoreau's contemporary and a founder of American ethnology, wrote in 1851, the "sentiment" that "*the destiny of the Indian is extermination*" was universal. Morgan found it "so wide-spread as to have become a general theme for school-boy declamation." It was, Morgan went on, both erroneous and prejudicial.[28] But as well as providing a fatalistic apologetic for white conquest, it also provoked an elegiac impulse. The Indian, the daemon of the continent, must be studied and honored while he was yet available.

Artists, authors, and historians of many dispositions, representing nearly all of what Thoreau rightly identified as his generation, did studies of Indians and "the Indian." Savagism was their common starting point and, in most cases, their conclusion, too. Where Thoreau differed from them, both in methods and conclusions, will be covered later. First we need to examine more closely the uses he made of savagism. For good books can sometimes be made from bad ideas, and in the next two chapters I want to study the uses of savagism in *A Week on the Concord and Merrimack Rivers* and *Walden*.

CHAPTER II

"As Long as Grass Grows and Water Runs"

TODAY, *A Week on the Concord and Merrimack Rivers* is probably the second or third most famous literary river trip in America, after *Huckleberry Finn* and *Life on the Mississippi*. But its fame far exceeds its number of readers. The river trip is less than half of the book, being interrupted time and again by digressions on religion, literature, history, and many other subjects which do not seem integral to the narrative. James Russell Lowell wrote in an early review that these digressions are like "snags, jolting us headforemost out of our places as we are rowing placidly up stream or drifting down."[1] One reason for them, we know now, is that Thoreau filled out the book with excerpts from his early journals, lectures, and essays, until it "became perilously like a library of the shorter works of Henry Thoreau."[2] More recently, Lawrence Buell has argued that the book's randomness is not only intentional but, by the standards of Transcendentalist aesthetics, a pleasing virtue.[3]

From a savagist perspective, however, the book has more order than these accounts of it recognize. It contains a condensed history, in an inferential, poetic form, of Indian-European relations in America, as represented in the little corner of northeastern Massachusetts and southern New Hampshire which is the book's microcosm. The history begins in the introductory chapter "Concord River" and the first day's trip "Saturday" with an evocation of the river and land as they were before the white man's coming. "Sunday" brings the Puritan settlers' arrival and the first conflict with the Indians over religion. In "Monday" the conflict expands into war. In "Tuesday" Thoreau concentrates on what was, in New England, a later development

28

than missions and battles, the extensive fur trade and commercial relations. "Wednesday," which contains the long, interpolated essay on Friendship, also shows rare, admirable examples of red-white friendship. In the last two chapters Thoreau examines the still more transcendental connections in art, which to him means imitation and is thus an inferior and fallen relationship ("Thursday"), and in poetry, which as a final, visionary subject provides the hope for new life and regeneration ("Friday"). The subjects run together a little at the edges, but on the whole they are so well defined that we could list them as alternative chapter titles:

Indian Prehistory	Concord River
Prehistory and White Arrival	Saturday
White Arrival, Religious Conflict	Sunday
War	Monday
Commerce	Tuesday
Friendship	Wednesday
Imitation and Art	Thursday
Poetry and Originality	Friday

Listed this way, we can also see certain similarities to the numbered steps in Emerson's Transcendental staircase in his first book, *Nature*. There he discussed Nature as, successively, Commodity, Beauty, Language, Discipline, Idealism, Spirit, and Prospects. Both books, coincidentally, have seven chapters plus introduction, and both move from the supposedly lower to higher views of their topic. Thoreau's exploration of New World "Nature" was made on a week's reenactment of a voyage of discovery.

My purpose is a literary explication of *A Week* that stresses its images and history of Indians. There may be some danger in implying that Indians are the major subject. They are not. But Thoreau's visions of them make a coherent story, which is one of the threads of the book's continuity. In addition, they are a reference point to which he repeatedly turns for criticism or insight on other topics. In his quest for an American aesthetic, he looks to the original Americans as predecessors who have been superiors in

29

some respects and inferiors in others. Collectively, these visions and references make up his initial literary savagism. It is drawn from the savagist mythology of other writers, but it is also his own.

PRE-WHITE AMERICA

Like many, or all American rivers, the Concord has its Indian name, and Thoreau's opening sentence begins with it. "The Musketaquid, or Grass-ground River, though probably as old as the Nile or Euphrates," did not, he says, receive the "kindred name of CONCORD" until white settlers arrived in 1635. But his reasons for starting with the earliest name are not merely those of the conventional travel writer. "It will be Grass-ground River," he says next, "as long as grass grows and water runs here; it will be Concord River only while men lead peaceable lives on its banks." The savagely poetic name Musketaquid has more permanence (the other, we might reflect, having been temporarily disproven by the battle in 1775), and ingeniously embodies the phrase used in Indian treaties, in Thoreau's time and before, as an expression for the furthest imaginable future: "as long as grass grows and water runs."[4]

To Thoreau, boldly attempting a book and a life of equal endurance in men's memories, the words had the status of an aesthetic ideal. Melville also used them in *Typee* and *Pierre*, but not with the same reverence.[5] Thoreau uses them as a refrain throughout the book. He repeats them in his digressions on classic authors, whose sentences "were written while grass grew and water ran" (p. 93). He adapts them to his critique of politics. "Most revolutions," he says, neither interest nor alarm him, "but tell me that our rivers are drying up, or the genus pine dying out in the country, and I might attend" (p. 134). The words epitomize his ideal of an "out-of-doors" sort of book, one which will come to life even when English is a dead language, because the words are for living things. (See *Journal*, June 29, 1851.)

The people who spoke such words are associated with the land and water, and as Thoreau tries to imagine pre-white America, he looks into the water. The major portion of "Saturday" is about fish. There is a Waltonian catalogue of the fish to be found in the Musketaquid, and he concludes with salmon, shad, and alewives, which both Indians and early white inhabitants caught in great numbers until dams stopped the fishes' migrations. But the dams and canals are ultimately doomed, and "after a few thousands of years, if the fishes will be patient, and pass their summers elsewhere meanwhile, nature will have leveled the Billerica dam, and the Lowell factories, and the Grass-ground River will run clear again" (p. 32). This eventual return of the fish would also bring the return of the Indians.

But his knowledge of pre-white America is limited, and "Saturday" ends with a short description of the camp the brothers made for the night and of their boat beached at the water's edge, "the first encroachment of commerce on this land." Their "port" is "our Ostia," and they, by extension, are the first Virgilian adventurers in a land they have never seen. Looking at the boat's still swaying mast, Thoreau says, "That straight, geometrical line against the water and the sky stood for the last refinements of civilized life, and what of sublimity there is in history was there symbolized." The coming story will be another account in the long engagement of civilization and the unknown, the wilderness (p. 39).

RELIGION

In "Sunday" Thoreau combines his classical and savage perspectives on early America. "It was a quiet Sunday morning, with more of the auroral rosy and white than of the yellow light in it, as if it dated from earlier than the fall of man, and still preserved a heathenish integrity." The dawn is Homeric rather than Christian. But mixed with the rosy-fingered dawn is the "white," which warns us of the coming white man, "pale as the dawn," while the "heathenish integrity" refers to both the Indians and the pagan Greeks and Romans (p. 42). And so the day describes the conflict between, on the one hand, the savage ages of Homer, epic

31

poets, and American Indians, who were all hunters, warriors, and representatives of natural religion, and, on the other, the modern ages of Christianity, farmers, and a civilized poetry.

Through the very early morning, Thoreau and his brother glide along in a landscape still unmarked by signs of civilization. They are even reminded "of the reed forts of the East-Indians" and of "trim Persian gardens" from The Arabian Nights. It is a timeless dream world, where only the frogs and minnows have "Sabbath thoughts" (p. 48). But as they pass the village of Billerica, the sound of the church bell comes through the woods. "No wonder that such a sound startled the dreaming Indian, and frightened his game, when the first bells were swung on trees, and sounded through the forest" (p. 49). And soon Thoreau begins to recreate the white man's arrival as it must have looked from that forest perspective. The white man built a house, made a clearing, and let in the sun. This dried the ground, and he planted apple trees. He built fences, bridges, and mills, cut the wild grasses, driving off the beaver and otter, and planted English grain, as well as the seeds of dandelion and wild trefoil, burdock, catnip, and yarrow. He even brought the honeybee, symbol of this energetic pastoral life, and it advanced into the woods and "stung the red child's hand, forerunner of that industrious tribe that was to come" (p. 52).

The white virtues, as Thoreau recites them in the magnificent paragraph beginning, "The white man comes, pale as the dawn," are a calculating intelligence, community, obedience, racial experience, and "wonderful, wonderful common sense." He is "dull but capable, slow but persevering, severe but just, of little humor but genuine; a laboring man, despising game and sport; building a house that endures, a framed house." With these traits, he buys the Indian "hunting-grounds," plows up Indian bones, and soon forgets all the old signs and records of the past, for he has also brought his English names and "strews them up and down this river," making New England. Yet to the Indians,

32

these are "not Angle-ish or English, but Yengeese, and so
. . . Yankees." Then, returning to the present time of a
Sunday morning in September 1839, Thoreau notes how
the Billerica schoolhouse stood meekly in the village, "en-
treating a long truce to war and savage life" (pp. 53–54).
He has thus characterized the Yankees as farmers and
orchard-growers and fully accepted the savagist notion of
the Indians as forest hunters. His only difference with the
usual eulogists of civilization is that "my genius dates from
an older era" and he has "a singular yearning toward all
wildness." He balances his catalogue of white virtues with
an equally long one of the red virtues, in which he goes
beyond pity to an impassioned defense of the Indian as he
supposedly was.

> We talk of civilizing the Indian, but that is not the name
> for his improvement. By the wary independence and aloof-
> ness of his dim forest life he preserves his intercourse with
> his native gods, and is admitted from time to time to a
> rare and peculiar society with Nature. He has glances of
> starry recognition to which our saloons are strangers. . . .
> We would not always be soothing and taming nature, break-
> ing the horse and the ox, but sometimes ride the horse
> wild and chase the buffalo. The Indian's intercourse with
> Nature is at least such as admits of the greatest independ-
> ence of each. If he is somewhat of a stranger in her midst,
> the gardener is too much of a familiar. . . . There are other,
> savager and more primeval aspects of nature than our poets
> have sung. It is only white man's poetry. Homer and Os-
> sian even can never revive in London or Boston. And yet,
> behold how these cities are refreshed by the mere tradition,
> or the imperfectly transmitted fragrance and flavor of these
> wild fruits. If we could listen but for an instant to the chant
> of the Indian muse, we should understand why he will not
> exchange his savageness for civilization. Nations are not
> whimsical. Steel and blankets are strong temptations; but
> the Indian does well to continue Indian. (Pp. 55–56)

I have quoted this passage at such length because it contains the essence of Thoreau's savagist speculations. Admir-
ing as they are, they are not nearly so specific as his previous

description of the white man. All Thoreau can do is develop imaginatively the themes of independence and wildness, and these are not portrayed in their own right but in contrast to white civility and refinement. Indian "society" is with nature, the white is in "saloons." The white tames the horse and ox, but should sometimes "ride the horse wild and chase the buffalo." Likewise with gardening and poetry: the white is too refined and intimate; the wild is healthier and stronger. It can refresh the cities. But Thoreau is also slightly evasive about Indian poetry, seeking to listen "to the chant of the Indian muse" because he does not know the poets themselves.

Despite its vagueness, this definition of savage life soon becomes the basis of Thoreau's praise of the classics and of myth and fable as wilder and more powerful than the literature of cities. When an encounter with some pious churchgoers sets off his attack on New England Christianity, he eventually returns to Indians for examples of a simpler and more sincere religion. At Wannalancet's conversion to Christianity, as recorded by Daniel Gookin, the Puritan Indian agent, Wannalancet told John Eliot,

> "'I must acknowledge I have, all my days, used to pass in an old canoe . . . and now you exhort me to change and leave my old canoe, and embark in a new canoe, to which I have hitherto been unwilling; but now I yield up myself to your advice, and enter into a new canoe, and do engage to pray to God hereafter.'" (P. 83)

The allegory is clear and apt, since Wannalancet had frequently canoed past the Puritan village. But a white man from Billerica asks Eliot to tell Wannalancet that the old canoe was bound for "'death and destruction'" and that though he will meet "'storms and trials'" his new journey will be towards "'everlasting rest.'" To Thoreau, the old religion was graceful, while this new one, Christianity, is stern and pompous.

He reenforces this judgment with records from other Indian conversions. In the Puritan's language, the converts

" 'did voluntarily submit themselves' " and " 'promise to be willing' " to be taught. The paradoxes of such phrases tell us a lot, which is evidently why Thoreau took such pains to quote them exactly. When the Indians are asked not to work on the Sabbath, their obliging way shines forth. They answer, " 'It is easy to them; they have not much to do on any day, and they can well take their rest on that day' " (p. 84). The Indian religions, Thoreau is implying, were tolerant and naturally pious, while the Puritans compelled piety. They imposed their intricate theology on the Indians and demanded an obedience which the Indians had customarily given freely.

At the end of these stories Thoreau exclaims, "What journeyings on foot and on horseback through the wilderness, to preach the gospel to these minks and muskrats!" He echoes the attitudes with which Puritan missionaries themselves regarded their errands in the wilderness, while also being sympathetic to the "minks and muskrats" rather than the missionaries. From such stories he further realizes that the country through which he is travelling has been "an old battle and hunting-ground" in several senses. It is "the ancient dwelling-place of a race of hunters and warriors," but more recently it has been a ground for the hunting of souls and battling of prayer and faith.

As Thoreau tries to recover the records of Indian life itself, we can see how his savagism, naturalism, and classicism were all related. The Indian fishing weirs, arrowheads, and mortars and pestles were only to be found, now, in the mud of river bottoms or in the earth. They seemed to be, therefore, a part of the land and vegetation, a chapter in natural history. Moreover, the stone implements endure, as more refined articles do not. Classical antiquity also endures in stones and in the *moving* words of poetry. Virgil's lines

"Jam laeto turgent in palmite gemmae;"
Now the buds swell on the joyful stem.

"Strata jacent passim sua quaeque sub arbore poma;"
The apples lie scattered everywhere, each under its tree.

35

contain "recognition of living nature." "These are such sentences as were written while grass grew and water ran" (p. 93). As an American writer, Thoreau overcomes the fact that American antiquity is not as picturesque as the Greek or Roman—no great tottering monuments or buildings—by stating his distaste for such moldy ruins and preferring the living past which is in poetry and nature. They are open to the sky, airy, and healthy. And by making the treaty phrase his standard by which to judge classical poetry, he admits it to America by an enduring native test. At the same time, he finds Virgil, Homer, Ossian, and a few more modern writers, like Sir Walter Raleigh, to be sufficiently wild and savage that their language and thought serve to suggest to him what savage American life may have been. And savage life, in being heroic, vigorous, and close to nature, was an enduring style by which Americans and American writers should continue to live and write. "The scholar may be sure that he writes the tougher truth for the calluses on his palms," says Thoreau. "The sentences written by such rude hands are nervous and tough, like hardened thongs, the sinews of the deer, or the roots of the pine" (p. 109).

Such a scholar, or example to scholars, is the old settler Jonathan Tyng, whom Thoreau recalls at the end of "Sunday." In 1675, during King Philip's War, Tyng fortified his house in Dunstable and held it as a garrison. He requested three or four men to help him, and they were sent. "But methinks that such a garrison would be weakened by the addition of a man," says Thoreau, emphasizing the value of one heroic volunteer over any number of men who have to be ordered (p. 115). For his fortitude Tyng was rewarded by the grant of Wicasuck Island in the Merrimack River. But this courage was so unusual—and necessary— that in 1694 Massachusetts passed a law that settlers who deserted a town from fear of Indians would forfeit their rights. This law provokes Thoreau into saying how today "the fertile frontier territories of truth and justice" are constantly deserted. It also illustrates how the Puritan attempts to force obedience in religion carried over into the need to compel obedience in war. Though the Puritans had not learned from the Indians in religion, they would have to learn from them in war.

WAR

Thoreau's account of New England's Indian wars is also inferential rather than comprehensive. He does not deal with King Philip's War, that most famous early conflict in which over half of the New England settlements were attacked and twelve completely destroyed; rather, he deals with just two small border skirmishes of 1724 and 1725.[6] Yet just as the Musketaquid-Concord is all rivers, "an emblem of all progress, following the same law with the system, with time, and all that is made" (p. 11), so can these battles stand for all battles. He is interested in the Transcendental history of Yankee-Indian warfare, which can be written of any encounter, properly examined.

He tries, therefore, to look at these battles from several angles and to give the emblematic, representative details. Lovewell's Fight in April 1725 was a victory, according to old ballads, in which thirty-four valiant English overcame about fourscore Indians. But in addition to quoting the ballads, in which the English dead and wounded are only memorialized and mourned, Thoreau consults other accounts, which give grim pictures of how the wounded had to survive for two weeks in the wilderness. One cut his moccasins into strings to use as fishing line. Another had had a hand shot off, but somehow survived. A third, who according to an old journal "'subsisted . . . on the spontaneous vegetables of the forest,'" watched the cranberries he had eaten come out of his wounds. Such is the difference, Thoreau implies, between a ballad writer's account of war and the soldier's experience. Finally, he also wonders about the wounded Indians, their adventures, and "how fared their cranberries." But of how they managed and what heroes' welcome and reward awaited them "there is no journal to tell." In war, and in these wars in particular, only one side is told, one set of records kept. But Thoreau does find an ironic note with which to end. Lovewell, the dead hero, had been warned beforehand of Indian ambuscades. For an answer he bent down a small elm and bragged he would do the same to the Indians. "'This elm is still standing,'" Thoreau closes the story, "'a venerable and magnificent tree'" (pp. 123–26).

Thoreau's other major subjects in "Monday" are reform and tradition and the differences between Eastern and Western philosophy. Nineteenth-century reformers annoy him because of their ignorance of history and "the true state of things" (p. 133). "Most revolutions in society have not power to interest, still less alarm us; but tell me that our rivers are drying up, or the genus pine dying out in the country, and I might attend" (p. 134). Neither reform nor revolution affects the Indian idea of eternity. Yet neither does government-as-is appeal to him. "I have not so surely foreseen that any Cossack or Chippeway would come to disturb the honest and simple commonwealth, as that some monster institution would at length embrace and crush its free members in its scaly folds; . . . while the law holds fast the thief and murderer, it lets itself go loose." Men as they are simply embalm tradition, execute "the wills of the dead, to the last codicil and letter" (p. 135). Thus tradition does not attract him either. The origin of "piety" is *pius Æneas'* bearing his father on his shoulders, and this symbol of tradition, found in both civilization and "some Indian tribes," is offensive to him (p. 136).

He turns to contemplate Oriental philosophy and finds a higher tradition. Here, as Menu said, "'Immemorial custom is transcendent law'" (p. 140). The Eastern religions are calm and intellectual, Christianity active and practical; and Thoreau hints that this philosophical conflict between East Indians and Europeans may underlie the physical conflict in America between Indians and Yankees. In Thoreau's geography the Yankees are "Occidental" and the Indians "Oriental," and the conflict universal:

> There is a struggle between the Oriental and Occidental in every nation; some who would be forever contemplating the sun, and some who are hastening toward the sunset. The former class says to the latter, When you have reached the sunset, you will be no nearer to the sun. To which the latter replies, But we so prolong the day. (P. 147)

This philosophical conflict is eventually demonstrated again in the second battle memory of the day, the skirmishes around Nashua, New Hampshire, in September 1724. Some Indians had captured two men who were out in the woods making turpentine. Ten men from Dunstable went to look for them, and, finding the spilled turpentine and marks of coal and grease on trees, tried to rescue them. The ten were ambushed, and the only one to escape was one named Farwell, who had advised against open pursuit. Then another party went out from Dunstable, but it was beaten back. So Thoreau uses this story to show how slow the English were in learning that the Indians were accomplished warriors. Only Farwell, he says, "had studied his profession, and understand the business of hunting Indians" (p. 176). Though he too was killed the following spring in Lovewell's Fight, he was the kind of cautious forest scout who became a New England hero.

These lessons of Indian warfare are by now familiar: the Americans had to give up European pride, break ranks and fight as scouts and woodsmen, as Indians. Richard Slotkin has recently shown how these lessons were first taught by Benjamin Church, a hero of King Philip's War, then repeated in the eighteenth century by men like Thomas Hutchins and Maj. Robert Rogers, and likewise Col. James Smith and Daniel Boone in the nineteenth century. They all espoused Indian endurance, resistance to pain, patience, and self-denial. Thoreau, we can see, not only respected them; as a kind of unarmed Ranger of Concord he also imitated them. He associated them with both the Indians who were their own examples and also the ancient epic heroes. But his further judgment was that these battles of Farwell and Lovewell were "incredible."

> I think that posterity will doubt if such things ever were,— if our bold ancestors who settled this land were not struggling rather with the forest shadows, and not with a copper-colored race of men. They were vapors, fever and ague of the unsettled woods. Now, only a few arrowheads are turned up by the plow. In the Pelasgic, the Etruscan, or the British story, there is nothing so shadowy and unreal. (P. 176)

The Indian-fighters, I understand him to be saying, were fighting something which they only glimpsed, perhaps a projection of their own unreal or unfulfilled imaginations, or the sickness they feared in the woods. Of necessity, his own images of this warfare are shadowy, too. He leaves it for higher relationships. But he has balanced the savagist unreality of the Indian with the equal enigma of the savage-fighter.

COMMERCE

Ordinarily, we do not think of Thoreau as liking commerce. He hated the ties of New England mills to Southern plantations, and in his own affairs he gave minimum attention to the family pencil and plumbago business. But in *Walden* he described commerce as "unexpectedly confident and serene, alert, adventurous, and unwearied." It succeeded where "fantastic enterprises and sentimental experiments" did not because it was realistic and natural. In "Monday," in his reflections on Oriental philosophy, he noted that it was the merchant-scholars of Europe who had discovered this treasure, not the professional scholars. In New England it was the early merchants and fur traders who, learning from the Dutch in New York and the French in Canada, came in the eighteenth century and helped drive out the "fantastic enterprises" of religion and war. So to Thoreau commerce was a historical and moral improvement.

The travellers in "Tuesday" rise before dawn and proceed upriver without their usual antagonism towards the
people on shore, like merchants who are out to do business,
not start quarrels. But not all merchants are so shrewd, and
the first Indian memory of the day concerns a fur trader
named Cromwell, who was a crook. Living near what became known as Cromwell's Falls, he " 'carried on a lucrative
trade [with the Indians], weighing their furs wth his foot.' "
The Indians became suspicious and decided to kill him.
But Cromwell learned of their plans, quickly buried his
wealth, and fled. Rumors about the wealth and its location
were still to be heard, and Thoreau uses the story as a cau-
tionary tale about the various follies of bad business. "The
truth is," he comments, "there is money buried everywhere,
and you have only to go to work to find it" (pp. 207–208).

Two tales from his own experience illustrate better relationships between merchant-travellers and natives. The first
is of a walk into the mountains from the Connecticut River.
The further west he went, the more uncivilized he expected
the inhabitants to be, and yet his host for the night, a hill
farmer named Rice, turned out to have a "sweet, wild way"
which was more civil than the ways of city folk. His mountain cottage even had running water—from a spring piped
indoors. Rice had, Thoreau says, "a long-suffering Saxon
probity." He had burrowed into the hills, and "he would
not let the race die out in him, like a red Indian." Thus
Rice was a kind of Saxon savage who had made himself
more native to the place than the Indians, because he had
cultivated the land. Such a judgment stemmed from Thoreau's own savagism. Yet Thoreau's further judgment that he
got along with Rice because he had come only "for novelty
and adventure, and to see what nature had produced here"
also reflects his attitude that the way to travel among savages, whether Indian or Saxon, is to carry an open mind
(pp. 217–18).

His other personal memory attempts to provide the native's view of the foreign traveller. When he was a boy in
Concord, he says, the news would spread every year or two

of a great canalboat coming up the river. It would moor
for a day or two at some wharf in a meadow, unload huge
cargoes of lime, brick, and cast iron, and then, its crew and
their wheelbarrows taken back aboard, it would disappear
as mysteriously as it had come. The awe which the youth
of Concord had for these "fabulous rivermen" is comparable
to the wonder of the Pacific islander.

> Such is Commerce, which shakes the cocoanut and bread-
> fruit tree in the remotest isle, and sooner or later dawns on
> the duskiest and most simple-minded savage. If we may be
> pardoned the digression, who can help being affected at
> the thought of the very fine and slight, but positive rela-
> tion, in which the savage inhabitants of some remote isle
> stand to the mysterious white mariner, the child of the sun?
> —as if *we* were to have dealings with an animal higher in
> the scale of being than ourselves. (P. 224)

This cheerful vision of European behavior in the South Seas,
which would have brought guffaws to Herman Melville,
results in part from Thoreau's own boyish wonder over the
canalboatmen. As they were benign and wonderful to the
boys of Concord, so must the Europeans seem to the "duski-
est and most simple-minded savage." Yet the equation de-
pends on the "poor savage's" being as inferior to the European as boys are to men. It assumes savagist theories of
racial inferiority.

Thoreau's ideal of this "white mariner," as seen in North
America, was the fur trader Alexander Henry, of whom he
will have more to say in "Wednesday." In the "Tuesday"
chapter he introduces Henry, stopped for two days on "the
shore of Ontario" in order to build two bark canoes in which
to cross to Fort Niagara. The incident illustrates how early
travellers adopted native techniques and also how experienced travellers make "a delay as good as much rapid
traveling." He compares Henry to Xenophon building rafts
to transport his army, and calls his *Adventures* "a great poem on the primitive state of the country." Henry's book is
rough and unfinished, but accurate and informational. It is
heroic material to inspire future heroic poets.

In its rough and natural expediency, commerce also engendered military alliances between whites and Indians, and Thoreau's next documents are some transcriptions—misspellings and mispunctuations included—of seventeenth-century military messages. As some white men like Tyng, Farwell, and Henry had become native in styles of fighting and travel, so had some red men like John Hogkins, a Penacook, learned English well enough to write to the English warning of the advancing "Mohogs" (p. 233). A synthesis of cultures developed from both sides, and Thoreau then goes on to introduce the lyrics of Anacreon as a synthesis of the wildness of Homer and the refinement of Horace and Latin authors. To Thoreau, the contrast between wildness and refinement is so fundamental in human history that it can be found anywhere. Moreover, classical literature and American experience are constant analogs.

For another synthesis, he tells of some wild apple trees which he and John found later in the afternoon. The trees, whose ancestral seed had been brought from England, had been abandoned by settlers and gone wild. The trees are images of what the two Thoreaus wish to be. As they went further up the River, they also found a deserted mill, where the "trout glanced through the crumbling flume" (p. 247). It was as if the prediction at the beginning of the book, that the decay of the milldams would bring the return of fish and Indians, had already come true; the brothers end their day's travel singing a boat-song about "the Indian hunter" of years ago. By going wild themselves, they have found nature wild and begun to revive "the spirits of the braves."

FRIENDSHIP

In Thoreau's savagism, friendship was a virtue in which Christianity and the refinements of civilization had made no improvements. Or so we judge from the fact that the only historical friendship to which he refers in his long "Wednesday" essay on friendship is the one between the fur trader Alexander Henry and Wawatam, the Chippeway who saved Henry's life. Better than any of the friendships of Christian-classical legend, this illustrates his ideal.

The friendship began in a dream. Wawatam dreamed of

a "white brother," and after fasting and reflecting on it, he went to tell Henry, whom he had just met, that Henry embodied it. Henry tells in his *Travels and Adventures* that just after the Michilimackinac massacre of 1763, he and other captives were about to be killed and eaten.[7] Wawatam gained Henry's release, found a place to hide him, and returned to drink whiskey and "Human broth" with the other victors. Then the two men retired to a long and happy winter of living with Wawatam's family and hunting and fishing in the wilderness. In the spring they had to separate, neither thinking they would never see each other again.

Those are the simple facts of this "almost bare and leafless, yet not blossomless nor fruitless" friendship. It is also bare and leafless because, though stories of noble Indians saving white men's lives are famous in American history (Pocahontas and John Smith, Squanto and the Pilgrims), they are fewer in history than in literature (where they blossom in Uncas and Natty Bumppo, Queequeg and Ishmael, and the many imitations). It also blossoms for Thoreau in that it represents the "free and irresponsible," gratuitous, "heathenish intercourse" of true friendship. ("To say that a man is your Friend means commonly no more than this, that he is not your enemy," Thoreau has said earlier, speaking of the ordinary friendships of village and farm [p. 282].) Thoreau is not so interested in the fact that Wawatam saved Henry's life as in the fact that the men united from some instinct higher than self-preservation and went on to live together with no idea, on either side, of changing the other. " 'Metals unite from fluxility; birds and beasts from motives of convenience; fools from fear and stupidity; and just men at sight,' " he quotes Henry (p. 291). When they cease to be simply " 'just men' " and begin to worry about charity and helping one another, then friendship is over.

> When the Friend comes out of his heathenism and superstition, and breaks his idols, being converted by the precepts of a newer testament; when he forgets his mythology, and treats his Friend like a Christian, or as he can afford,— then Friendship ceases to be Friendship, and becomes char-

44

ity; that principle which established the almshouse is now beginning with its charity at home, and establishing an almshouse and pauper relations there. (P. 293)

. As many readers of the *Week* have noted, the book as a whole and the friendship section in particular are also a memorial to Thoreau's brother John, who died in January 1842, two and a half years after the trip itself and some seven years before the book's publication. Very little is known about John, however, other than that he shared Henry's love of nature, love of solitude, and political and religious independence. The formal eulogy read at his funeral, Walter Harding has said, "twenty years later could have just as appropriately been read for Henry Thoreau."[8] Yet something else they shared was an affection for Indian ways and legends. In the summer and fall of 1837 they hunted arrowheads together (*Journal*, October 29, 1837). Their boats were named "Red Jacket" and "Musketaquid." And in November 1837 Henry wrote a letter to John, who was off teaching school, in which he addressed him as "his brother sachem—Hopeful of Hopewell" and then expressed all his thoughts and news in the Indian talk of treaties and speeches.[9] Like Wawatam and Alexander Henry, John and Henry Thoreau were Savage Brothers.

Or rather, they had romantically imagined themselves that way, and Henry, with John dead, preserved the illusion. I will have more to say about this uniquely important relationship in a later chapter, but it must be recognized here because of its obvious bearing on the portrait of friendship. "The Friend," Thoreau says in another revealing passage, "is some fair floating isle of palms eluding the mariner in Pacific seas." Friendship, in this image, is an object of quest, but of a faintly phantom kind. The quest is dangerous, he goes on, "but who would not sail through mutiny and storm, even over Atlantic waves, to reach the fabulous retreating shores of some continent man?" (p. 278). The figure of the "retreating shores" leaves us to wonder whether the quest can ever be accomplished. In the poem following, "The Atlantides," friendship is compared to the lost continent

Atlantis. Yet the images of American discovery imply that this "continent man" was once discovered, becoming a New World. Then, a few lines after the poem, the discoverer is compared to a "shipwrecked mariner," a Robinson Crusoe, who "has not seen a footprint on the shore."

Yet Thoreau is not merely idealizing the red-white, Savage Brother relationship. The chapter's epigraph, "Man is man's foe and destiny," from Charles Cotton, suggests fraternal rivalry as well as comradeship, and the other references to Indians also acknowledge that in America red-white friendship was the exception, not the rule. As Henry and John are rowing past Manchester, New Hampshire, for instance, the author alludes to the story in Gookin's *Historical Collections of the Indians of New England* about old Pasaconaway, a sachem who lived to be 120 years old. He could " 'make water burn, rocks move, and trees dance, and metamorphose himself into a flaming man; . . . in winter he could raise a green leaf out of the ashes of a dry one, and produce a living snake from the skin of a dead one.' " With this great influence among his people, he urged them not to quarrel with the English (p. 267). In King Philip's War his son Wannalancet (the convert to the new canoe) followed his advice and withdrew his people from the fighting. Afterwards, when Wannalancet visited an English minister in Chelmsford, he asked the minister whether Chelmsford had suffered in the war. The minister answered that it had not and that God should be thanked. Wannalancet only replied, "Me next" (p. 268).

To further emphasize white ignorance and ingratitude, Thoreau then lists the names of the famous citizens of the area who are remembered in books and monuments. Breaking this seeming patriotic catalogue is one short paragraph: "The graves of Pasaconaway and Wannalancet are marked by no monument on the bank of their native river" (p. 269). For totally different reasons, from savage pride and restraint rather than white ingratitude, the name and dates of John Thoreau are not given in his brother's memorial to him.

46

ART

"Thursday," the short next-to-last chapter of the *Week*, is also one of the most complex. Its major subject is art and its differences from nature and poetry, or what the nineteenth century commonly called the difference between talent and genius. In remarks on Goethe at the end of the chapter, Thoreau tells us that the "Man of Genius . . . is an originator, an inspired or demonic man, who produces a perfect work in obedience to laws yet unexplored. The artist is he who detects and applies the law from observation of the works of Genius, whether of man or nature" (p. 350). Here Thoreau also covers the whole second week of his and John's vacation, during which they set off overland and climbed Mt. Washington. For its "Indian" material it has the incredible story of Hannah Dustan, the frontier mother who with her nurse and an English boy surprised their sleeping Indian captors, scalped ten of them, and fled down the Merrimack by canoe. The challenge to the reader is to figure out what the vindictive Hannah Dustan is doing here, when Thoreau has finished with warfare and gone on to the peaceful aspects of white-Indian affairs.

His version of the story is so powerful that it has recently attracted the attention of such different literary scholars as Leslie Fiedler, that old chief of "Redskin" critics, and Richard Slotkin, the author of *Regeneration Through Violence*.[10] To Fiedler, Thoreau has made Hannah Dustan an American Eve, who broke the natural bonds of friendship between white and Indian males. To Slotkin, the story is more enigmatic, and yet takes its place in the mythology of white initiation into the wild and renewal by partaking of the Eucharist of blood and sacrifice. Yet neither Fiedler nor Slotkin read the story in the context of the rest of the "Thursday" chapter or the still larger structure of the book. The story concerns one of the most contested issues of white-Indian history: who started scalping and cruelty in frontier war?

47

The most general quality that is common to all the parts of this chapter, and to the book as a whole, is the direct or implied presence at all times of two states of mind, two ways of looking at things, and two ways of being in the world. In "Sunday," for example, we had two ways of worship and honoring the day, the Puritan and the pagan or Indian. In war, commerce, and friendship there were similar polarities between the wild and the civilized, between the river way and the land way. Here, if we take this chapter's general subject to be art and the artist, and the Hannah Dustan story to represent, as Fiedler has suggested, a Fall, then it seems reasonable to suggest also that we will have two kinds of art and artists, one original and the other fallen. We will also have original and fallen nature.

"Thursday" opens with the only rainy morning of the *Week*. "The rain had pattered all night, and *now the whole country wept*," the writer tells us (emphasis added). Still, this in itself is not bad for Thoreau, and in place of a rainbow he is cheered all morning by the trill of a hair-bird; rain is just a matter of how one adjusts to it. The next few pages are a short essay on the pleasures of rain in the woods, punctuated with such maxims as " 'Nothing that naturally happens to man can *hurt* him, earthquakes and thunder-storms not excepted' " (p. 319). Arriving in Concord, New Hampshire (which these travelers from the other Concord "persisted in calling *New* Concord," and which had once been called by the Indian name of Penacook), the author makes another short digression on the frontier. The first white family moved into this region just a little over a hundred years before, in 1727, and the "frontiers were not this way any longer" (p. 323). His conclusion is that the "frontier" is also a matter of how one looks at it.

> The frontiers are not east or west, north or south; but wherever a man *fronts* a fact. . . . Let him build himself a log house with the bark on where he is, *fronting* IT, and wage there an Old French war for seven or seventy years, with Indians and Rangers, or whatever else may come be-

tween him and the reality, and save his scalp if he can.
(Pp. 323–24)

In the first literary digression ·of this chapter, Thoreau
takes up the Roman satiric poets, whom he regards as de-
cidedly inferior to epic, lyric, and dramatic writers. They
"are measured fault-finders at best . . . and so are concerned
rather about the monster which they have escaped than the
fair prospect before them." In contrast, he decides that "the
divinest poem, or the life of a great man, is the severest
satire; as impersonal as Nature herself, and like the sighs
of her winds in the woods, which convey ever a slight reproof to the hearer" (p. 329).

Leaving the river, Thoreau now begins his very short
account of climbing the highest mountain in New England.
In a book called *A Week on the Concord and Merrimack
Rivers*, this extra week of climbing is an interruption, but
it belongs because it is a point of transcendence, a place
and time where the travellers rose to something above both
river and land, something original and permanent. To illustrate the transcendence, and also hint at the name of the
mountain, he spends one half of this account on a description of a pathetically cold and encumbered "soldier lad"
whom they pass in the woods, "going to muster in full regi-
mentals." He is the ghost, as it were, of the father of his
country, suffering the trials of war in the wilderness, yet
bound for his own kind of glory. Then, listing all rivers and
streams by their Indian names, Thoreau traces his own
climb up the Pemigewasset to "its fountain-head, the Wild
Amonoosuck," till he reaches "the summit AGIOCOCHOOK"
(pp. 333–35). Mountains are unfallen nature; only the Indian name can be used.[11]

The return to the river is now a return to civilization,
except that by this time Thoreau is prepared to find "the
fresh and primitive and savage nature" even in an "Oriental
city." His vision is now that double.

> Art is not tame, and Nature is not wild, in the ordinary
> sense. A perfect work of man's art would also be wild or

natural in a good sense. Man tames Nature only that he may at last make her more free even than he found her, though he may never yet have succeeded. (P. 337)

The ensuing descriptions of afternoon on the river make it out to be nature's work of art. The boughs of pine trees are seen in the water as "worn into fantastic shapes, and white and smooth, as if turned in a lathe." "The landscape contains a thousand dials which indicate the natural divisions of time. . . . The haze over the woods is like the inaudible panting, or rather the gentle perspiration of resting nature, rising from a myriad of pores into the attenuated atmosphere" (pp. 339–41).

Into this perfectly calm and yet haunting scene come "two white women and a boy" on a March afternoon from nearly a hundred and fifty years before, paddling for their lives. They are cold—and lying in their canoe are "the still bleeding scalps of ten of the aborigines." Then Thoreau identifies them: Hannah Dustan and her nurse, Mary Neff, and an English boy, Samuel Lennardson. Indians had attacked the Dustan home two weeks before, frightened off Hannah's husband and seven older children, and captured her in bed, where she had just delivered a child. She had watched "her infant's brains dashed out against an apple tree," and her house burned (p. 342). Hannah and her nurse had then been taken to an island up the Merrimack, the home of an Indian family of two men, three women, and seven children, and been told that they would soon "be taken to a distant Indian settlement, and there made to run the gantlet naked." Hannah determined to escape and told the English boy—a previous prisoner—to find out from one of the Indian men how to kill and scalp.

So, on the morning of March 31, Hannah quietly got up before dawn and directed her two companions in killing all the Indians except a woman and boy. Then they loaded one canoe with food, destroyed the rest, and started their escape to Haverhill, sixty miles downstream. But soon realizing they would never be believed, they turned back, cut the scalps from their ten victims, and taking this bleeding proof in a bag, they resumed their flight.

Continuing to tell the story from Hannah Dustan's viewpoint, Thoreau now imagines their blood-stained clothes, their resolution and fear, their exhaustion, and their "hasty meal of parched corn and moose-meat."

> They are thinking of the dead whom they have left behind on that solitary isle far up the stream, and of the relentless living warriors who are in pursuit. Every withered leaf which the winter has left seems to know their story, and in its rustling to repeat it and betray them. An Indian lurks behind every rock and pine, and their nerves cannot bear the tapping of a woodpecker. Or they forget their own dangers and their deeds in conjecturing the fate of their kindred, and whether, if they escape the Indians, they shall find the former still alive. (P. 343)

Then, considering the swift March current and the occasional falls around which they carry their canoe, Thoreau provides a fuller description of the ice in the river, the beaver and muskrat "driven out of their holes by the flood," the deer, the fishhawk overhead, and the geese flying past "with a startling clangor." These pictures from the grey spring day bring the escape to life—as something which happened as the snow melted and the river ran. "But they do not observe these things, or they speedily forget them. They do not smile or chat all day."

> On either side, the primeval forest stretches away uninterrupted to Canada, or to the "South Sea;" to the white man a drear and howling wilderness, but to the Indian a home, adapted to his nature, and cheerful as the smile of the Great Spirit. (P. 344)

Referring again to himself and his brother and their leisurely selection of a camping spot, Thoreau imagines the opposite situation of Hannah Dustan, gliding on through the night until she reached "old John Lovewell's house on Salmon Brook." The escape succeeded, and they were paid

51

fifty pounds for "their trophies." "The family of Hannah
Dustan all assembled alive once more, except the infant
whose brains were dashed out against the apple tree, and
there have been many who in later time have lived to say
that they have eaten of the fruit of that apple tree" (p. 345).

That Thoreau saw Hannah Dustan as an American Eve
seems provable by the two references to the apple tree and
by his own comment: "This seems a long while ago, and
yet it happened since Milton wrote his Paradise Lost." Me-
dea or Judith might have been equally appropriate models,
however, while the story also seems so unique and told with
such attention to its particulars that we will be wrong if
we fix mythic identifications on it quickly. Better to forget
about Hannah for a minute and think of the story itself:
an American Paradise Lost.

Thoreau makes no judgment of Hannah Dustan. Cotton
Mather, one of the first to record the story, saw her as a
magnificent frontier heroine, as did many tellers of the
story down into the 1930s. Hawthorne, that tireless reex-
aminer of New England morality, called her "this awful
woman," "a raging tigress," and "a bloody old hag"—having
pointed out that most of her victims were little children.[12]
But Thoreau takes neither side and instead lets Hannah and
her two companions judge themselves. They find judgment
in their feelings of fear and estrangement from nature as
they glide down the river. "Every withered leaf . . . seems
to know their story, and in its rustling to repeat it and be-
tray them. An Indian lurks behind every rock and pine, and
their nerves cannot bear the tapping of a woodpecker."
They cannot see the wonder of the early spring day, and
the forest is to them "a drear and howling wilderness."
Whether or not Hannah Dustan was right in what she did,
the result is that she and her companions are now terrified,
and their fear has made nature hostile and cold. They and
their countrymen who go on eating the fruit of her anger
and revenge now live in a fallen world, where they can have
no peace of mind until they have burned every leaf and

silenced every woodpecker. Nature to them is now dangerous and wild and must be tamed. Such, for Thoreau, is their loss and fall.[13]

Hannah Dustan's terror and estrangement also illustrate Thoreau's definition of satire. She has heard "the sighs of [Nature's] winds in the woods, which convey ever a slight reproof to the hearer." Such a nature is *not* "wild," but very refined and subtle and certainly very moral. It is a "howling wilderness" only to the frightened and guilty murderer, who in taking up the Indian tomahawk, has paradoxically become an Indian hater and imitator. And this is what relates Hannah and her companions to, of all people, Goethe and the artist. All are imitators and, in their different ways, killers—a category in which Thoreau also includes himself. "The talent of composition is very dangerous," he says in his remarks on Goethe, "—the striking out the heart of life at a blow, as the Indian takes off a scalp. I feel as if my life had grown more outward when I can express it" (p. 351). What makes Thoreau of two minds about Goethe is that the German traveller possessed this talent in such a perfect form. In his *Italian Journeys* Goethe tells of describing an old stone tower so accurately that Italian peasants, who lived right beside it, gathered around him " 'that they might behold with their eyes, what I had praised to their ears.' " That exactness and integrity of description commands Thoreau's respect. "Above all," he continues, Goethe "possessed a hearty good-will to all men, and never wrote a cross or even careless word." But this artistry and civility have been obtained at the price of "the unconsciousness of the poet." Goethe is a "city boy" who has been "defrauded of much which the savage boy enjoys." "He was even too *well-bred* to be thoroughly bred" (pp. 348–49). And these deficiencies are to Thoreau decisive. The artist's great and dangerous talent for "striking out the heart of life at a blow" must be respected, as, we realize, the dauntless Hannah Dustan must be respected. But this is not poetry; it is fatal imitation.

So to Thoreau, the Indian had taught scalping, but the

white imitation of it, putting it to different purposes, is what was immoral. The immorality, furthermore, was felt by the doers themselves and began their alienation from nature. Conventional savagist writers readily condemned white scalping and bounty-paying also, but they usually went on to accept it as an evil inevitability—a fact of savage warfare—and to look ahead to the day when civilization of the frontier would end it. Thoreau's emphasis, we can see, is totally different. Civilization might end the act but not the consequence. To imitate and to civilize, to civilize and become estranged from nature were all the same.

Thoreau's materials in this chapter are so different that they make shocking commentary on each other. No well-bred artist would equate scalping and composition. But the problem for the reader is to grasp the inferences of these combinations. In the concluding pages of this chapter, describing the night at their campground along the river, Thoreau seems to be saying that such unforeseen relationships and correspondences are part of the method of nature herself and, thereby, of the true poet. One series of reflections, for instance, describes trees as "rivers of sap," the heavens as "rivers of stars, and milky ways," and rocks in the earth as "rivers of ore." "Let us wander where we will, the universe is built round about us, and we are central still." The American who has really made his peaceful camp on the banks of the Merrimack now feels whole and content here as neither Hannah Dustan nor Goethe, neither Washington nor a satirist ever would. It does not bother him that behind him are killers and heroes and old women stretching back to Eve. Regenerating sleep comes from lying so close to the river and grass that the river is flowing all around and through them.

> With our heads so low in the grass, we heard the river whirling and sucking, and lapsing downward, kissing the shore as it went, sometimes rippling louder than usual, and again its mighty current making only a slight limpid, trickling sound, as if our water-pail had sprung a leak, and the water were flowing into the grass by our side. (Pp. 354–55)

This is how an original relation to nature might begin: in sleeping peacefully where the grass grows and the water runs.

ORIGINALITY

Thoreau's desire for an original American poetry was certainly not uncommon. Many of his contemporaries had called for it, like Emerson in "The American Scholar" address. And the condition which made this kind of call possible (and not just necessary to national pride and self-realization) was the tacit assumption that Indians had not been poets. As hunters and warriors, they might supply abundant material for poetry, but they supplied, so far as white Americans knew, neither forms nor legends nor tales which would benefit a civilized poet. This condition changed, to be sure, in the 1840s, with the publication of Henry Rowe Schoolcraft's pioneer translations of Ojibway tales; Longfellow's *Hiawatha* (1855) was based on them. But Thoreau did not know of these until the 1850s, and even then had little idea what to make of them.[14] Having already made up his mind that Indian poetry must be wild and Homeric, he and many other Americans (including Longfellow) were ill-prepared to deal with the reality. He might, as we have seen, suppose good things, "*if* we could listen but for an instant to the chant of the Indian muse." But no one knew what the muse was. The song itself, he assumed, was merely the war dance; and that was worthless to literature.

Moreover, the savagist theory of impending Indian extinction meant that the poetry, if there was any, would disappear along with the people. So that if some really native American poetry were still extant, it soon would be no more, and white Americans would still have upon themselves the burden and the excitement of creating a new literature. The *aboriginal* literature was dead or dying, and *original* literature was to replace it.

As we have seen, however, Thoreau found one very suggestive clue to the aboriginal poetry in the immortal words for immortality itself, and the passion unto desperation with which he listened on Thursday night (how did he keep his blankets dry?) to the river flowing in the grass beside him is the passion with which he wakes on Friday morning: "We lay awake long before daybreak, listening to the rippling of the river and the rustling of the leaves" (p. 356). These two (or three) forces—the river, the grasses and leaves, and the new autumn wind (first north wind of fall) —are the dominant and directing themes of the day's events and reflections. He is headed downstream towards home, with a fresh breeze behind him; and the changing season, with the new colors and the dry leaves driven by the wind, is like a new life, a new life after the fall, after the eviction from paradise of Indians, missionaries, soldiers, and grim Mrs. Dustan.

One of the first thoughts is of village fairs and cattle shows, a new American tradition in harmony with the ancient autumn festivals of Greece and Rome. The very wind which gleans the fields also seems to blow the farmers into town to show their produce and socialize with their neighbors. The poet, who is a country boy, "toughest son of earth and of Heaven," relishes and celebrates such fairs. But this very association, we can hardly fail to note, is based upon the savagist's assumed replacement of the hunter by the shepherd and farmer. Poetry is possible in America because the wilderness has given way to the pasture and pastoral. Meanwhile, Thoreau can celebrate such shows and rude country life because they are close to the rude, essential life of Homer and Ossian. The savage has just been displaced, and "inside the civilized man stands the savage still in the place of honor" (p. 368).

Further down the Merrimack, Henry and John return to Tyngsborough, which was mentioned before in "Sunday" and "Monday." But now he sees an apple tree, where a nail in the trunk marks the height of a flood in October 1785. It is named "'Elisha's apple tree,'" after an Indian who worked for old Jonathan Tyng, but who was killed by another Indian. Elisha was buried near the tree, and during

56

the flood the weight of the water depressed the earth above the grave, so that the grave, once lost, could be seen. Later, the grave filled in again, but the nail in the tree was still there and could have warned a railroad surveyor who failed to locate tracks high enough to be safe against later floods. Such a story, of course, is just what Thoreau enjoys, for it unites his love of Indian memories and respect for Indian eternities. Had the railroad surveyor had a similar respect, his track would not have been flooded. But only poets listen to the legends and the Indians, the river and the trees. Meanwhile, the tree continued to bear "a native fruit," prized by the present owners (and Thoreau). Elisha's bones had been transmuted into "the white man's sinew," as Thoreau had predicted of the Indians in "Wednesday" (p. 251).

Passing Wicasuck Island (which, we remember, was an Indian campground until Wannalancet sold it in 1663 to get his brother out of jail, whereupon it went to Jonathan Tyng), Thoreau and his brother are suspected by a canal-boatman of having "a claim on it." The Island has become "disputed property," and it is, therefore, another symbol—symbol of the different Indian and white attitudes towards land and of the unending disputes which occur when it is treated as property.

But to develop an original poetry of the land, Thoreau cannot rely on the Indians. He must rely on his own powers of observation and must study the examples of other poets. So he briefly considers "the poetry of mathematics" and repeats his belief that there can be no knowledge apart from its ethical implications. "The Tree of Knowledge is a Tree of Knowledge of good and evil" (p. 387). Then he repeats his conviction that "the purest science is still biographical" and that the senses will yet provide this basis of wisdom. Turning to Chaucer, he finds another poet with some savage wit and power—Chaucer reminds us "that flowers have bloomed, and birds sung, and hearts beaten in England"— but this is about as far as wildness can come in civilized poetry (p. 396).

Consequently, he turns towards the mystical, natural

sources within himself. They are "behind the rustling leaves, and the stacks of grain, and the bare clusters of grape." They are in "the hues of October sunsets" and in the heavens themselves (p. 403). But ultimately, they are in silence.

> As the truest society approaches always nearer to solitude, so the most excellent speech finally falls into Silence. Silence is audible to all men, at all times, and in all places. She is when we hear inwardly, sound when we hear outwardly. Creation has not displaced her, but is her visible framework and foil. All sounds are her servants, and purveyors, proclaiming not only that their mistress is, but is a rare mistress, and earnestly to be sought after. (P. 418)

The praise of silence is, of course, sufficiently universal to be both classical and savage. Thoreau was aware, like most literate Americans, of Father Le Jeune's praise of Indian councils, where men "do not all talk at once, but one after the other, listening patiently." He was also aware of the Indian visionary's respect for silence. And the grass grows and water runs not only with a rustling and a sucking, but in silence. But silence, too, is the stillness after the extinction of the aboriginal and the beginning of the original. Having been all the way to Agiocochook, he and John returned to Concord, now originals themselves, and slipped their boat into its groove in the Concord mud and fastened it to a native "wild apple tree."

CHAPTER III

The Vision Quest—*Walden*

You have noticed that everything an Indian does is in a circle, and that is because the Power of the World always works in circles, and everything tries to be round.

BLACK ELK[1]

For the first time I perceive this spring that the year is a circle. I see distinctly the spring arc thus far. It is drawn with a firm line. Every incident is a parable of the Great Teacher.

THOREAU, *Journal*, APRIL 18, 1852

MANY reasons have been given for Thoreau's famous retreat (or advance) to Walden Pond in the spring of 1845 and his life there for two years and two months, beginning July 4. Some readers, picking up on his remark that his "fellow-citizens were not likely to offer me any room in the court house, or any curacy or living any where else,"[2] have stressed the problem of the literary vocation in America— the absence of jobs for authors and his choice of life in the woods over life as a schoolteacher, pencil-maker, or handyman to the Emersons and tutor to their children. Others have seen it as an act of protest—a move *away* from the town and all it represents *towards* nature and independence. "I went to the woods because I wished to live deliberately, to front only the essential facts of life, and see if I could not learn what it had to teach, and not, when I came to die, discover that I had not lived" (p. 90). Others have concentrated less on the social significance of the gesture and more on the "private business" the author said he went to transact. It was a radical fulfillment of Emersonian self-reliance. One more reason sometimes given is that in 1845 Thoreau had his first book to finish, and a cabin in the woods was both a place to work on it and potential material for a second. All these reasons surely have some validity. Thoreau's self-advertised private act was one which could be made to bear great public significance as well as controversy, and one suspects it of having been chosen as deliberately as it was later executed, with further motives becoming clear in time.

True as all this is, what has not been sufficiently recognized by Thoreau's critics and biographers is that for any American to go live in the woods immediately calls to mind living like an Indian. The forest life of fishing and simple farming, of watching the animals, of being wild and free is the stereotypical Indian life. In Thoreau's time, when many a New England village still had one or two old Indians, Negroes, and half-breeds living on its fringes—some of whom he visited on his travels and to whom he refers in *Walden*—this connection would have been even more obvious.[3] Moreover, even before the Walden experiment, friends of Thoreau's like Nathaniel Hawthorne had recognized that he was "inclined to lead a sort of Indian life among civilized men."

In particular, Hawthorne was impressed by his Indian refusal to work, "the absence of any systematic effort for a livelihood." But, carefully recording his detailed first impressions of Thoreau, just after they had met in September 1842, Hawthorne attributed a large number of Thoreau's most remarkable traits to this strange association. "Mr. Thorow," as he phonetically spelled the name, "is a keen and delicate observer of nature . . . and Nature, in return for his love, seems to adopt him as her especial child, and shows him secrets which few others are allowed to witness." Thoreau had "strange stories to tell" of his friendships with fish, birds, and animals, as well as herbs and flowers. He could give very accurate predictions of the weather. He could handle his boat with only one paddle, a skill he had learned on his own but then verified with some Indian

60

visitors to Concord. And strangest of all was his skill in finding arrowheads and relics. It was, Hawthorne believed, as if the red men's "spirits willed him to be the inheritor of their simple wealth."[4]

So to Thoreau's Concord friends it apparently came as no surprise that a man with these red gifts should wish, for a while, to lead a life even more emphatically Indian. Neither does it surprise people reading *Walden* today for the first time. Thoreau's life in the woods seems to carry out the popular American fantasy of going off to live like an Indian, in a basic and primitive fashion, close to nature. The savagist image of the Indian as a solitary and self-sufficient forest hunter makes this association almost inevitable.

Yet some clarification is therefore all the more important. What traditions did the tribes which Thoreau knew have for this kind of forest isolation? Did he know of them and was he consciously imitating them? Or was he basing his experiment more on white notions of how "the Indian" ideally lived? Simple as these questions are, they are not easy to answer.

The nearest Indian equivalent for Thoreau's two-year solitude is the adolescent's vision quest, of which Claude Lévi-Strauss has written as follows, summarizing the studies of modern anthropologists:

> Some young men set themselves adrift on solitary rafts without food; others seek solitude in the mountains where they have to face wild beasts, as well as cold and rain. For days, weeks or months on end, as the case may be, they do not eat properly, but live only on coarse food, or fast for long periods and aggravate their impaired physical condition by the use of emetics. Everything is turned into a means of communication with the beyond. They stay immersed for long periods in icy water, deliberately mutilate one or more of their finger-joints, or lacerate their fasciae by dragging heavy loads attached by ropes to sharpened pegs inserted under their dorsal muscles.[5]

None of this was Thoreau's intention. It is clear from his notes in his "Indian Books" that as late as 1854, when

61

Walden was published, he was unaware of the vision quest as a rite of passage of North American natives. Not until the twentieth century have anthropologists systematically identified and described it.[6] The nearest thing which he knew to self-tortures such as Lévi-Strauss describes were the penances of East Indian Brahmins, "sitting exposed to four fires and looking in the face of the sun," etc., which he compared to the unconscious self-tortures of average farmers and tradesmen (pp. 4-5). The more sensible purposes of the vision quest as such were unknown to him, and he ridiculed such excesses. Moreover, no traditional North American vision quest would have been as long as Thoreau's stay at Walden, without a woman and without constant companions. That would have been regarded only as a punishment for the asocial or a misfortune of the old survivors who remained on the fringes of white villages. "No good thing can be done by any man alone," was Black Elk's pronouncement to John G. Neihardt, as he made an offering to the "Spirit of the World" and included his friends in the dictating of his autobiography (*Black Elk,* p. 2). Only a mistaken but passionately imitative savagist white man would have undertaken such a prolonged voluntary exile as Thoreau's.

Yet some deeper purposes in Thoreau's experiment are similar to a vision quest. Lévi-Strauss compared the North American vision quest to the twentieth-century European youth's need to travel outside Europe, and indeed, to the young anthropologist's fieldwork. The quest is undertaken because the "institutions and customs [of one's original society] seem . . . like a mechanism the monotonous functioning of which leaves nothing to chance, luck or ability." To the quester, "the only means of compelling fate is to venture into those hazardous marginal areas where social norms cease to have any meaning, and where the protective laws and demands of the group no longer prevail; to go right to the frontiers of average ordered living, to the breaking point of bodily strength and to the extremes of physical and moral suffering" (Lévi-Strauss, p. 40). This, too, may overstate the physical sufferings of the quester, but they symbolize Thoreau's spiritual adventure. "Old deeds for old people, and new deeds for new," he said, indicating his need to break free of convention and to find the new life on the frontier. His savagist image of "the Indian" as the figure beyond the frontier—the aboriginal uniquely American—made an imitation of this life a way of escaping civilization and discovering what was wild and original in himself.

Walden, therefore, is the record of the vision quest of a Transcendental savage, and I would like to study it in this way, rather than in reference to the European, Puritan, or Emersonian traditions to which it has often been compared. I am not arguing that it corresponds to any particular quest form of American Indians. On the contrary, I will sometimes point out how different it is or how, to some Indians, Thoreau's activities might have seemed very strange or comical, obvious or pathetic. I will simply show how he begins with a primitivist critique of civilization and then attempts wild meditations. Thirdly, I will dwell on some of the visions and discoveries he made, and finally I will describe his renewals, represented in his kind of creation tale. It is a white quest. But it bears comparison with Indian ones because the white fictions of Indian life helped inspire it. Sometimes it penetrates beyond these fictions into truth.

PRIMITIVISM

At the outset of *Walden*, "savages" are exemplars of the economically simplified life. The score of references to the "uncivilized" native people of America, from the arctic to Tierra del Fuego, nearly all make this point. They live hardier and more rational lives than the mass of New Englanders. The other great exemplars of "simplicity, independence, magnanimity, and trust" are the "ancient philosophers, Chinese, Hindoo, Persian, and Greek" (pp. 14, 15). Unlike modern philosophers, they showed their wisdom in practical solutions to the basic problems of life. As he represents his own quest to live a simple and wise life, Thoreau repeatedly turns to the philosophers and savages to learn from them and to ridicule civilized complexity from their position.

Such a critique of civilization is, of course, in the tradition of philosophical primitivism. But where the traditional noble savages of Rousseau and Diderot criticized the institutions of civilization—such as marriage, education, justice, and religion—Thoreau's Indians represent simpler relations to the basic necessities of life: "Food, Shelter, Clothing, and Fuel" (p. 12). Since he is living alone, these are what matter. As he insistently shows, the ordinary New Englanders' failure to examine their relations to these necessities is what makes their life inwardly poor, even if outwardly luxurious.

Coming out of a still agrarian economy, Thoreau treats food most briefly. It could be grown, foraged, or caught near at hand, and, we can see from hindsight, it was a necessity for which European and Indian solutions differed least. From the beginning, Europeans had adopted Indian foods —the wild animals like deer and turkeys, the shellfish and seafoods, the berries and nuts, and also Indian corn, melons, beans, and pumpkins. European and Indian ways of preparing these differed, owing to the different cooking methods and spices (of salt, Thoreau says later, "I do not learn that the Indians ever troubled themselves to go after it" [p. 64]). But in many of the most common items of diet, New Englanders in the 1840s were eating Indian foods: succotash, cornbread, hasty pudding, cranberries, beans, fish, clams, and birds and game. The notable non-Indian foods were beef and pork, butter and cheese, and fruits like apples and pears. In his own diet, it is clear from the *Journal*, Thoreau continually preferred the wild native foods, especially berries. But he can say little about Indian food here because, by the very definitions of savagism, Indians were hunters and their foods gross and undesirable from both the civilized and the ideally primitive viewpoints. His problem, which is taken up in the chapters "The Bean-Field," "Baker Farm," and "Higher Laws," is to refine the savage

64

diet. Therefore, it is difficult to make that diet a standard by which to mock civilized luxury.

As for fuel, white New Englanders were again like the natives. They burned wood. Every farmer had his wood lot, and Emerson's was where Thoreau built his hut (though he does not tell this). The woodchopper was an essential person in the economy, as shown in the portrait of the French Canadian (Alek Therien) in the chapter "Visitors." Yet it is relevant to our own fuel-conscious times that throughout the 1840s and 1850s the price of firewood was steadily rising. It eventually became so expensive that people robbed woodpiles, and Thoreau noted in his *Journal* (Oct. 12, 1855) that he heard farmers were putting gunpowder under the bark as a threat and reprisal to thieves. This rise in cost also explains his preference for scavanging driftwood and stumps and his study of tree growth. Gradually people turned to coal. His foresight also appears in his satire here on the civilized waste of fuel. Europeans are not hardy; they shiver around a fire while "naked savages" stand further off sweating. They "go to the other side of the globe . . . and devote themselves to trade for ten or twenty years, in order that they may live,—that is, keep comfortably warm,—and die in New England at last. The luxuriously rich are not simply kept comfortably warm, but unnaturally hot . . . they are cooked, of course *à la mode*" (p. 14).

On clothing the opportunities for irony are greater. Since the European is taught from childhood that savages are either naked or else impractically overdressed in feathers, beads, and fancy furs, Thoreau equates savage and civilized foppery. "We are amused at beholding the costume of Henry VIII., or Queen Elizabeth, as much as if it was that of the King and Queen of the Cannibal Islands." The English are not superior or inferior to cannibals, but like them, and, perhaps, in more than clothes. "The childish and savage taste of men and women for new patterns keeps how many shaking and squinting through kaleidoscopes that they may discover the particular figure which this generation requires today. . . . Comparatively, tattooing is not the hideous custom which it is called. It is not barbarous merely because the printing is skin-deep and unalterable" (p. 26). Savages may be simple like philosophers in other things, but in clothing they are simple like children, and civilized men and women, whatever their pretensions, or because of them, are the same.

Thoreau is also deprecatory in his story of the Indian basketmaker who expected people to buy his baskets merely because he had made them. "He had not discovered that it was necessary for him to make it worth the other's while to buy them, or at least make him think that it was so, or to make something else which it would be worth his while to buy." Such an Indian is a silly Indian, a type he expected his readers to recognize. Yet he went on, in a veiled reference to people's not buying *A Week on the Concord and Merrimack Rivers*, his "basket of a delicate texture," to equate that Indian's mistake with his own. So, "instead of studying how to make it worth men's while to buy my baskets, I studied rather how to avoid the necessity of selling them" (p. 19).

The necessity which Thoreau studies longest is shelter. Here his own solution was the most unusual, as judged by the ordinary standards of Concord, but also most American, because similar to the frontier cabin. Yet what he emphasizes are the advantages of the Indian wigwam or tent, the shelter most unlike the white man's and which best symbolized the differences between their cultures. "Here . . . where wretched wigwams stood, the miserable abodes of savages," wrote John Filson, the propagandist of Daniel Boone and Kentucky, "we behold the foundations of cities laid," and Filson spoke the sentiments of all white America.[7] Wigwams, in the literature of savagism, are drafty, cramped, fouled with smoke, dark, and filthy. All the poverty and pity of the unimproved savage state came together in the lowly wigwam, while all the promise of civilization was in the house. Be it ever so humble, home sweet home was a house. But Thoreau takes a different view. Indian tents prove how little shelter we need, even in winter, while

66

Gookin's description of the ancient dwellings shows how practical the Indians were.

"The best of their houses are covered very neatly, tight and warm, with barks of trees, slipped from their bodies at those seasons when the sap is up, and made into great flakes, with pressure of weighty timber, when they are green. . . . The meaner sort are covered with mats which they make of a kind of bulrush, and are also indifferently tight and warm, but not so good as the former. . . . Some I have seen, sixty or a hundred feet long and thirty feet broad. . . . I have often lodged in their wigwams, and found them as warm as the best English houses." He adds, that they were commonly carpeted and lined within with well-wrought embroidered mats, and were furnished with various utensils. The Indians had advanced so far as to regulate the effect of the wind by a mat suspended over the hole in the roof and moved by a string. Such a lodge was in the first instance constructed in a day or two at most, and taken down and put up in a few hours; and every family owned one, or its apartment in one. (Pp. 29–30; ellipses Thoreau's)

Not only were wigwams larger and more comfortable than generally thought, a man did not have to work half his life to buy one. With only modest exertion every family had shelter. From this Thoreau deduced that Indian life permitted a great deal more freedom, for the individual could go his own way without having to pile up "superfluous property." Civilized life, on the contrary, is "an *institution*, in which the life of the individual is to a great extent absorbed, in order to preserve and perfect that of the race" (pp. 31–32).

On the same evidence—the simplicity and equality of Indian wigwams—he could have reached the opposite conclusion, that tribal life was more institutional and devoted to racial rather than individual welfare. And he would have been more correct. But he was thinking as a savagist, and the false conclusion was the one he drew and went on to live by. He rejected what he believed to be the civilized institutional life in favor of the savage individual life.

What he took to be "the very simplicity and nakedness of man's life in the primitive ages" also implied to him the life of "a sojourner in nature." The savage lived closer to nature because he had thinner walls between it and himself. "He dwelt, as it were, in a tent in this world, and was either threading the valleys, or crossing the plains, or climbing the mountain tops," says Thoreau, rewriting his Harvard essay on "Barbarities of civilized States" and still echoing the conventional ideology (p. 37). Wigwams meant both simplicity and closeness to nature, and the only reason he did not build one, he explains, is that in his neighborhood "boards and shingles, lime and bricks, are cheaper and more easily obtained than suitable caves, or whole logs, or bark in sufficient quantities, or even well-tempered clay or flat stones" (p. 40). The philosophical savage, the Transcendental Indian uses the materials at hand and so tries to "make our civilization a blessing."

After describing the hut he built, Thoreau then finds his symbol for his primitivist rejection of civilized excesses in the Mucclasse (or Creek) custom of the busk. The busk, as described by the naturalist William Bartram, was a " 'feast of first fruits' " before which everyone in a town cleaned house and burned all old clothes and equipment, leftover grain and provisions. Next, people fasted for three days and granted amnesty to all former offenders. On the fourth day, the high priest made a new fire, and people began a feast on their new year's food. It appeals to Thoreau because it would celebrate his own easier solutions to the necessities of life, but he also proposes it as an alternative to the civilized custom of the auction, where old possessions are not burned but taken out of one man's garret and moved on to another's. The busk is a ceremony of renewal, and so a perfect one for him to adopt.

But his retreat from civilization is not yet thoroughly defended. It can be said that he has run from the vices of civilization, but left the virtues of it too, that he has been selfish and not fulfilled his Christian responsibilities. Thus in the latter pages of "Economy" he returns to the subject of philanthropy, one of the major points of alleged pagan inferiority. Characteristically, his method is to attack, to say that philanthropy as a virtue "is greatly overrated; and it is our selfishness which overrates it" (p. 76). He even takes the point of behavior on which savages were believed to be most merciless and suggests that they had virtues as yet inconceivable to the Christian mind.

> The Jesuits were quite balked by those Indians who, being burned at the stake, suggested new modes of torture to their tormentors. Being superior to physical suffering, it sometimes chanced that they were superior to any consolation which the missionaries could offer; and the law to do as you would be done by fell with less persuasiveness on the ears of those, who, for their part, did not care how they were done by, who loved their enemies after a new fashion, and came very near freely forgiving them all they did. (P. 75)

Neither would he have missionaries and philanthropists coming to him. "If I knew for a certainty that a man was coming to my house with the conscious design of doing me good, I should run for my life" (p. 74). A man can do as much for the poor by his example, though it "leaves them far behind," as by his money. He will be like the Indians, therefore, and neither give nor receive charity. Or, as his Persian (*East* Indian) sage Sheik Sadi of Shiraz put it, he will "be an azad, or free man, like the cypress" (p. 79).

MEDITATION

In this reading of *Walden*, I am arguing that the book follows the pattern of a Transcendental Indian vision quest: rejection of village society, meditation, visions, and finally renewal or a sense of creation and re-creation. The beginning and end of this pattern or cycle are in the first two chapters, "Economy" and "Where I Lived, and What I Lived For," and the last two, "Spring" and "Conclusion." The more-meditative chapters are the third through seventh ("Reading," through "The Bean-Field") and the more openly visionary are the eighth through sixteenth ("The Village" through "The Pond in Winter"). I must hasten to add, though, that this division of the book is not rigid. The internal and organic structure of the book is the cycle of a year: from spring, when the building of the hut began; to summer, when Thoreau moved in; to autumn, when he completed the hut; and through winter to the following spring. Significantly, he did not number the "chapters," which are really more like interconnected individual essays. He wished his readers to see the annual process of renewal and the integrity of each event in his experience, not a numerical sequence of actions. He certainly did not proceed by a programmatic order of meditation and vision, like the stages of the cross. Equally important is the fact that each essay on the experience has its own large and small cycles of withdrawal (or encounter), meditation and discovery. The process of simplification and renewal had to go on constantly. " 'Renew thyself completely each day; do it again, and again, and forever again,' " the motto which king Tching-thang (Confucius) had engraved on his bathing tub, is a major precept, as important to Thoreau as his wish to brag like Chanticleer in the morning. Simplification is purifying; purification brings renewal. It was as daily an endeavor as bathing; and the day and the year, on the Transcendental calendar, were correspondent cycles.

Indian symbolism, coincidentally, makes a similar equation of day and year. Morning is like spring and noon like summer; fall is like evening and winter like night. And since each day or year has four parts and four is also the number of the directions, in the numerology of many American tribes four stands for completeness. In classic stories a person who is gone four days, or four years, has gone around the world and come back. Vision quests, traditionally, lasted four days, or as long as one could sensibly fast and with time enough to see everything. A person who has looked in four directions (and the contrasting and balancing ways symbolized by four directions) has, by the same logic, looked everywhere; he has, in the white man's game, "tagged all the bases." If he had been aware of this numerology, I am sure Thoreau would have appreciated it. Its diurnal, seasonal, and directional sense would have fit his own observations. And this, I confess, is another reason for my four-part organization of *Walden*. Withdrawal and meditation, vision and renewal make a whole; and they are both Thoreauvian and Indian.[8]

What Thoreau wished to meditate on at Walden, any college sophomore can say, was nature. Or, as Hawthorne summarized the "secrets" of nature in which Thoreau had special familiarity, beast, fish, fowl, and reptile; herb and flower; clouds and storms. Add trees, insects, ice, and pond, and you have a good list. But the nature he sought was wild or savage nature, and he wished to learn from it in the appropriate way, which was again Indian. He could have observed domestic nature from a corner in any garden or barn; he could have studied wild nature in a civilized way on a laboratory field trip. As he wrote in his early essay, "Natural History of Massachusetts," which was a critical review of just such scientific reporting, minute and factual but utterly lifeless and amoral, he sought "a more perfect Indian wisdom."

Thus the problem in Thoreauvian meditation is the proper attitude, and the chapters which I have singled out as the ones where the mood of meditation is dominant are, in effect, essays on *how* to observe and meditate more than on the subjects and discoveries made. And for this method, the examples given in the literature of savagism are paramount.

> I lived like the Puri Indians [a tribe of eastern Brazil, described by Ida Pfeiffer], of whom it is said that "for yesterday, to-day, and to-morrow they have only one word, and they express the variety of meaning by pointing backward for yesterday, forward for to-morrow, and overhead for the passing day." This was sheer idleness to my fellow-townsmen, no doubt; but if the birds and flowers had tried me by their standard, I should not have been found wanting. A

71

man must find his occasions in himself, it is true. The natural day is very calm, and will hardly reprove his indolence. (P. 112)

The leisure of the savage, then, is one prerequisite. Another, as this quotation implies, is silence, using just one word and gesturing in order to make the rest of the meaning clear. Still another is alertness, a component of being *awake*, and a regularly mentioned virtue of the independent hunter. In this patience, silence, and alertness he has learned from the very woods in which he lives and the animals which he hunts. Nature and her creatures are objects of meditation because, first and last, they teach it.

The chapter "Sounds" provides some excellent instruction in the method. It is, as Sherman Paul has written,[9] representative of the book, a vision quest in miniature. Coming just after the chapter "Reading" and before "Solitude," it presents a day of absolute leisure and solitude, a summer day when "I sat in my sunny doorway from sunrise till noon, rapt in revery," revery which continued through the whole afternoon and evening. Previously, he has been occupied with building the house and "burrowing" into the landscape (p. 98). Now he emerges, to look and listen. And yet, silent and relaxed as he is, alertness is still essential. "No method nor discipline can supersede the necessity of being forever on the alert" (p. 111). This is also an activity superior to work and reading, the "broad margin" to his life, a time "much over and above my usual allowance."

So situated, he records and composes the particular meditations of the summer afternoon, in which the progress of his thoughts and perceptions is relentlessly away from civilization and towards savage nature. As he begins, the loudest sound is the railroad rattling in the neighboring hills. Late in the evening, when he closes, the railroad has given way to far-off bells and the lowing of a cow; those domestic sounds have given way to whippoorwills, and the whippoorwills to screech owls and hoot owls. One by one the sounds and symbols of domestic nature die or are excluded. Even the rooster which might crow in the dawn is imaginatively replaced by the desired crowing of the cockrel, the "once wild Indian pheasant." "Instead. of no path to the front-yard gate in the Great Snow,—no gate,—no front-yard,—and no path to the civilized world!" (p. 128).

Thus time itself is one ally in this meditative retreat to wildness. Darkness, which brings the thought of winter and the Great Snow, a Thoreauvian metaphor for isolation and the ultimate endings, is also on the side of savagery. But he assists and presides over the process by being attuned, at every moment, to each wild sound and sight, and also by describing the most civilized intrusions in a wild manner. The railroad, as he first mentions it, has been "now dying away and then reviving like the beat of a partridge" (p. 114). The locomotive whistle sounds "like the scream of a hawk sailing over some farmer's yard" (p. 115). The loco-motive he refers to as "the iron horse" (pp. 116, 117). The sound of bells "at a sufficient distance over the woods . . . acquires a certain vibratory hum, as if the pine needles in the horizon were the strings of a harp which it swept" (p. 123). By a reverse of the same method, the wild sounds of late evening are compared to mournful or decadent human sounds: the screech owls to "midnight hags" and "fallen souls" (p. 124), the hoot owls to "dying moans" (p. 125), and the bullfrogs to "ancient wine-bibbers and wassail-ers" and drunken aldermen so paunchy that they can only belch, "tr-r-r-oonk, tr-r-r-oonk, tr-r-r-oonk" (p. 126). By this hour, too, Thoreau has begun to imitate the sounds, learning to make the noises of pond and forest. In his "more perfect Indian wisdom," one does not know an animal or bird until one can sound like it and talk to it.

One consequence of the prolonged meditations illustrated in "Sounds" is the secure discovery in "Solitude," the next essay, that "every little pine needle expanded and swelled with sympathy and befriended me" (p. 132). With visions, with a "natural society" all around, "we are never alone." And so, with his world better known, he can make his typical cheerful and ironic comments on the pleasures of his retreat. "I have a great deal of company in my house; especially in the morning, when nobody calls" (p. 137).

He has also become more sensitive to human presence. He has developed the skill which all Indians were supposed to have (at least, Cooper's) for detecting the slightest signs of people having been around his hut, "by the bended twigs or grass, or the print of their shoes, and generally of what sex or age or quality they were" (pp. 129–30). He can smell the scent of a cigar or pipe a thousand feet away. So he feels a sort of native authority about his premises and looks to the early Massachusetts natives for models of behavior. He tells how Edward Winslow of Plymouth Colony once went to visit Massasoit and was given nothing to eat. At night Winslow had to sleep on a plank, squeezed in between Massasoit, his wife, and two other men. The next day they were offered nothing but two small fish, which had to be divided among about forty people. So they soon departed, fearing they might not even have the strength to get home. Thoreau's judgment, however, is that the Indians had not been inhospitable. "They had nothing to eat themselves, and they were wiser than to think that apologies could supply the place of food to their guests; so they drew their belts tighter and said nothing about it." On another visit, when they had plenty, they fed Winslow well (p. 143). This kind of silence about his inconveniences and shortages, this sharing of both his feasts and his hunger is to be Thoreau's style of hospitality.

He also has respect for the French Canadian woodchopper, who is a later kind of native of the woods, an eater of wild meat and a person of strong opinions. At the end of "Visitors," having adopted these original habits, he is ready to greet the new "pilgrims" who have come "out to the woods for freedom's sake, and really left the village behind" with the words " 'Welcome, Englishmen! welcome, Englishmen!' " According to legend, these were Samoset's words to the Pilgrims at Plymouth.

Another consequence of his savage engagement is that

work itself has become a form of meditation, and so of discovery and renewal. We find this in the essay "The Bean-Field," as Thoreau found it in the planting and hoeing, by his calculation, of the "seven miles" of rows. Nothing could be less like the Thoreau of popular legend, certainly, than his undertaking this tedious labor, growing not just beans but also potatoes, corn, peas, and turnips. It is the life of a farmer, the antithesis of the hunter's. And, as he says, he gave it up the next year, to plant "such seeds, if the seed is not lost, as sincerity, truth, simplicity, faith, innocence, and the like." But plant and hoe the beans he did, and the gains were much more than the $8.71 1/2 of "pecuniary profit" which he prankishly figures for the editor of a farm journal.

It was, as he says, "a small Herculean labor." It attached him to earth, "and so I got strength like Antaeus." In the cultivating, he turned up arrowheads and firestones which proved to him that Indians had used the same field and grown the same crop (pp. 156, 159). It also brought him closer to the dews and rain which helped him and the woodchucks which ate the young shoots. It gave him contact with the "sacredness" of the farmer's calling, "its sacred origin" and the ancient festivals of the fields. On another level, it provided humor, as he overheard passersby gossip about his unorthodox practices and as he made up mock-heroics about his battles with weeds. He played by hoeing barefoot in the early morning and taking periodic breaks in the shade of the neighboring woods. The hard work is also proof of the pain that attends necessity. In all these ways the bean field and beans were teachers. They taught him, provoked these meditations; and he taught himself, invoking the meditations to relieve the labor.

From an Indian perspective, "The Bean-Field" is, in curious ways, a trickster tale. Tricksters, such as the Winnebago "Wakdjunkaga," the Chippewa "Manabozo," and the Cheyenne "Vihio," are gods remarkably like the Hercules Thoreau refers to. They set themselves impossible tasks, like boring through mountains and flying on eagles. They have herculean personal attributes, like great penises which could cross lakes for intercourse and bowels which could unloose catastrophic farts and mountains of dung. Morally, they mark the excesses of life and show how things came to be as they are now. On most occasions, therefore, the trickster god himself is less of a trickster than are the plants and animals who trick and teach him. He sticks his penis in a log, and a chipmunk bites it off; he makes a feast of ducks, and foxes steal it. Through these hilarious and yet instructive adventures, the trickster god is for the most part comically stupid, which is a nominal difference from Thoreau. Yet we can wonder at how stupid Thoreau was to plant seven miles of beans—and note that he, like the trickster, learned not to repeat his folly. Thoreau also studied his lessons more carefully than the trickster, but this is what listeners to the legends are meant to do with the trickster. When he wrote *Walden*, he knew little or nothing of these tales; and there are no trickster tales of bean fields. The connection is coincidental, the result of his naive encounter. The bean field taught him lessons, so he recited them for his own and his readers' edification, and for not a little self-mockery. "What shall I learn of beans or beans of me?" he asks innocently. The answer is, of course, a great deal— but not without work and meditation.[10]

VISIONS

Having established his familiarity with the woods, his relations with the human family are utterly changed. In the opening of "The Village" is a long balancing of the two, with a new vision of human society.

> As I walked in the woods to see the birds and squirrels, so I walked in the village to see the men and boys; instead of the wind among the pines I heard the carts rattle. In one direction from my house there was a colony of muskrats in the river meadows; under the grove of elms and buttonwoods in the other horizon was a village of busy men, as curious to me as if they had been prairie dogs, each sitting at the mouth of its burrow, or running over to a neighbor's to gossip. I went there frequently to observe their habits. (P. 167)

Birds and squirrels, men and boys; a colony of muskrats or a village of men are equal attractions. The writer is halfway between them, and they are similar. He observes the civilized "habits" as a civilized scientist would observe the wild. Telling of the village's appetite for "gossip," he uses the style of a scientific traveller describing some new-found tribe.

> I observed that the vitals of the village were the grocery, the barroom, the post-office, and the bank; and, as a necessary part of the machinery, they kept a bell, a big gun, and a fire-engine, at convenient places; and the houses were so arranged as to make the most of mankind, in lanes and fronting one another, so that every traveller had to run the gantlet, and every man, woman, and child might get a lick at him. (P. 168)

Running the gantlet was an Iroquois way of torturing prisoners (one also known in Europe, to be sure), and he goes on to say that his recourses were to run through as rapidly as possible, or to keep his thoughts on higher subjects, like Orpheus drowning the voices of the sirens, or to bolt aside and disappear over a fence or erupt into a friendly house. Afterwards come more extended similes describing his trips back home at night. He is like a ship sailing "for my snug harbor in the woods" (p. 169). Travellers who get lost are like ships which have sailed beyond "well-known beacons and headlands." "Not till we are lost, in other words, not till we have lost the world, do we begin to find ourselves, and realize where we are and the infinite extent of our relations" (p. 171). Then to conclude the chapter he describes his imprisonment for not paying his tax to "the state which buys and sells men, women, and children, like cattle at the door of its senate-house." Justifying his mode of disobedience, he uses the Malay word for a "furious attack." "It is true, I might have resisted forcibly . . . might have run 'amok' against society; but I preferred that society should run 'amok' against me, it being the desperate party" (p. 171).[11]

These complex comparisons, with their underlying theme

of village and state as savage and desperate, nature as familiar and gentle, signal the change of vision which his nesting in the woods has brought. He cannot speak of slavery as only a white and European-American custom, since he knew that it was practiced, in various forms, by many societies, including the American natives, but he now can feel more dissociated from it. It is not practiced in his quarter of the forest, where slaves (of all kinds) come for freedom. As if to emphasize this escape, in the next chapter, "The Ponds," he ranges "still farther westward," the direction of freedom (p. 173). On such rambles, he also makes his supper on huckleberries and blueberries and resumes his wild ingestions. On Walden, he breaks the silence by thumping his paddle against the side of the boat, or by playing his flute and charming the fish. Historically, the pond has various Indian associations. But since every pond, river, or hill in America has comparable legends, his way of *looking* at Walden is more important. It is as an ideal reflection of himself. He notes its colors at different seasons, at different distances from shore, and in different weather. He notes its rise and fall over the seasons and years. These means of study, in turn, enable him to see its reflections of the surrounding forest and forest life and further reflect them in himself. On a bright day in September or October, it is "a perfect forest mirror." He and it both reflect what is around them. That we are what we see is a universal aphorism, but the American Indian shamans, with their subtle experiential knowledge of vision and character, understood it well. He is now as deep and pure, sensitive and wild as the pond, his other self.

"Baker Farm" and "Higher Laws" bring to mind another ancient (and Biblical) aphorism, that we are what we eat. From different perspectives, these essays return to the necessity of food and the civilized and savage diets. In the first, Thoreau tells of a visit, during a rainshower which interrupted a fishing trip, to the hut of John Field and his family, an Irish immigrant who works at "bogging," i.e., turning over meadow for a farmer. Field is an example of the "degraded poor" who would be better off living in a wigwam. He works hard but has no security and freedom. The annual rent for his dismal hut is almost as much as the total cost of Thoreau's, and he finds it necessary to use tea, coffee, milk, butter, and beef, believing that "a gain in coming to America" is having these things daily. But the only true America, lectures Thoreau, "is that country where you are at liberty to pursue such a mode of life as may enable you to do without these" (p. 205). Their meeting is the more involved because Thoreau once thought of living at Baker farm himself, and is now rejoicing he did not. Field's sorry life discloses what the poetry of rural life neglects, and as Thoreau resumes his fishing trip, on which Field later joins him, he praises wild life instead. "Grow wild according to thy nature, like these sedges and brakes, which will never become English hay. . . . Enjoy the land, but own it not" (p. 207).

Having responded to John Field as might a hunter, in "Higher Laws" Thoreau tries to reach an ethic above the hunter's. In the opening of the chapter, wildness reappears in "a woodchuck stealing across my path," making Thoreau wish to "devour him raw; not that I was hungry then, except for that wildness which he represented." "I found in myself, and still find, an instinct toward a higher, or, as it is named, spiritual life, as do most men, and another toward a primitive rank and savage one, and I reverence them both. I love the wild not less than the good." He attributes this, and his initial acquaintance with nature, to the hunting he did as a boy. Hunters know nature "practically or instinctively," and Thoreau terms such knowledge "a true *humanity*, or account of human experience" (pp. 210–11). Hunters are also the more *humane* of humans, and he believes that "there is a period in the history of the individual, as of the race, when the hunters are the 'best men,' as the Algonquins called them" (p. 212).

Nevertheless, he now objects to the "uncleanness" of animal food and wishes to pass beyond this stage of life. "The gross feeder is a man in the larva state; . . . I have no doubt

79

that it is a part of the destiny of the human race, in its gradual improvement, to leave off eating animals, as surely as the savage tribes have left off eating each other when they came in contact with the more civilized" (pp. 215–16).

The whole argument is within the structure of savagism. For Christian Americans to have a moral right to succeed the Indians, they must live a purer life, and a fleshless diet is basic to it. He has not been able to moderate the issue with the proverb, "Not that food which entereth into the mouth defileth a man, but the appetite with which it is eaten." Eating and drinking is still a "slimy beastly life" (p. 218). So in the end he can only look forward to the day when a New Englander named "John Farmer" bathes after a hard day's work, plays the flute, and thinks of "some new austerity" which will redeem his body. It is a very Puritan and Brahminic solution.

Obviously, Thoreau was not acquainted with the Indian practice, in which not only did people hunt for no more than was needed, but they also honored the animals which sustained them. They made their food animals part of tribal ritual, examples of generosity. Dekanawida, the law-giver of the Five Nations, instructed his Royaneh, a society of "bereaved chiefs" who were counselors and wise men, to wear deer antlers, because "their strength came from the meat of the deer."[12] Deer were the gift which supported the people, the source of food, clothing, and wisdom. For like reasons the Plains Indians placed a buffalo skull on the center pole of their sun-dance lodges. To the missionaries and other European visitors such customs seemed so depraved that they made no effort to understand or report them fairly, and so Thoreau could not learn. The Indian hunter's ritual (and practical) expression of purity came in his sweat baths and chastity before hunting; Thoreau's idea of purity was chastity and avoidance of meat-eating altogether. It is a noble but unrealistic consequence of his savagism. Frowning on farmers because they were so often drudges and not free hunters, yet frowning on hunters because he wished something "Higher," he left himself, as his preferred diet, only clams and berries. He became a wild gatherer.

Surely another reason why he did not like to eat meat, though, was his exquisite delight in the living animals. They were as much a part of his vision quest as of any traditional one, and he was too fond of them to eat them. He studied them less as a hunter than as a poet and shaman, learning about himself and his environment. As he says in "Brute Neighbors":

> Why do precisely these objects which we behold make a world? Why has man just these species of animals for his neighbors; as if nothing but a mouse could have filled this crevice? I suspect that Pilpay & Co. have put animals to their best use, for they are all beasts of burden, in a sense, made to carry some portion of our thoughts. (P. 225)

The basis of animal stories, red and white both, is that animals are teachers. They exemplify various kinds of human behavior, and different people, in turn, resemble different animals. We recognize this in daily speech when we say that someone is "brave as a lion," "quiet as a mouse," or "cunning as a fox." We also regard some species as favorably or unfavorably instructive in their social forms: the crowding and discipline of the anthill, the status in the chickens' pecking order, the industriousness of beavers, the tribal solidarity of the wolf pack. Learning these associations is such an essential part of one's upbringing that even urban children are given them—in story books, television, zoos, and so on. It is as necessary as language. Without references to animals we would have difficulty talking about human beings; we would have, to use Thoreau's words, no "beasts of burden . . . to carry some portion of our thoughts." And it may very well be, as Thoreau suggests, that these metaphors and the animal fables, like Pilpay's Sanskrit ones, are the "best use," better than for food or work.

As he further says, the precise aggregation of animals which we behold around us makes our world. Ecologically, regions of the earth support different animals, and the ani-

81

mals, in turn, participate in those regional food chains and cycles of fertility. Psychologically and anthropologically, people vary according to the animals they favor and use. Before the white man's coming, Thoreau learned from his reading, native American people had domesticated only one animal, the dog. White men's horses seemed marvelous and changed the whole way of life on the American plains, but frail chickens and sheep, smelly cows and pigs seemed unnecessarily burdensome and ravenous. Their dependence on man was strange, too. Even today some Indians refer to cattle as "slow elk."[13] Older Indians did not make the white man's distinctions between wild and tame.

> We did not think of the great open plains, the beautiful rolling hills, and winding streams with tangled growth as wild. Only to the white man was nature a wilderness and only to him was the land infested with wild animals and savage people. To us it was tame. Earth was bountiful and we were surrounded with the blessings of the Great Mystery. Not until the hairy man from the east came and with brutal frenzy heaped injustices upon us and the families we loved was it wild for us. When the very animals of the forest began fleeing from his approach, then it was for us that the Wild West began.[14]

Animals were brothers and sisters, parents and grandparents. They were, as Thoreau knew, "totems" designating different clans and associations. Or, as Thoreau did not know (though he grasped the general idea), they were "medicines."[15] They were observed closely because they could give warnings of changes in the weather, of an approaching fire, or of other animals who were near. And the "ways" of different animals expressed the "ways" of different people. One's animal medicine showed in everything one did: walking, seeing, listening, getting up in the morning or going to bed at night.

In European traditions these vital animal metaphors have become overly codified. The European usages are also, obviously, foreign to America. We thoughtlessly say "hungry as a wolf"; a native American might say, as did the

Sioux writer Charles Eastman, "hungry and thirsty as a moose in burned timber."[16] Children's (and adults') expensive picture books pay great attention to large or exotic animals from far away, but relatively little attention to those of America, like ringtail cats, wapiti, jumping mice, and pronghorns. Yet if white Americans were ever to discover their land and know themselves, they would have to know these native teachers in their full complexity. Having regarded so many of them as dangerous or as pests, because they eat crops, or farm animals, or occasionally attack a person, white men have supposed them wild in the sense of ferocious. But to Thoreau, who saw in his reading of the Hannah Dustan story that it was the white man who thought nature a wilderness, they were wild only in the sense of free and undomesticated. They were not dangerous, if known and respected, and they could teach a person to be free and undomesticated too.

The other great difference between European and native attitudes towards animals seems to derive from the Biblical instruction that Adam and Eve were to "subdue" the earth and "have dominion over the fish of the sea, and over the fowl of the air, and over every living thing that moveth upon the earth." This sets human beings up either as stewards over animals (to say it most positively) or as killers (to say the worst), and supposes animals inferior. Being more pantheistic and less authoritarian in their models for relationships, Indian religions tended to regard all nature as in the image of the Creator and Great Mystery. Therefore, once one gets outside the European value systems that dominated the early immigrants, the idea that only man is in God's image is foolish. Man is not at liberty to subdue nature and behave imperiously, condescendingly, or sentimentally towards animals. If there is any subduing that must be done, it is that man must subdue himself. He is the dangerous creature to other creatures and to himself. And animals can help people to subdue, know, and laugh at themselves. Some of these assumptions are, to be sure, present in the fables of Aesop, La Fontaine, and others; but over the centuries in which Europeans have become increasingly estranged from animals, the fables have become reductive moral allegory and the animals' traits simplified and stylized. Indians could not reduce to simple moralisms animals, whose behavior was so intricate and wonderful, a full mirror of human behavior. Nor could they be sentimental; they had to hunt and eat.

For Thoreau, therefore, completely seeing each animal— wondering that "nothing but a mouse could have filled this crevice"—was essential to seeing America, his world, and himself. He wished the native knowledge and more—"a more perfect Indian wisdom." One of the most neglected parts of *Walden* is the repeated study of animals, which comes to a peak in the four fall and winter chapters, "Brute Neighbors," "House-Warming," "Former Inhabitants; and Winter Visitors," and "Winter Animals." The first is about the partridges, raccoons, woodcocks, otters, woodchucks, runaway domestic cats, loons, and ducks seen around the pond, and also the war of red and black ants which he studied for most of a day. "House-Warming" primarily describes his finishing off of the chimney and walls, as he prepares for winter—a seasonal move also marked by the coming indoors of wasps, the southbound flight of geese, and the nesting of moles in his cellar. The next, though more engaged with people, carries forward the comparisons and balancings of people and animals made before in "The Village" and the summer "Visitors" chapter. Since he had human visitors less frequently, he would still go to town, "like a friendly Indian" now, or would tramp "eight or ten miles through the deepest snow to keep an appointment among the pines" or stand for half an hour in the snow feeling "a slumberous influence" from a drowsy barred owl (pp. 265–67). In "Winter Animals" we are again aware of winter as a test of survival, developing foresight and endurance, memory and intellect. Here the animals are examples of how to stay warm and store food or continue to travel and forage.

In these chapters the difference between Thoreau's animal wisdom and the Indians'—actual or imagined, according to the prejudices of savagism—is that he presents his in the form of discovery. He was, after all, still an explorer; his observations were new to him. The older Americans had built up their knowledge over the ages, and it was passed on in traditional stories and learned by children. In "Brute Neighbors" Thoreau tells with pleasure how he befriended a mouse while building his hut, feeding it crumbs from his lunch and letting it run up his clothes and along his sleeve. On the other hand, Charles Eastman says in a book for white children that between the ages of seven and ten he and other boys used to snare mice and then set them loose on a tiny island or enclosure where they could play with them.[17] Eastman also played with crows and magpies, squirrels, gophers, and rabbits; he and his friends made pets of "young foxes, bears, wolves, raccoons, fawns, buffalo calves and birds of all kinds."[18] At the end of "Brute Neighbors" Thoreau recounts at length the game he played one afternoon on the pond with a loon. (See also *Journal*, Oct. 8, 1852.) The loon would dive, he would expect it to go one way, and it would come up having gone another. It seemed to laugh at him, "a long-drawn unearthly howl . . . perhaps the wildest sound that is ever heard here, making the woods ring far and wide. I concluded that he laughed in derision of my efforts, confident of his own resources" (p. 236). Eastman tells a different story.

> Up on Seine Bay [in Ojibway country] the favorite sport was hunting the loon, which scarcely ever takes to the wing, but dives on being approached. Most people would be put to it to guess in which direction he would reappear, at a distance of from a quarter to half a mile, but [the Ojibway] have learned his secret. As soon as he goes under, the canoes race for a certain point, and invariably the bird comes up among them. He is greeted with derisive laughter and cheers and immediately dives again, and the maneuver is repeated until he is winded and caught.[19]

Thoreau, having his first experience with a loon, could not yet think like one and laugh back at it. He was awed by it.

Yet neither would he simply come out to the pond like the hunters from the village, "at least ten men to one loon," then lose patience and "beat a retreat to town and shop and unfinished jobs" (pp. 233–34). He had the patience and quiet of the Indian hunter as celebrated in white legend.

One of Thoreau's most interesting animal studies is the ant war. As he rather pedantically informs us, there is European literary precedent for such descriptions, but his own seems to go beyond the usual mock-heroic. One moral is pretty obvious: men and ants are the creatures most alike in the ferocious arts of war. But in most parts of his description Thoreau does not use the red and black ants simply to satirize men, or praise them only ironically to show the pettiness of war. Their battles are so absorbing and their sufferings and heroism so genuine that satire drops out. Thoreau instead enlarges the reader's sense of wonder at the fullness of life, even in so minute and neglected an arena. Yet for a dig at his own enemies he does conclude with the satirist's reference to monarchs and human events. "The battle which I witnessed took place in the Presidency of Polk, five years before the passage of Webster's Fugitive-Slave Bill" (p. 232).

Neither is Thoreau inclined towards the most extreme practices of the Indian shaman. In the interesting modern occult books of Carlos Castaneda, *The Teachings of Don Juan, A Separate Reality*, and *Journey to Ixtlan*, Don Juan, a Yaqui Indian, can assume animal identities—can, for instance, become a crow. Such assertions have been made by many mystics, Indian and non-Indian, for centuries. But in his "Indian Books" Thoreau showed little credence in these acts of the "jugglers" or "pow-wows." "It is astonishing how few facts of importance are added in a century to the natural history of any animal," he had said in "Natural History of Massachusetts," and this is one standard in his judgment of the jugglers and powwows. Do they add to "the natural history of any animal"? He is also skeptical out of respect for reality itself. "Shams and delusions are esteemed for soundest truths, while reality is fabulous," he said earlier, echoing Emerson's rejection of Christian miracles (p. 95). Thoreau, coming from democratic and Protestant traditions which had long considered mystification the device of charlatans and priestly overlords, wanted to expand his personal power and sense of self in ways interpretable to other men and women. Whether the shamans in the Indian nations of Thoreau's time were egotistical mystagogues or sincere servants using their knowledge as best they could for the benefit of their people, is a point which can probably never be answered. However, Thoreau, as a Transcendental Indian, sought visions of birds and wild animals in order to expand his reality with theirs, not to reach a "nonordinary reality." To him reality was not ordinary.

Operating in this way, Thoreau does make some extraordinary discoveries, at least for an immigrant American. The ant war does prove that men and ants are the most warlike creatures in the forest. His study of foxes leads him to the equally unusual discovery that foxes are not as cunning as alleged. Experienced hunters tell him "that if the fox would remain in the bosom of the frozen earth he would be safe, or if he would run in a straight line away no fox-hound could overtake him; but, having left his pursuers far behind, he stops to rest and listen till they come up, and when he runs he circles round to his old haunts, where the hunters await him" (p. 277). So the tricky fox tricks himself. With the help of another old hunter and the records of a Concord merchant, Thoreau also recalls the time when bears and wildcats were hunted in the area and skins were traded for rum. But it is finally the hares and partridges which gain his respect as the true spirits of the woods. Looking one winter evening at a hare just six feet from his door, he begins to pity it. But when he takes a step, it lightly and gracefully springs off across the crusted snow. It is slender for a purpose. Rabbits and partridges, he says, "are still sure to thrive, like true natives of the soil, whatever revolutions occur" (p. 281). They are safe both in the forest and in the bushes which grow up when a forest is cut. They are not so noble as the vanished bigger animals, but they go back to that era and will survive into new eras. They are suitable medicine for a wild New Englander.

CREATION TALES

In *The Savage Mind*, Claude Lévi-Strauss, in speculating about the intellectual method of prescientific people, introduced the anthropological profession to the French word *bricolage*. It derives from the old verb *bricoler*, which was "always used with reference to some extraneous movement: a ball rebounding, a dog straying or a horse swerving from its direct course to avoid an obstacle." Another derivative, *bricoleur*, is a modern French word which Lévi-Strauss says could be translated as a "jack of all trades or a kind of professional do-it-yourself man," someone very skilled at making ingenious repairs and improvements out of whatever tools and materials are at hand. On a manual level, then, bricolage is the activity of such a clever fix-it man and wizard of the shop, and Lévi-Strauss uses it to describe a similar kind of ingenious intellectual activity. "Mythical thought is," he proposes, "a kind of intellectual 'bricolage.'" "Like 'bricolage' on the technical plane, mythical reflection can reach brilliant unforeseen results on the intellectual plane." It catalogues diverse materials and observations. It is constantly receptive to new insights. It is systematic, though not systematic in the way the scientist is, just as the bricoleur is not systematic in the way the engineer is. The engineer, says Lévi-Strauss, in another illuminating contrast, "is always trying to make his way out of and go beyond the constraints imposed by a particular state of civilization while the 'bricoleur' by inclination or necessity always remains within them."[20]

The terms bricoleur and bricolage apply very well to Thoreau. In *Henry Thoreau as Remembered by a Young Friend*, Emerson's son Edward Waldo Emerson provides wonderful testimony of Thoreau's skill at fixing pumps, grafting fruit trees, repairing doors and windows, and improving the graphite used in the family business. He could turn himself to any domestic or village task. He had, said

Edward, what New Englanders used to call "faculty,"[21] which seems like a better term than the now trite "Yankee ingenuity," since it doesn't apply just to industrial inventiveness but to skill in garden, orchard, and woods as well. Thoreau was one of Concord's most sought-after bricoleurs, we could say. And the descriptions in *Walden* of all the phases of building the hut, from obtaining the used boards to bricking up the chimney and plastering the walls, are more illustration of his manual bricolage. His vast collection of Indian arrowheads, mortars, pestles, bowls and other stone and clay implements, along with the repeated study of Indian techniques of building canoes, fish-weirs, and lodges proves that he was equally curious about the skills of native bricoleurs. "How much more we might have learned of the aborigines," he wrote in his *Journal* on March 20, 1858 (having found a willow creel in the sluiceway of a brook and wondered whether it was Indian or English),"if they had not been so reserved! Suppose that they had generally become the laboring class among the whites, that my father had been a farmer and had an Indian for his hired man, how many aboriginal ways we children should have learned from them!" New England children of his generation had not had the Faulknerian Sam Fathers so important to the white children of the frontier South, and Thoreau wished that he could have acquired "aboriginal ways" more directly.

But as he puzzled out Indian methods of building, so did he develop for himself the intellectual bricolage of native America, and the concluding chapters of *Walden* show how this process worked. It is, to use Lévi-Strauss's language again, a matter of mythical reflection and a matter of using facts symbolically, while looking for the signs in nature which stand suggestively between fact and general truth.

His further studies of Walden Pond are one example. The middle of "The Pond in Winter" is devoted to the survey he made late in the winter of 1846 by cutting through the ice and taking soundings with "a cod-line and a stone weighing about a pound and a half." The resulting chart that he made—which is printed in some editions of *Walden*, including the new Princeton edition—shows seventy-two different soundings ("more than a hundred" is his statement of the total he made [p. 289]), and these are evenly spaced along eleven directional lines. Some readers of Thoreau who have felt that his mere data-gathering increased as his Transcendental vision dimmed may cite this survey as an instance of his coming decline. But Thoreau's purpose was not merely to gather scientific data; it was, initially, only to disprove the local legends that the pond had no bottom, had holes as wide as a load of hay and "reached quite through to the other side of the globe." He was, he says mischievously, "desirous to recover the long lost bottom of Walden Pond." So he was scientific only in the sense that he preferred accurate facts to marvelous ignorance. But as he looks over his findings, what seizes his imagination is that the pond's "line of greatest length intersected the line of greatest breadth *exactly* at the point of greatest depth" (p. 289). This and other generalizations about the continuity of points and sandbars, coves and their depths, then lead on to generalizations about human character and ethics. The depths and dimensions of the pond are mythologized.

With his nineteenth-century surveyor's instruments, his pencils and notebooks, Thoreau is technologically a long way from the people who stood on the Walden ice two hundred years and more before him. But even though his instruments and specific information are different, his ways of thought seem coincidental. We know, unfortunately, very little about the minds and mythology of the Wampanoags and other people of what is now New England. Their culture was destroyed before this mythology could be learned, before there was even open-minded interest in it. But we can still safely assume that in general outline the mythologies and bricolage of all the people of the northeastern woodlands were roughly similar. Besides, by the early 1850s Thoreau's interest in Indians had spread far beyond interest in the natives of Massachusetts and New Hampshire. By this time he had also increased his reading of

East Indian and Asian philosophy, and had no resistance
to unifying ideas which were Indian, Asian, Emersonian,
and his own. It pleases him, for instance, when an occasional Walden ice cutter falls in the water: this is Squaw
Walden's revenge on these men for stripping off her winter
coat. And it pleases him that some of the ice these men cut
is shipped around the world to Bombay and Calcutta. This
completes a circle. He bathes his intellect in the Bhagavad-
Gita; the residents of India "drink at my well." "The pure
Walden water is mingled with the sacred water of the
Ganges" (p. 298). As "bricoleur," he uses whatever materials fit, something American Indians themselves did when
they mingled Christian stories and teachings with their
own. These are the intellectual methods of the handyman,
not the engineer.

Thoreau's most elaborate myth-making occurs in "Spring."
There, from observations of the slight changes in Walden's
ice and its cracking and thundering he discovers that the
pond is still sensitive even when frozen. He also realizes:

> The phenomena of the year take place every day in a
> pond on a small scale. Every morning, generally speaking,
> the shallow water is being warmed more rapidly than the
> deep, though it may not be made so warm after all, and
> every evening it is being cooled more rapidly until the
> morning. The day is an epitome of the year. The night is
> the winter, the morning and evening are the spring and
> fall, and the noon is the summer. (P. 301)

The idea that "the day is an epitome of the year" is, as I
have said, basic in American Indian stories, and, of course,
in other cultures. But Thoreau presents it as a personal discovery, a natural insight from a natural life.

Then, from the observation of the ice on Walden, he
looks for other first signs of spring, finding his earliest delight in the tracings made by thawing sand and clay in a
steep bank above the railroad tracks. With the lavalike
flows of the little globules of colorful sand and clay making
patterns which resemble leaves, vines, the claws of animals
and birds, the cords of brains and bowels, this thawing

91

seems to him to express an essential form found everywhere in the universe.

> When I see on the one side the inert bank,—for the sun acts on one side first,—and on the other this luxuriant foliage, the creation of an hour, I am affected as if in a peculiar sense I stood in the laboratory of the Artist who made the world and me,—had come to where he was still at work, sporting on this bank, and with excess of energy strewing his fresh designs about. (P. 306)

Thawing, therefore, is not just a sign of spring, it is the act of creation. The world ("and me") began with an "Artist" melting frozen sand and clay, releasing them and the very atoms inside them to break out into these designs of lobes and leaves. With the excitement of the Original-Artist, Thoreau traces the patterns himself: into language and the shapes of the mouth forming words like "λείβω, *labor, lapsus*" and "λοβός, *globus*, lobe, globe" into the patterns of birds' wings, grubs and butterflies; and into the shapes of trees and river systems ("whose pulp is intervening earth, and towns and cities are the ova of insects in their axils").

> Thus it seemed that this one hillside illustrated the principle of all the operations of Nature. The Maker of this earth but patented a leaf. What Champollion will decipher this hieroglyphic for us, that we may turn over a new leaf at last? This phenomenon is more exhilarating to me than the luxuriance and fertility of vineyards. True, it is somewhat excrementitious in its character, and there is no end to the heaps of liver lights and bowels, as if the globe were turned wrong side outward; but this suggests at least that Nature has some bowels, and there again is mother of humanity. This is the frost coming out of the ground; this is Spring. It precedes the green and flowery spring, as mythology precedes regular poetry. I know of nothing more purgative of winter fumes and indigestions. It convinces me that Earth is still in her swaddling clothes, and stretches forth baby fingers on every side. Fresh curls spring from the baldest brow. There is nothing inorganic. These foliaceous heaps lie along the bank like the slag of a furnace, showing that

Nature is "in full blast" within. The earth is not a mere fragment of dead history, stratum upon stratum like the leaves of a book, to be studied by geologists and antiquaries chiefly, but living poetry like the leaves of a tree, which precede flowers and fruit,—not a fossil earth, but a living earth; compared with whose great central life all animal and vegetable life is merely parasitic. Its throes will heave our exuviæ from their graves. You may melt your metals and cast them into the most beautiful moulds you can; they will never excite me like the forms which this molten earth flows out into. And not only it, but the institutions upon it, are plastic like clay in the hands of the potter. (Pp. 308–9)

A typical Indian creation story is much more of a story, with narrative and characters, and not necessarily so lyrical as this; but in important other ways it is remarkably similar. One of the most common is the story of a creator asking various birds and animals to dive under water and bring up earth, and in the reading recorded in his "Indian Books" Thoreau found at least two versions of it. The first he found in E. G. Squier, *The Serpent Symbol, and the Worship of the Reciprocal Principles of Nature in America* (New York: Putnam, 1851), and he copied it out in the fourth volume of his "Indian Books," as nearly as can be determined, in early August 1851. The second version, on which he made briefer notes, in "Indian Book," vol. 6, he found in the *Jesuit Relations*, 1633, which he borrowed from the Harvard Library on October 5, 1852.[22]

In Squier's "Serpent Symbol in America," [Thoreau's note begins] I find an "Algonquin Tradition of the Evil Serpent" —describing a contest between their Great Teacher Manabozho, and a Great Serpent, the spirit of evil, which involves the destruction of the earth by water, . . . from which I extract the following. Manabozho having actually wounded the Great Serpent with his arrow the latter in revenge deluges the earth.

"Then he (Manabozho) gathered together timber, and made a raft, upon which the men & women, and the animals that were with him, all placed themselves. No sooner had they done so, than the rising floods closed over the mountain, and they floated alone on the surface of the waters. And thus they floated for many days, and some died, and the rest became sorrowful, and reproached Manabozho that he did not disperse the waters and renew the earth, that they might live. But though he knew that his great enemy was by this time dead, yet could not Manabozho renew the world unless he had some earth in his hands wherewith to begin the work. And this he explained to those that were with him, and he said that were it ever so little, even a few grains of earth, then could he disperse the waters, and renew the world. Then the beaver volunteered to go to the bottom of the deep, and get some earth, and they all applauded her design. She plunged in; they waited long, and when she returned, she was dead; they opened her hands, but there was no earth in them. Then said the otter, 'Will I seek the earth;' and the bold swimmer dived from the raft. The otter was gone still longer than the beaver, but when he returned to the surface, he too was dead, and there was no earth in his claws. 'Who shall find the earth,' exclaimed all those on the raft, 'now that the beaver & the otter are dead?' And they desponded more than before, repeating, 'Who shall find the earth?' 'That will I' said the muskrat, and he quickly disappeared between the logs of the raft. The muskrat was gone very long, much longer than the otter, and it was thought he would never return, when he suddenly rose near by, but he was too weak to speak, and he swam slowly towards the raft. He had hardly got upon it, when he too died from his great exertion. They opened his little hands, and there, closely clasped between the fingers, they found a few grains of fresh earth. These Manabozho carefully collected and dried them in the sun, and then he rubbed them into fine powder in his palms, and rising up, he blew them abroad upon the waters. No sooner was this done than the flood began to subside, and soon the trees on the mountains and hills emerged from the deep, and the plains and the valleys came in view and the waters disappeared from the land, leaving no trace but a thick sediment, which was the dust Manabozho had blown abroad from the raft." (4/97–99)

Nineteenth-century collectors of Indian stories such as Squier repeatedly missed the lesson that the creation here is continuous and still happening. Taking the analogous Biblical stories of the Creation and the Flood as literal historical fact, they assumed that Indians believed the same of their stories. But this is not only a story of the Creation, it applies to creation all around us. First there is flux, a floating point in a flood, until by diving into the flux, someone establishes a dimension and reaches an opposite. There is earth to balance against water, and with care and inspiration, touch and imagination, the earth displaces the water. Such might be one reading of it. Another truth in the story may be that otters dive deeper than beavers and muskrats deeper than otters. People are the same, which the story emphasizes in referring to the animals as having hands, not front feet. As the attempt to create goes on, the less patient people give up and die. It takes a strong person to keep the faith and sustain the operation.

We may also suspect that the story is garbled because most versions of it have four divers rather than three. Three is a European-Christian totality—past, present, and future; Father, Son, and Holy Ghost—and it is likely that Squier or his informant, accustomed to sequences of threes in all jokes, try-try-again, prayers and punctuations, lost patience after two trials and shortened it. But even with suspicious features, the story is still of creation, and Thoreau liked it well enough to copy it out—and to observe muskrats with great care ever after. (See *Journal, passim*. He also came to call them by the Indian word musquash.)

There are, however, many more questions. Did he read this story before or after making up his own creation tale of the sand foliage? The sand foliage myth is very short in *Walden*'s "First Version."

> As I go back and forth over the rail-road through the deep cut I have seen where the clayey sand *like lava* had flowed down when it thawed and as it streamed it assumed the forms of vegetation, of vines and stout pulpy leaves—unaccountably interesting and beautiful—which methinks I

95

have seen imitated somewhere in bronze—as if its course were so to speak a diagonal between fluids & solids— and it were hesitating whether to stream in to a river, or into vegetation—for vegetation too is such a stream as a river, only of slower current.[23]

And in the *Journal* for January 29, 1852, it is still only in embryo.

I have come to see the clay and sand in the Cut. A reddish tinge in the earth, stains. An Indian hue is singularly agreeable, even exciting, to the eye. Here the whole bank is sliding. Even the color of the subsoil excites me, as if I were already getting near to life and vegetation. This clay is fæcal in its color also. It runs off at the bottom into mere shoals, shallows, vasa, vague sand-bars, like the mammoth leaves,—makes strands.

He would have read at least the Squier version of the Algonquin story before seeing the Artist in the Cut. But would he have thought of the Algonquin story as an allegory of continuous creation and re-creation? One thing sure is that in the winter and spring of 1852 he was beginning to see Indian hues frequently.

I love that the rocks should appear to have some spots of blood on them, Indian blood at least; to be convinced that the earth has been crowded with men, living, enjoying, suffering, that races passed away have stained the rocks with their blood. (*Journal*, March 4, 1852)

A month and a half later, looking at dwarf andromeda leaves across a pond, with the sun behind them:

. . . from this position alone I saw, as it were, through the leaves which the opposite sun lit up, giving to the whole this charming, warm, what I call *Indian*, red color,—the mellowest, the ripest, red imbrowned color. (April 17, 1852)

Four days later, hearing a robin in the woods, he suddenly

heard him even as he might have sounded to the Indian, singing at evening upon the elm above his wigwam, with which was associated in the red man's mind the events of an Indian's life, his childhood. Formerly I had heard in it only those strains which tell of the white man's village life; now I heard those strains which remembered the red man's life, such as fell on the ears of Indian children. (April 21, 1852)

The result was that later in "Spring" in *Walden*,

> I heard a robin in the distance, the first I had heard for many a thousand years, methought, whose note I shall not forget for many a thousand more,—the same sweet and powerful song as of yore. (P. 312)

He had Indians on the brain. He was seeing their color in the clay of the railroad embankment, the blood on the rocks, and through the leaves of the dwarf andromeda. And as he heard the robin, its song was suddenly wild again, a *red* robin!

We are, admittedly, in a realm of speculation, trying to imagine the currents running along the wires of the writer's brain and out to the tips of his fingers, the lashes of his eyes, wondering whether he could transcend the errors and limitations of the garbled sources he used, cut through the errors in his own savagist prejudgments, and see an Indian legend's electric correspondence with his most skillful and naked perceptions. Indian he was trying to be. We hear the echoes of Indian speech in "The earth is all alive and covered with papillae," "There is nothing inorganic," and, from the concluding chapter, "The life in us is like the water in the river." They are sentences as universal as the grass. Within recognitions that the year is a circle and "the day is an epitome of the year" are the tightly folded buds of the whole structure of *Walden*. Without this Indian order and concision, the book would have been a two-year journal, reporting on economic makeshifts and hectoring the Concord villagers. But the latinate abstractions are still there, in the little word "epitome" and in the extensive etymologies of *labor* and *lobe*, the bristling metaphysical *written* style. He is a white Indian who saw red in the

97

woods, refracting it through the lens of English and classical literature. Indian creation tales are narratives; Thoreau's were transcendental allegories.

But however different his own creation allegories and his own year, the Indian material provided him with precedents and confirmations for his own views. Towards the end of the second volume of his "Indian Books," which he appears to have completed in June 1850, is the brief note, "Names of the moons in Thatcher's *Indian Traits* 2nd vol." But he did not copy them out. By January or February of 1852, taking notes on Baron de la Hontan's *New Voyages to North America*, he seems to have become more curious.

> "The year of the Outaouas, Outsjamas, Houron, Sauteurs, Minois, Oumamis, and some other savages, is composed of 12 synodic lunar months, with this difference that at the end of 30 moons they let one pass as supernumerary, which they call the Lost Moon; afterwards they continue their count as usual. Moreover all these lunar months have names which belong to them. They call that which we name March, the Moon of Worms (aux Vers) because these animals are accustomed to come out of the holes of trees at that time where they shut themselves (se remberment) up during the winter. That of April the Moon of Plants, May the Moon of the Swallows—& the like." (5/91)

Later in February 1852, he copied the Sauk names of almost all the months (from Jonathan Carver's *Three Years Travel Throughout the Interior Parts of North America*, 1794).

> April the month of Plants — May of Flowers — June the Hot Moon — July the Buck Moon — August the Sturgeon Moon — September the Corn Moon — October the Travelling Moon. (Leave their villages & travel toward their winter hunting grounds.) November the Beaver Moon. (Beavers retire to their houses.) December the Hunting Moon — January the Cold Moon. (6/29)

In later volumes of his "Indian Books" Thoreau copied out all thirteen of the Moons of other tribes. He had obviously come to like them. The names of English months, like the days of the week, bear the stamp of Roman deities and Roman numbers, which is why Whitman preferred the Quaker names "Ninth Month," "Twelfth Month," etc. But neither bear any relation to the seasons. The Indian names are not only more natural, they also remind one more of the year's circular form, of the annual returns and renewals in the American world: Moon of Plants, Moon of Flowers, Hot Moon, Buck Moon, Sturgeon Moon, Corn Moon, and so on.

The spring of 1852, therefore, was a crucial time in Thoreau's larger conceptions of *Walden*. At this time, when he was seeing "Indian red" and revisiting the railroad cut, he was also learning the Indian calendar. The *Journal* entry of April 18, 1852, when he records realizing "that the year is a circle," honors the Indian god who played a part in the realization:

> For the first time I perceive this spring that the year is a circle. I see distinctly the spring arc thus far. It is drawn with a firm line. Every incident is a parable of the Great Teacher.

According to Lyndon Shanley, who made a searching investigation of the manuscripts of *Walden*, it was not until this time that Thoreau began to round out the book's full cycle of the seasons.

> Though the cycle of the seasons was in the work from the start, it was incomplete in the early versions: they lack most of "Brute Neighbors" and "House-Warming," all of "Winter Visitors," and considerable portions of "Winter Animals" and "The Pond in Winter." Thoreau added all this material in the versions written after 1851. . . . With the additions and with Thoreau's careful and extensive reordering of a considerable amount of material, the cycle is fully set out.[24]

Walden ends with yet one more story of rebirth, one which is reminiscent of other Indian legends of tribes which once lived underground and then came to live aboveground, or, like the Kiowa, were originally born out of logs.[25]

Every one has heard the story which has gone the rounds
of New England, of a strong and beautiful bug which came
out of the dry leaf of an old table of apple-tree wood,
which had stood in a farmer's kitchen for sixty years, first
in Connecticut, and afterward in Massachusetts,—from an
egg deposited in the living tree many years earlier still, as
appeared by counting the annual layers beyond it; which
was heard gnawing out for several weeks, hatched perchance by the heat of an urn. (P. 333)

This is the perfect ending for Thoreau's vision quest because it unites so many of his themes and symbols. Here is
a surprising awakening from the tomb, from the wood of
a foreign tree made native to New England. Creation and
renewal can happen even after decades of sleep. The legend
is white, and Thoreau learned of it from John Warner Barber's *Historical Collections* (Worcester, Mass., 1839), but
he jotted it down on the first page of what became the second volume of his "Indian Books": "Bug ate out of a table
in Williamstown 73 years after the egg was laid."

CHAPTER IV

A Book about Indians?

THOREAU died on May 6, 1862, not quite 45 years old and having published only two books, *A Week* (1849) and *Walden* (1854). His only other publication had been in magazines, reviews, and newspapers. There had been a considerable amount of such material, however, and towards the very end of his life there was also rapidly growing interest in his work. Therefore, in 1861 and 1862, when his tuberculosis kept him indoors and an early death became increasingly likely, he spent more and more time getting his work in order and preparing it for his sister and friends to publish. Between 1863 and 1866 they published five posthumous volumes, a very impressive list.* It was not a half of what was yet to come. From 1881–1892, Thoreau's friend Harrison Blake brought out excerpts from the *Journal* in seasonal arrangements—*Early Spring in Massachusetts, Summer, Winter,* and *Autumn*—and in 1906 Bradford Torrey and Francis H. Allen published the *Journal* in 14 volumes, as part of the Walden Edition of Thoreau's works, which had a total of 20 volumes.

Despite these five books in the 1860s and the 14-volume *Journal,* an idea persists that Thoreau's powers declined after *Walden,* that he was a romantic who peaked young, and that, if he had more to write, he could not find a form. He died, as Emerson said at the memorial service for him in 1862, leaving "his broken task which none else can finish." Why should he have written no books, but only maga-

---

* *Excursions,* ed. Sophia Thoreau and R. W. Emerson, 1863; *The Maine Woods,* ed. Sophia Thoreau and Ellery Channing, 1864; *Cape Cod,* ed. Sophia Thoreau and Ellery Channing, 1865; *Letters to Various Persons,* ed. R. W. Emerson, 1865; and *A Yankee in Canada, with Anti-Slavery and Reform Papers,* ed. Sophia Thoreau and Ellery Channing, 1866.

zine pieces in the last eight years of his life? If there was a "broken task," other than the general work and joy of life itself, what was it?

Various answers and theories have been given, and one which has had wide acceptance is that he was working on a book about American Indians. Thus, Franklin Sanborn, one of the originators of this theory, wrote in 1864 in a review of *The Maine Woods*:

> This constant celebration of the Indian and his native characteristics should be carefully attended by all readers of the book, for it is the only result we are likely to see of Thoreau's researches into the history and qualities of the North American Indian. It was his purpose to write a book on this topic, and he collected great heaps of matter relating to it.[1]

A year later, reviewing *Cape Cod*, Sanborn praised the last chapter for its compressed essay on early European navigators and colonists as "a fragment of that web of researches into the early history of the Indians which would have been so priceless had Thoreau lived to complete it."[2] Indeed, to Sanborn this was no theory; it was a fact. Thoreau intended to write a book about "the history and qualities of the North American Indian." Sanborn repeated the point in his biography in 1882, and the English biographer Henry S. Salt repeated it in 1890. After *Walden*, Thoreau was "engaged in various literary plans, chief among which was his projected book on the Indians."[3]

That Thoreau had such intentions is in many ways an appealing thought. As we have seen, in the first two books Indians are the personifications of prehistoric America, ideals of simple economy and heroic poetry, holders of an intimate knowledge of nature which he sought himself, and representatives of his own nonconforming attitudes towards the white village. Given the old American battle line between the village and the forest, civilization and savagery, his choices were clear. The frontier divided the world so that Indians were to be expected to be everything the whites weren't. Rejecting civilization and the ordinary means of getting a living meant embracing the Indian way and becoming a white Indian, with the result that a book about Indians would be, in the last analysis, a new book about himself. *Walden* was one "letter from a distant land," the next might be from a still more distant one—from beyond the frontier, from the silent forests of prehistoric America, from the wilderness dreamland of an undiscovered consciousness, an undiscovered continent. Mirrors to all Americans, Indians were still more intricate and inviting mirrors to Thoreau. They were opposites, doubles, projections, and ideals of a staggering number of shapes and voices. Add to this Thoreau's instincts for irony and moral indignation, his patience in observation and in historical research, and you have an intriguing possible book. Its impact on readers and so on American literature and life might have been stunning. It might have done far more than merely answer the biographer's and the literary critic's questions about what happened to Thoreau after 1854.

But he did not write it, and a skeptical critic must also recognize that no evidence has so far turned up of his explicitly saying he intended to. Sanborn's remarks in the reviews of *The Maine Woods* and *Cape Cod* were made after Thoreau's death, and he did not say whether he had the information from Thoreau himself or whether he (and probably other members of the Thoreau circle) deduced it on discovering the many books of notes and quotations about Indians. William Ellery Channing, who was closer to Thoreau than Sanborn was, wrote in his biography that Thoreau never spoke to him of "his collections on the subject," that is, the "Indian Books."[4] If he did not mention them to Channing, there is little reason to think he mentioned them to anyone else, and they must have been quite a surprise to friends and family after his death. The notion that he planned a book about Indians could have quickly sprung up to account for them.

On the other hand, Thoreau was notoriously reserved about his writing. Channing also says that he declined trying or pretending to do what he had no means to execute. He forebore explanations.[5] Emerson had no idea of the extent of the *Journal* until Sophia loaned it to him after Thoreau's death.[6] From time to time, however, Thoreau did write or tell someone when he was working on something, and it is reasonable to suppose that at least once in the course of fourteen years or more there might have been mention of a book about Indians—if there was to be one. All we have is a letter from Hawthorne, February 19, 1849, about Thoreau's being engaged to lecture in Salem, which included the words, "or perhaps that Indian lecture, which you mentioned to me, is in a state of forwardness." The editors of Thoreau's correspondence add that there is no record of an Indian lecture, that Hawthorne might have been referring to one about Maine, and that what was delivered, February 28, 1849, was a lecture about Walden.[7]

Some evidence about Indian research appears in Thoreau's famous answer, in 1853, to a questionnaire and membership invitation from the Association for the Advancement of Science. In the blank after *"Branches of Science in which especial interest is felt,"* he wrote, "The Manners & Customs of the Indians of the Algonquin Group previous to contact with the civilized man."[8] But he did not return the form until December 19, declining the invitation which had come nine months before, when he had written in the *Journal*:

> I felt that it would be to make myself the laughing-stock of the scientific community to describe or attempt to describe to them that branch of science which specially interests me, inasmuch as they do not believe in a science which deals with the higher law. So I was obliged to speak to their condition and describe to them that poor part of me which alone they can understand. The fact is I am a mystic, a transcendentalist, and a natural philosopher to boot. Now I think of it, I should have told them at once that I was a transcendentalist. That would have been the shortest way of telling them that they would not understand my explanations. (March 5, 1853)

104

We have to realize, then, that his interest in "The Manners & Customs of the Indians of the Algonquin Group" was merely "that poor part of me which alone they can understand." It was true, but it did not express him and the language was not his. "The history and qualities of the North American Indian," as Sanborn stiffly described the book which might have been, has the same un-Thoreauvian sound.

The reason why it is necessary to scrutinize this theory of "A Book about Indians" is that it makes a great deal of difference in how we read Thoreau. It acknowledges his interest in Indians and that he took them as seriously as did contemporaries like Irving, Cooper, Parkman, and Melville. It also implies, to most of his readers, that he liked them and wished to present them more favorably and personally than did other writers. But the effect of the theory, paradoxically, is to push the interest into a special place, a kind of undeveloped literary reservation. If there was to be *one* book about Indians, then the other books are less so. People can speculate about that book and continue to neglect the references to Indians in the finished work. Indians remain, in Thoreau as elsewhere, "forgotten Americans."

On the other hand, if he did not plan "A Book about Indians," then the thousands of pages of notes on Indians must be construed more broadly as self-education and preparation for what he *did* write. Every reference to Indians must be recognized as backed by all that thought and research and should be taken more seriously. Indians come off the literary reservation and will be found—as they are—in prominent places in Thoreau's most important books.

If there is an answer to the question, the best place to look is in the so-called "Indian Notebooks"—the "Indian Books" as Thoreau called them. We need to know when he kept them, and how he used them. We need to know what is in them and the pattern or order of their contents. Are they, as Sanborn called them, simply "great heaps of matter?" Does their evolution tell us useful things about the development of Thoreau's interests? Do notes or the beginnings of lectures or essays in them tell us more about his intentions?

Thoreau's name for them, collectively, was "Indian Book" or "Indian books." He referred to them by number, for example "*vide* Indian books, No. 6, p. 13," and there were 12 of them, not 11, as generally believed. (See Appendix, "On the Name and Number of the 'Indian Books.'") For all we know, this somewhat ambiguous name may have been partially responsible for people's thinking he planned to write *an* Indian Book, but "Indian [Commonplace] Books" or "Indian [Fact] Books" is clearly what he meant, as can be seen by comparing them with his various other commonplace books and "Fact Books." In the Berg Collection at the New York Public Library is a commonplace book which he started at Harvard on English Poetry, as did many other students then and for generations back. The first 74 pages contain neatly written quotations from Elizabethan and seventeenth-century lyrics, along with notes on such classic academic studies as the relation of "Lycidas" to the pastoral tradition. Pages 75–86 are blank, for further entries. Pages 87–123 are largely on Gaelic poetry, which he also studied in college and continued to like. Then on page 127 appears the title *Confucius et Mencius, Les Quatres Livres De Philosophie Morale et De La Chine*, Paris, 1841. In 1841, if he read this book new, he was already four years out of college, so we know that this material (about the sayings and sacred books of Confucius) is all later. There are more notes and quotations on oriental drama and philosophy, and then some poems by William Allingham dated 1850. A commonplace book is an open-ended form which a person suits to his own taste and expanding curiosity. The Berg Collection has another which is labeled "Extracts, mostly upon Natural History." Another, which he referred to now and then in the *Journal* and also in the "Indian Books," he called his "Fact Book" or "Book of facts." He did much of his reading in books borrowed from friends and libraries.

Commonplace books were a means of compiling a condensed personal library, a personal anthology.

The twelve "Indian [Fact] Books" contained many more pages than these others, but this is not necessarily reason to think that he used them differently. From the poetry book he drew many things English, Gaelic, and Oriental which he used in *A Week* and *Walden*. It does not suggest that he planned someday to write a history of poetry, nor does the "Book of facts" suggest he was going to write an almanac. Poetry and facts both were recurrent passions in his life and writing. The peculiar status given "Indian Books" may tell us more about Sanborn and a hundred years of Thoreau scholarship than it does about Thoreau. Indians! All the excitements of nativism, guilt, tragedy, and the exotic come leaping to the biographer's or scholar's mind. This becomes a special subject because it is America's peculiar anxiety, her daemon. Thoreau was going to write a book on *Indians!* And perhaps he was. Lacking evidence that an author clearly did not plan something, it is impossible to disprove a theory that maybe at sometime or other he did think about it or that if he had lived longer he might have eventually completed it. A writer has many ideas, and some stay with him even though he may never write a word or tell anyone about them. Perhaps he even thought now and then of a book about poetry or a book about facts. But neither poetry nor facts stimulate the ordinary American imagination as Indians do, the oldest poets and the most stubborn facts. They are made the subject of grand folios, paintings, and epics, of special programs and investigations; or they are ignored entirely. In this, Sanborn and many Thoreau scholars (including possibly the present author) are no different from everyone else. Confine and ennoble "the Indian," make him the subject of a masterpiece; or ignore him. By not going ahead with such a masterpiece, Thoreau showed a modesty and sobriety we might all learn from. We need balance.

The issues of how he used his "Indian Books," and of when he started them and how they developed are all related. Richard Fleck, one of the Books' readers, has shown that the passage on Pasaconaway's magic in *A Week* and two important passages in *Walden* (on Massasoit's hospitality to Edward Winslow and Daniel Gookin's description of wigwams) are based on quotations in "Indian Books" numbers 2 and 3.[9] Since "the great bulk" of the *Week* was written at Walden Pond between 1845 and 1847 and *Walden* itself started there, Fleck suggests that the "Indian Books" must have been started there too. This seems possible. Many of the kinds of things noted in the early volumes are similar to things said about Indians in *A Week* and the "Economy" chapter of *Walden*. However, these two books and Thoreau's essays of the late 1840s and the 1850s contain fewer direct quotations from them than one might expect. He did not generally use the "Indian Books" as a notebook from which to draw facts and anecdotes to reshape in print. As a result, we cannot use them very often for the kinds of precise annotations on his books and essays that some scholars might like. His Indian reading was a wilder raw material that seldom went straight into his finished work. It was like a pile of fine logs drying behind a carpenter's shop —uncut, maybe for use someday, and meanwhile a joy to possess and go to for certain jobs. Just looking at it could, on occasion, inspire and reassure him, as I suggested at the end of the last chapter.

The place where Thoreau did write about this wild wealth was his *Journal*. Writing only to himself, he often noted the finding of a new book or author or meditated on something which was especially provocative. As I try to show in the next chapter, the "Indian Books" and *Journal* connect in many ways. They make fascinating combined reading. They, along with the other later commonplace books, grew together. Consequently, references in the *Journal* are normally very good clues to when he read something, and the sequence of these references provides a chronology of his study. In later volumes of the "Indian Books" Thoreau also wrote a few dates, like when he made special visits to a library or museum. Moreover, a large number of the books which he used were borrowed from the Harvard Library, where records exist of the charges. These were published in 1945 by Kenneth Walter Cameron.[10] Correlated, this evidence gives a history of the "Indian Books," indicated in Table 1.

The correlations between what Thoreau was copying into these "Indian Books" and what he was doing and writing from week to week and month to month over the 14 years or so that he kept them are continuous. They were not an isolated research project. They grew and fluctuated, changed content and direction with the evolution of the rest of his life and work. As I will show later, the life and work were also affected now and then by these books. They were, despite their superficial resemblance to "great heaps of matter," very sensibly and conscientiously compiled, in the same way Thoreau compiled his *Journal*. Regular journalizing and regular keeping of commonplace books both require a special blend of discipline and delight. One can do them by fierce discipline alone—strong resolutions to write a page a day, and so on—but then one's own pleasure ends and there is no more variety and sense of personal discovery in them. They become a chore to write and are dull to read. Conversely, they cannot be kept merely by sporadic impulse. They must become habitual—good habits that are comfortable to keep and yet can be broken and changed or improved as opportunities arise.

Thoreau, with his leisurely habits of writing in the morning, walking in the afternoon, and reading at night, was a preeminent journalizer and collector. Collections of arrowheads, of leaves, plants, flowers, birds' eggs and birds' nests, as well as temporary collections of live turtles, squirrels, and other animals filled his attic room in the family house. Those were "natural history" collections to file and to write about in the *Journal*. The reading, another kind of collecting, was filed in the commonplace books and written about in the *Journal*. This collecting and recording made a system of study. It trapped what was observed and provoked new observation and study.

109

TABLE 1.

Chronology of "Indian Books"

Book Number	Pages	Date Started	Date Completed	Approx. No. of Mos.
Canada &c.	102	Sept. 1850	Dec. 1850 (date Nov. 18, 1850, on p. 5 in back—book having been filled from back)	3
2	86	1847, or with last drafts of A Week & first drafts of Walden	May 1850, at latest; probably earlier	?
3	63	June 1850, or near the completion of No. 2	Oct. 1850	5
4	121	Nov. 1850 (Cartier, Roberval & Champlain, qtd. pp. 6–49, drawn from Harvard, Oct. 28, 1850)	Sept. 1851 (Kalm, qtd. at end, drawn from Harvard, Aug. 11, 1851)	11
5	126	Sept. 1851 (ref. to Kalm in Journal Sept. 5)	Feb. 1852 (Lahontan, pp. 76–104, drawn from Harvard, Feb. 2)	6
6	166	Feb. 1852	Oct. 1852 (Jesuit Relation for 1633 borrowed from Harvard, Oct. 5)	8
7	167	Oct. 1852	Dec. 1852, or Jan. 1853	3–4
8	507	Nov. 1852 (Jesuit Relation for 1636 drawn from Harvard, Nov. 11)	Jan. 4, 1855 (date on p. 504, "In Worcester")	24
9	437	Jan. 1855	Dec. 10, 1855 (date on p. 436—in Cambridge)	11
10	667	Jan. 24, 1856 (date on p. 1)	Feb. 1858	25
11	198	Feb. 1858 (Rasles' Dictionary drawn from Harvard, Feb. 15)	Feb. 28, 1859 (date on p. 197)	12
12	352	Mar. 1859	Apr. 1861	26

"Indian Books" 2, 3, and 4, kept between 1847 and 1851, contain the kinds of information used in *A Week* and *Walden*, though it would be impossible to summarize. (One can summarize an argument or a novel, but not a commonplace book!) There are over 40 different authors and particular sources, and an even larger number of particular subjects. But these are the kinds of things gathered: the idea of using clams for seasoning, instead of salt, which bears out the observation in *Walden* that Indians didn't bother with salt; the first appearances of Indians to Columbus and various explorers and settlers of New England, which was a fascination in *A Week*; an Indian account of Indian origins —"They say themselves that they have sprung and grown up in that very place, like the very trees of the wilderness"; methods of catching birds on Cape Cod; the design of fish weirs; the burning of forests to clear the brush or provide space for planting; seasonal migration between the shore and places inland, and how the simplicity of Indian houses facilitated it. Almost all of this concerns New England, and the sources are mostly Puritan historians or Puritan records. Their number is large, but investigation reveals that Thoreau found the majority of them in volumes 1, 3–5, and 8–10 of the *Collections of the Massachusetts Historical Society,* 1st series. The Puritan historians themselves had performed the same function of gathering many accounts and printing them in a single book. Most of these books were probably available to Thoreau in Concord, from Emerson or other friends. So he began not only with the Indians who had lived nearby but also with the books that were nearby. (There is a story of Thoreau's being asked at dinner which dish he would like. "The nearest," he said. And it was the same here.)

In numbers 3 and 4 he also began recording information about Canadian Indians—a study which tied in with his trip to Canada in the fall of 1850 and the starting of "Canada, &c." In number 3 are some pages from Rev. William Kip's *The Early Jesuit Missions in North America* and Charlevoix's *History of New France*. Number 4 has about forty pages from the explorers Cartier, Roberval, and Champlain. Number 5 is half about Canadians and half material taken from *The Collections of the New York Historical Society* (ser. 2, vol. 1), a sign that he was beginning to reach out beyond New England and Canada. Number 6 opens with 14 pages from Sir John Richardson's *Arctic Searching Expedition* . . . (1852), an account of Richardson's search for the lost explorer John Franklin. Yet Thoreau's interests are not changed: techniques of hunting and gathering food, the building of "dome-shaped snow houses," clothing, the various uses of the bark of "the sweet cedar" and "the spruce fir." What is also significant in number 6 is that it has about 15 pages from Samuel George Morton's *Crania Americana; or, A Comparative View of the Skulls of Various Aboriginal Nations of North and South America* and 80 pages from Schoolcraft's *Historical and Statistical Information . . . ,* vol. 1. His reading of these two "scientific" studies, in nineteenth-century terms, indicates the development of a more general ethnological interest.

"Indian Book" number 6 ends and number 7 begins with a total, between them, of 141 pages from the *Jesuit Relations* for the years 1632–1636. In succeeding years, up to June 21, 1858, when he wrote in "Indian Book" number 11 that he was in Cambridge and had examined "unbound added *Relations,*" he took nearly 200 pages more of notes on these many volumes, until he stopped with the ones for 1693–1694, apparently the last ones available to him. The *Jesuit Relations* are epical: the missionaries' year-to-year history, in the form of accounts written back to their superiors, of their apostolic sufferings and successes. Thoreau was not concerned with what the fathers preached or their struggles to build churches, but he did admire their sincerity and the practicality of many of the things they learned about life in the wilderness. In travelling by canoe, " 'it is necessary to be prompt to embark & disembark, & tuck up so one's clothes as not to wet onesself & not carry water or sand into the canoe.' " One can wear shoes in passing rapids and shoes and socks around portages, but otherwise it is better to be barefoot and barelegged. One's big cap is a disturbance in a canoe; better to wear one's night cap: "'There is no impropriety among the savages.'" And don't begin to paddle unless you wish to row always. (Father Brebeuf's advice to new missionaries, in the *Relation* for 1637, qtd. 8/51–52.) That, as Thoreau might say, was written while the canoe travelled and the water ran. Moreover, he himself copied it out probably in the winter of 1853, or not long before his own canoe trip in Maine the coming summer. The Indians with whom the Jesuits had most contact were the Hurons, who lived in what is now Michigan and southern Ontario. Thoreau took pages of notes on their farming, hunting, marriage and sexual practices, burial customs, house-construction, medicine, games, magic, and so on —the same subjects, in general, that he pursued in his other reading. Jesuits met resistance from the "jugglers" and from the rival Iroquois, and this provided particular material here which he weighed carefully. Were the Iroquois really as cruel in their tortures as men like Father Vimont reported? Thoreau had much different reports from other sources of Iroquois eloquence, diplomatic finesse, and republican institutions. While he seems to have shared the Jesuits' criticism of the jugglers' magical tricks, he also shared the jugglers' belief in the value of remembering and trying to act out dreams.

Therefore, it is not hard to see why he read the *Jesuit Relations* so comprehensively. They combined travel, history, and the culture of Indians, and raised various questions to which he began to seek answers. But his pleasure and fascination with the *Relations* still does not reveal whether or not he read them to use in a special book. He read them as systematically as someone doing research, yet checking through all of them could have become a project carried on for its own sake, the way many people read all the works of a great novelist. Thoreau hated novels; the Jesuits and Schoolcraft, whom he also went through indefatigably, were his preferred kinds of substitutes.

Just after the long quotations from the Jesuits in "Indian

Book" number 7, however, is some evidence that Thoreau at this time may have begun to think of writing a book or essay on Indians. There are about six pages which are mostly his own thoughts and comments on what he had read. They are worth quoting in their entirety.

The medicine man is indispensable to work upon the imagination of the Indian by his jugglery, and of like value for the most part is the physician to the civilized man.

Men lived and died in America, though they were copper colored, before the white man came. Charlevoix states that the Otchagros, commonly called PUANS—who gave their name to the *Baye de Puans* (Green Bay)—already much reduced, lost 600 of their best men in a single squawl on Lake Michigan as they were going against their enemy the Illinois. All were swallowed up in the Lake, their fleet being struck by a sudden squawl.

Whence is it that all nations have something like a drum? Charlevoix speaks of the *tambour* of the Indians. There would appear to be a kind of necessity in human nature to produce this instrument. In London & Paris you hear the sound of the unmusical drum—which has come down from antiquity.

The trader's price for a handkerchief or string of beads in California is all the gold the Indian has got, be it more or less. A thousand dollars is not too much nor one dollar too little. Accordingly the Indian learns to put this gold into separate little socks, and say that one contains his all. So was it with the fur traders.

Hontan returning from his somewhat fabulous expedition up the River *Longue* in 1688 says, "We arrived therefore the 24th at *Chekakow* (Chicago), the place where the re-embarkment was to be made." Thus the white man has but followed in the steps of the Indian. Where the Ind. made his portages the white man makes his—or makes the stream more navigable. The New Englander goes to Wisconsin & Iowa by routes which the Indians discovered & used ages ago—and partly perchance the buffaloes used before the Indians. At the points of embarkation or debarcation on the route where was once an Indian is now in many instances no doubt a white man's city—with its wharves.

Labor among the Indians was to a certain extent merely mechanically divided between men & women—the former making their canoes and nets, traps &c.—whatever war, hunting & fishing required. The women made the utensils of the house &c.

Each savage feels the necessity of being governed by reason in the absence of law. Hence gives of his game to his old relations, &c.

The Indian is like the muskrat [seen?—word unclear] on freshwater dams apparently. Both had a strong hold on life naturally—but are alike exterminated at last by the white man's improvements. He was hardy & supple & of a cold temperament like the muskrat whose feast he shared and whose skins he often used.

What a vast difference between a savage & a civilized people. At first it appears but a slight difference in degree—and the savage excelling in many physical qualities. We underrate the comparative general superiority of the civilized man. Compare the American Family (so-called by Morton) with (his) Toltecan. Consider what kind of relics the former have left—at most rude earthen mounds, pottery, & stone implements; but of the latter Morton says, "From the Rio Gila in California, to the southern extremity of Peru, their architectural remains are everywhere encountered to surprise the traveller and confound the antiquary: among these are pyramids, temples, grottoes, bas-reliefs, and arabesques; while their roads, aqueducts and fortifications, and the sites of their mining operations, sufficiently attest their attainments in the practical arts of life."

How different the evidence afforded by an earthen mound containing rude fragments of pottery & stone spearheads—and that afforded the remains of a public or military roads.

Morton (in his *Crania*) quotes Mr. Wm. Jones (indirectly) as saying, "The Greeks called all the southern nations of the world by the common appellation of Ethiopians, thus using Ethiop and Indian as convertible terms." —The origin of the word Indian? Perhaps what the Orientals were to the Greeks—barbarians—the Indians are to some extent to us.

We have a voluminous history of Europe for the last

115

1800 years. Suppose we had as complete a history of Mexico
& Peru for the same period—a history of the American
Continent,—the reverse of the medal. It is hard to believe
that a civilized people inhabited these countries unknown
to the old world! What kind of poets—what kind of events
are those which transpired in America before it was known
to the inhabitants of the old world?

Thoreau next copied a concise definition of the ages of
stone, bronze, and iron and two items about Viking warfare,
all found in the appendix to Samuel Laing's *Chronicles of
the Kings of Norway*. Then he concluded with two more
thoughts of his own:

> The Indians having no Sunday-feasts, games [and] dances,
> &c. are the more important to them.
> The recent ('52) persecution in Persia of the Sect of the
> Babis equals in the atrocity of the tortures employed—
> the lingering deaths at which all people assist—the prac-
> tices of our Indians. (7/112–118)

Afterwards he left two and a half pages blank, probably
for further comments.

In these reflections, which were written late in the fall of
1852, Thoreau had come up against some dilemmas which
still trouble North Americans. One line of associations led
him to see the similarities and continuities between red and
white life: medicine men and physicians both worked on
the imaginations (a connection he had already made in the
Week); men died in storms and battles just as now; "All
nations have something like a drum"; trade, travel, and
labor were much the same, or at least by similar routes and
by the same principles. But then, with the contrast of government by reason and government by law, he began to
think of differences and saw both Indian and muskrat as
"exterminated at last by the white man's improvements."
And that set him off on the "vast difference," which he illustrated and developed not by contrast between red and
white North Americans, but between the cultures of North
and South America. The one had left fragments of pottery

and stone spearheads, the other had left roads and temples and aqueducts. By this means he avoided a jingoistic enumeration of the differences between red Americans and white, but he only established more solidly a fundamental difference between high cultures and low cultures. The North American Indians were not Greek, as apologists had argued and as he had written in college and in portions of his first book; they were more like the Ethiopians or Orientals as known to the Greeks. "Perhaps what the Orientals were to the Greeks—barbarians—the Indians are to some extent to us." Once more he turned the picture and tried to imagine a history of Mexico and Peru as long and as detailed as the history of Europe—one, perhaps, in which North Americans would look to South Americans as barbarians did to the Greeks. Mexico and Peru would be the center of the world and Europe would be a remarkable, previously unknown other civilization. "The reverse of the medal" that definitely was; it inverted his world.

For Thoreau these reflections were especially hard to pursue because they undercut much of the American cultural mythology he had taken as his own. The Europe-America dichotomy, in which Europe stood for age and civilization, America for youth and nature, did not work when one introduced Mexico and Peru. There had been improvements in America just as civilized as those in Europe. About improvements he was more divided than were any of his contemporaries. But, prefer reason and nature and simplicity though he did, he could not deny the superior accomplishments of civilization. He did not wish to view the Indians, or the muskrats, with disdain, but when he looked at differences like this he felt forced to.

Further evidence that he was here beginning to think of writing a book, in which he might try to work out these problems, is that "Indian Book" number 8, begun in November or December of 1852, is much longer than numbers 2–7. They, along with "Canada, &c.," have a total of 831 pages. The new one alone had over 500. Number 9, started two years later, in January 1855, has over 430 pages, while number 10, started in January 1856, has over 660. He had learned that he filled the shorter ones very quickly, and some excerpts from single authors were now so long that a short copybook would hold but one or two of them. In March 1853, he began using a larger copybook of identical format for his *Journal*, which could indicate that these big ones were now simply the nearest available, but which more likely indicates that he had now committed himself to both projects more deeply.[11] Reading, collecting, and journalizing were to be an even bigger part of each day.

Another revealing fact is that in "Indian Book" number 8 he regularly listed, after each series of extracts from a book, the page numbers from which he had taken the material. In number 9 (and 10, 11, and 12) he wrote the page numbers beside each passage. His identifications of author, title, edition, and publisher are still rather brief (particularly to a reader a hundred years later), but they too began in this period to become a little fuller. It was not Thoreau's custom to use footnotes or cite page numbers when he referred to a book in one of his own writings, but he had probably learned that the page numbers were helpful here: they made it much easier to relocate something. And he had begun to reread some authors, sometimes because he now had them in better or more complete editions, sometimes because he apparently wanted to recheck them. Finally, December 1853, when he was about to page 140 of number 8, was the time of his telling the Association for the Advancement of Science—though with private qualifications—that his interest was "The Manners & Customs of the Indians of the Algonquin Group previous to contact with the civilized man."

I think, therefore, that the period when Thoreau most seriously regarded himself as working on a book about Indians (as well as the "Indian Books") was from December 1852, through February 1858. Depending on how serious one supposes Thoreau to have been, one might lengthen or shorten the period, and perhaps also question some of the months in between. Thoreau clearly wasn't working on such

118

a book when he was in the thick of final revisions of *Walden*, or in the midst of other projects. But this period of the biggest Indian commonplace books seems to be the best place for his future biographers to look for further evidence. Even more suggestive is the fact that this period includes his trips to Maine in September 1853, and July-August 1857. The trips to Maine were to study Indians and the wilderness, and Thoreau did not make long excursions like these without thinking of books and essays. In that, he was like any modern traveller-writer, and he also knew, as any author would in the 1850s, that Indians were a subject people wanted to read about.

But why, after these two successful trips, did Thoreau give up or put aside a book about Indians early in 1858? And why did he yet continue with the "Indian Books"?

Evidently he had run into two problems. The first was that, from the standpoint of a book or article, the second trip to Maine had been too successful. He had learned so much from his Penobscot guide Joe Polis that Polis would have to be reported at great length—and Polis knew how to read. Thoreau explained this in a letter to his old college acquaintance James Russell Lowell, who had recently become editor of the *Atlantic Monthly* and had asked Thoreau to contribute. He wrote Lowell, January 23, 1858:

> The more fatal objection to printing my last Maine-wood experience, is that my Indian guide, whose words & deeds I report very faithfully,—and they are the most interesting part of the story,—knows how to read, and takes a newspaper, so that I could not face him again.[12]

Instead, Thoreau offered "Chesuncook," his account of the 1853 excursion. The faithful reporting of Polis was, at this point, probably only in field notes or a first draft, but he recognized that to print it—or something like it—would infringe on Polis's privacy and their friendship. No account of that trip was published until it appeared as the last part of *The Maine Woods* in 1864.

If he could not report in detail on Polis or another Indian

guide and informant, then the book about Indians would
have to be based largely on his reading. What kind of book
would that be? That this too was a problem is plain from
a list of subjects which Thoreau made at this time. It is a
list comparing "Loskiel's Subjects" and "Adair's Subjects,"
on one side of a sheet with "Subjects of Schoolcraft's Vol.
V" and "*My own*" on the reverse side. The lists must date
from February 1858, or later, since this is when Thoreau
extracted from volume 5 of Schoolcraft's . . . *History, Condition and Prospects* . . . , the last of these three authors
to be read. (In "Indian Book" 11/34–72. The books quoted
just before Schoolcraft were drawn from Harvard, January
13, 1858, and the one begun one page afterwards was drawn
from Harvard, February 15, 1858.) Adair, Loskiel, and
Schoolcraft were three of America's Indian Experts, and
Thoreau's lists of their "subjects" were gleaned from their
tables of contents, so it is quite likely he was thinking about
his chapter titles. It is longer than any of the other three
lists, and it accurately represents the great variety of subjects covered in his "Indian Books."

My Own

Ante Columbian History	Dress
First Aspects of Land & People	Painting
Welch in America	Money
Dog indigenous?	Naming
Travelling	Government
Physique	Treatment of Captives
Music	Manners
Games	Woodcraft
Dwellings	Hunting
Feasting	Food &c
Food	Fishing
Charity	Superstitions & Religion
Funeral Customs	Medicine &c
Tradition or history	War
Morale	Language
Marriage customs	Ind. relics
Manufactures	Arts & uses derived from
Education	the Indians

It is also clear that as recently as early January 1858, at the end of book number 10, he was still contemplating a book about Indians. There, following a passage from Thomas Hariot's *A Brief and True Report*, telling how Indians around the Roanoke colony in the 1580s died of English diseases, Thoreau wrote, "It is pathetic to read—is told more at length—and will be *worth quoting fully.*" The only place to quote it fully, since he had already quoted over half of it, would be some longer book or essay. And yet his failure to do so here, when he had the opportunity, already suggests some waning of interest. He wanted to quote it *"fully"* but didn't quite have the time, place, or will.

January and February 1858, were months of decision about a book on Indians. He could still have wanted to write one, but the very intimacy of his relation to Polis and Polis's literacy were problems. Build an essay or part of a book around Polis, and Thoreau "could not face him again." But without him Thoreau would have to rely mainly on material in his Indian commonplace books, and it all came from other writers. That was not his kind of book. Six years before (March 16, 1852), after a day at the Cambridge Library, he had written a brilliant, derisive note on the three hundred years of books on Canada which he had seen.

> [I] could see how one had been built upon another, each author consulting and referring to his predecessors. You could read most of them without changing your leg on the steps.

Experience with the hundreds of books on Indians surely proved the same thing. In his own "Indian Books" he often noted to himself when an author had borrowed or stolen, and he had little truck with derivative writers like Drake, Thatcher, and McKenney and Hall. Nor did he bother with the countless biographies of famous chiefs and the repeated tales of massacres and captivities, of Indian vengeance and white perfidy which were the contents of the popular books. He could surely have done better than they, but he would still have been derivative. In his own writing Thoreau introduced other authors for insights and facts which suited his purposes. He did not serve them up as a stew. Writing thirty-four chapters on the subjects in his list of February 1858, would be thirty-four warmed-up stews. He hastily put the list aside, not even stopping to cross out a repetition.

Yet the question remains: if he gave up or put aside serious thought of a book on Indians at this time, why did he go on keeping Indian fact books for three more years? I believe he did so for the same reasons he started them. They were stimulating and pleasurable to keep. They were a means of discovery, not only about Indians but about the natural history of America. Such discoveries, in turn, provoked him, while on his walks and travels, into fresh observations and a keener sense of the world, an Indian eye. Ten or eleven years' experience and habit with them had proven their value, and there were scores of places in the *Journal* and his essays where he had used them. They aided all his writing. Thus, there was no reason to give them up entirely, and he might, eventually, find time and occasion to write the more personal and original book on Indians which was in his line. Finally, as he turned to new projects and the completion of old ones, the "Indian Books" continued to be useful. In late February and March, 1858, he enthusiastically took notes on Father Sebastien Rasles' "Dictionary of the Abenaki Language," which confirmed what Polis had taught him about that language. In June he finished his survey of the *Jesuit Relations.* In December, as he thought hopefully of a lecture trip to the Middle West, he began copying extracts from the voyages of Marquette, La Salle, and other explorers and early historians of Louisiana. In January 1859, he took additional notes on Samuel Champlain, a hero of his essay on American discovery in *Cape Cod.* And as he went on with "Indian Book" 12, he took extracts from herbals and books on botany for his new task, "Wild Fruits" and "The Dispersion of Seeds."[13] The "Indian Books" had very practical value.

CHAPTER V

Beyond Savagism

The man came down,
a crouching dwarf with rainwater eyes,
and spoke to us. He promised
that life would go on as usual,
that treaties would be signed, and everyone—
man, woman and child—would be inoculated
against a world in which we had no part,
a world of wealth, promise and fabulous disease.

JAMES WELCH, "THE MAN FROM WASHINGTON"*

To COME back to fundamentals: why was Thoreau so occupied with Indians, and what did he learn? These are more important questions for most Americans than whether or not he intended to write a book. They get to the other basic and controversial questions of why he lived as he did —"inclined to lead a sort of Indian life among civilized men," as Hawthorne put it—and what he wished to be. Was his devotion to learning from and about Indians a romantic primitivism, an expression of guilt over their treatment by other white men, a rejection of civilization, or what? What did he learn from the hundreds of books which he read and thousands of pages he tirelessly copied?

Readings of *A Week on the Concord and Merrimack Rivers* and *Walden* have already supplied some answers to these questions. The *Week*, as we have seen, is a unique history of red-white relations in New England and a vision of what they might become. Conflicts with Indians in religion and war, associations with them in commerce and

* From *Riding the Earthboy 40*, copyright © 1971, 1976 by James Welch, by permission of Harper & Row, Publishers.

friendship were the essence of early Anglo-American history and helped form New England character. Indians like Wannalancet and Wawatam and the whites like Jonathan Tyng, Farwell, and Alexander Henry, who knew, fought with, and were adopted by these Indians as friends, were clearly greater heroes to Thoreau than were the New England "saints" like Bradford, Winthrop, and the Mathers. When he read the journals and histories of these theocrats, it was only rarely that he found one whose style and character he liked. Primarily, he read them for the information they gave about the new land and native people. With this information, combined with his classical reading, he had turned to his own use the eighteenth- and nineteenth-century image of Indians as savage Homeric heroes. As the painter Benjamin West exclaimed on seeing the Apollo Belvedere, "My God, a Mohawk!" so we can imagine Thoreau exclaiming, when he read Indian speeches and stories of Indian warfare, "My God, a Homer! An Achilles!" This identification, in turn, enriched American nature for him. It was not an artificially preserved English park. It was wild nature, sustaining itself and sustaining him. In *Walden* we see that quest of and by the Transcendental Indian continued.

And the quest could not stop with the Walden years. The Indian meant renewal, and renewal could not stop. If the true poetry of the American experience was to be written, it would, according to the aesthetics of the *Week*, have to be original. It could not be imitation of Indian poetry any more than fashionable European poetry. Imitation was "scalping"—taking someone else's head as your own. It led, as Thoreau imagined happened to Hannah Dustan, to fearing the spirits and kin of the people scalped. It led to alienation. If there was any Original Sin in Thoreau's theology, leading back through sixty generations of 100-year-old women to Eve herself, it was this—doing what someone else did. But imitating the Indians was also to a great degree unavoidable, just as it had been for Hannah Dustan. She wanted revenge for their murder of her infant, she wanted

124

to escape captivity; so she killed them with their own weapons and bagged their scalps in order that the New Englanders downstream, including her cowardly husband, could believe what she'd done. Like her or not, she was an artist, an American Goethe! For the artist Thoreau, Indians were the old masters who had to be imitated until they were surpassed. Better to imitate them than imitate Goethe, just as American warriors had been wiser in imitating Indian warfare. Learn the country, follow the rivers, read and write while the grass grows and the water runs.

In this campaign, reading and taking notes on the Indians was like receiving intelligence reports on the military enemy. Indeed, some of the books Thoreau read actually were War Department publications: reports of Army surveys of the West in which the nominal interest was exploration of geography and resources and mapping of possible roads and railroads, but in which accurate knowledge of the inhabitants loomed in the background, a military necessity. Today an uninitiated reader may be startled to realize this, but it also puts him in touch with the realities of American expansion. The planners of the Pacific Railway, whose voluminous reports were published in the early 1850s, were meticulously thorough. And "Mr. Thorow," sitting in Concord with these big volumes, some sent to him personally by Senator Charles Sumner, kept up-to-date.[1]

But unlike the military strategist, Thoreau was interested in the past as well as the present. He wanted intelligence on the condition "of the Indians of the Algonquin Group previous to contact with the civilized man," as he wrote the Association for the Advancement of Science, because they were the true natives, uninfluenced by white men. As he also wrote, in a brilliant *Journal* passage, the dark and decaying books containing this information were like a peat bog, "a humus for new literatures to spring in."

> While we are clearing the forest in our westward progress, we are accumulating a forest of books in our rear, as wild and unexplored as any of nature's primitive wildernesses. The volumes of the Fifteenth, Sixteenth, and Seventeenth

Centuries, which lie so near on the shelf, are rarely opened, are effectually forgotten and not implied by our literature and newspapers. When I looked into Purchas's Pilgrims, it affected me like looking into an impassable swamp, ten feet deep with sphagnum, where the monarchs of the forest, covered with mosses and stretched along the ground, were making haste to become peat. Those old books suggested a certain fertility, an Ohio soil, as if they were making a humus for new literatures to spring in. I heard the bellowing of bullfrogs and the hum of mosquitoes reverberating through the thick embossed covers when I had closed the book. Decayed literature makes the richest of all soils. (March 16, 1852)

Getting to such valuable bogs was a process he found offensive. He hated, he said, going to the city and dealing "with men and institutions with whom I have no sympathy." He would rather a library were in the jungle of Central America than in "the well-preserved edifice, with its well-preserved officials on the side of a city's square" (February 3, 1852). And most books, he commented while surveying ones on Canada, simply built on other books. "You could read most of them without changing your leg on the steps." On any given subject, only three or four books in a thousand "contain all that is essential" (March 16, 1852).

So, drawn to the "wilderness" inside the libraries, he pursued his research, and he was exacting in his demands that the authors he read be original and reliable, as a few examples from the "Indian Books" will illustrate. Of Captain Jonathan Carver's *Three Years Travels through the Interior Parts of North America* (1797), once a well-known book on the Great Lakes region, he wrote: "Little or nothing in the narrative of his travels, & for the 2nd part or account of the Indians it is an imposition, being an adoption in all important particulars of Hontan's statements, to whom he gives no credit but merely calls some of his stories delusions. No original observations of value" (6/24). He copied only ten pages, on subjects where Carver seemed most trustworthy. In notes on Heckewelder's *Account of the History,*

Manners & Customs (1819), Thoreau began with a page of quotations from the introductory parts testifying to Heckewelder's qualifications. But he also spotted inconsistencies. The editor said Heckewelder resided " 'more than 40 years' " among various Indian nations; yet Heckewelder himself said he got his information " 'from the mouths of the very people I am going to speak of, and from my own observations . . . while residing among & near them, for more than 30 years.' " Under that Thoreau wrote, "NB———yet, he admits, he occasionally quotes other authors, especially Loskiel & Post." In another place on the page, Thoreau squeezed in the words, "H. has the tone of a partisan of the Indians—esp. the Delawares—to some extent" (9/139). Thoreau made 175 pages of extracts from Heckewelder, which surely indicates that he found him informative, but he was still suspicious. Thus several years later, he made fifteen pages of notes on General Lewis Cass's attack on Heckewelder, John Dunn Hunter, and John Halkett (12/37–51, from *North American Review* of January 1826). In such early nineteenth-century literary battles between the pro-Indian and anti-Indian white experts, Thoreau dutifully read both sides.

Working with this kind of careful, critical attention, Thoreau took from the literature of savagism a composite picture of Indian life in North America which disproves savagism. This was not his explicit or implicit intention, and neither did he assess the results of his research in this way, for he was still not far enough above the ideology to see to its edges. His general interest was also broken down into many particular ones, as revealed in the list of over thirty subjects on which he had taken his notes, and he never had a chance to pull all his intelligence together. Consequently, it is hard—and risky—for a twentieth-century reader of his notes and quotations to generalize about them.

But the risk is worth taking, and it is exciting. We can be guided by Thoreau's *Journal* entries where he commented on what he had read, and we can also refer to other biographical sources from time to time. For a structure we can use, in shortened form, Thoreau's own list of "subjects," tying them together in another visionary history such as he wrote in *A Week on the Concord and Merrimack Rivers.* Beginning with the question of Indian origins, we can move on through the white man's arrival as Indians saw it, the life they were living at the time, their villages and farming, their warfare and diplomacy, to the causes of their decline. This obviously will not be the history he himself could have composed, but it will be a picture made from his selections, a kind of mosaic for which he chose the stones, and whose design we guess, on the basis of his isolated sketches of the parts.

Thoreau's speculations about the origins of native Americans were provoked primarily by the theories of James Adair, an eighteenth-century Indian trader who contended that the Indians were descended from the Jews. Adair's evidence, which fills a great part of his *History of the American Indians* (1775), is based on such things as the similarities between Hebrew and the languages of the people he lived with (the Cherokee, "Chikkasah," and other Southern tribes) and his experience that these people were not naturally of a red skin. Thoreau called this Adair's "folly" (10/43), but disproving it forced him to examine other answers. From David Cusick, an English-speaking Tuscarora, he took an Iroquois legend of how the world began as an underworld inhabited by monsters and an upperworld inhabited by mankind. When a woman was about to bear a child, she sank into the lower world and was supported by a great turtle. This was the origin of both the world as we know it and of men as they now are. Here Thoreau was also skeptical, writing "Almost entirely fabulous & puerile—only valuable as showing how an Ind. writes history!" But later—possibly from a recognition that the white histories were not much better on this point—he added ". . . and perhaps for some dim on the whole interesting and suggestive traditions" (10/109).

From Cusick and Adair he went on to the speculations of

Benjamin Smith Barton, once a professor of Materia Medica, Natural History, and Botany at the University of Pennsylvania. Barton, in *New Views of the Origin of the Tribes and Nations of America* (1798), suggested that Indians were descended from "'the Persians, and other improved nations of Asia.'" His racial argument was, as Thoreau summarized it, that the Indians were therefore susceptible to improvement again. Barton was also one of the first people to suggest a trans-Pacific migration, but Thoreau noted that his evidence still did not show "which was the parent stock—old or new world men" (10/140). After studying yet another theory—George Burder's argument that Indians were of Welsh descent, sailing from Wales in 1170 with Prince Madoc—and finding this "mere rumor without foundation or definite statement" (10/155), Thoreau wrote in his *Journal*,

> It is most natural, *i.e.* most in accordance with the natural phenomena, to suppose that North America was discovered from the northern part of the Eastern Continent, for a study of the range of plants, birds, and quadrupeds points to a connection on that side. Many birds are common to the northern parts of both continents. Even the passenger pigeon has flown across there. And some European plants have been detected on the extreme northeastern coast and islands, which do not extend inland. Men in their migrations obey in the main the same law. (Sept. 27, 1857)

Thoreau copied contradictory and yet equally persuasive evidence about Japanese boats found in the Straits of Juan de Fuca (6/90) and the resemblances between the people of northern Canada and the people of Siberia (12/135). And reading David Crantz's *History of Greenland* (1767), he wrote, "I am struck by the close resemblance in manners and customs bet. the Greenlanders and our Ind. If they are proved to be distinct races, it will show that similarity of manners and customs is no evidence of a common origin" (12/310). Still later, having read Herodotus' accounts of Scythian scalping and burial practices, he wrote that they

129

"remind one most of our Indians" (12/351). The similarity
of Scythian and Indian practices did not mean common ancestry, however; it was further evidence that similar cultures could evolve independently of one another. Voltaire's
witty remark that "it was no more surprising to find men in
America than it is to find flies there" (Thoreau copied it
from Barton's book) might have put an end to the whole
question—or at least put it in perspective. Do other Americans know their racial ancestry beyond a particular country
of emigration? But Thoreau was with his generation in finding this a significant puzzle. Lewis Henry Morgan, beginning
in 1857, spent thousands of dollars and over twenty years
of work in establishing the theory of Asiatic origins, based
on common kinship patterns.[2] Moreover, Thoreau was fun-
damentally curious about the origins of humanity.

He had surer information, however, about first contacts
between Indians and Europeans. Heckewelder's story, received from the Delaware, was that some Leni-Lenape
who had been out fishing first saw a large canoe or house
coming towards them over the water and returned to shore
to tell their countrymen. Chiefs and counselors assembled
and decided the large canoe or house must be bringing the
great Mannitto himself. They went and waited on the shore
as the Mannitto, with white skin and dressed in lace and
red clothes, came up in a smaller canoe, accompanied by
other men. These apparent servants brought out a big
gourd, poured a cup, and the Mannitto drank. The cup was
filled again and passed to a chief, who smelled it and passed
it around the circle. Finally one brave man tried it, saying
that to return it undrunk might displease or provoke the
Mannitto. Everyone watched him as he drank, then stag-
gered, fell down and appeared to be dead. But in a while
he jumped up, declared he had never felt better, and asked
for more. His wish was granted, and the whole assembly
joined him, till they were all intoxicated. This place became
known as "Mannahattanink . . . *the place of general in-
toxication.*" The rest of the story told how the Dutch asked
for as much land as would be encircled by the hide of a bul-

lock, and then cut the hide into a long thin string (5/25–35).

To Thoreau, who cared as little for Manhattan as for alcohol, the story could hardly have been more appropriate! Like the Hannah Dustan story, it was one story, one sequence of incidents, each part of which was transcendental history. As the Dustan story *told how* the English became estranged from American nature, this *told how* the Indians became estranged from themselves and the land, how they became poisoned. (Nowhere in the "Indian Books" did he copy the story everyone knows today of the Dutch buying Manhattan; he either did not know it or considered it insignificant.) Yet this also established their original innocence and good will, motifs Thoreau found repeated. The white men appeared as gods and were received as gods.

The following is Marquette's account of his first contact with Indians living along the Mississippi in 1673:

> When they approached the cabin where they were to be received, an old man stood up naked by the door. "Holding his hands extended, he raised [them] toward the sun, as if he had wished to defend himself from its rays, which nevertheless passed between his fingers to his face. When we were near him, he made us this compliment: 'How beautiful is the Sun, when thou comest to visit us. All our town expects thee & thou wilt enter in peace into all our cabins.'
>
> "After we had taken our places, they make us the usual civility of the country, which is to present the Calumet. You must not refuse it if you do not wish to pass for an enemy, or at least for uncivil, though if you only make believe smoke, it is enough." When they proceeded by invitation to the Chief's town, "we went there in good company, for all these people, who had never seen French among them, did not cease regarding us; they lay down on the grass along the ways, they went before us, then they retraced their steps in order to see us again. All that was done without noise, & with marks of a great respect which they had for us."

When Marquette had finished his speech the Chief answered, "holding his hand on the head of a little slave which he wished to give us. 'I thank you Black Robe, & you Frenchman (addressing M. Jollyet), that you take so much pains to come to see us. Never has the earth been so beautiful, nor the Sun so bright as today; never has our river been so calm nor so clear of rocks, which your canoes have removed in passing; never has our tobacco had so good a taste, nor our corn appeared so fair (beau) as we see it now.'" (11/151–52. Copied from John Gilmaury Shea, ed., *Historical Collections of Louisiana*, pt. 4 [Redfield, N. Y., 1853], pp. 242–44.)

The land itself attracted the first sailors, who knew it was near when they smelled the scent of fires in the woods. Thoreau copied this from David Pieterszoon de Vries:

"The 2nd [of December, 1632] threw the lead in 14 fathoms, sandy bottom, & smelt the land, which gave a sweet perfume . . . as the wind came from the northwest which blew off the land, and caused these sweet odors. This comes from the Inds, setting fire, at this time of year, to the woods & thickets, in order to hunt; and the land is full of sweet-smelling herbs, as sassafras, which has a sweet smell. When the wind blows out of the north-west, the smoke too is driven to sea. It happens that the land is smelt before it is seen." (11/8. Copied from de Vries, *Voyages from Holland to America*, in William Lewis, *New York Historical Collections*, vol. 3, pt. 1 [New York, 1821], p. 22. Thoreau used this image himself in describing a spring walk, May 4, 1859, in the *Journal*.)

The scent of sassafras as a first sign of the New World intrigued Thoreau. He loved finding its fragrance of "Oriental Summers" deep in the winter woods (*J.*, February 9, 1852), and he easily imagined its power over the first explorers.

No wonder that men thought they [these spices] might have some effect toward renovating their lives. Gosnold, the discoverer of Cape Cod, carried home a cargo of sassafras. What could be more grateful to the discoverer of a new country than a new fragrant wood? (*J.*, April 1, 1852)

The kindliness of the people continued in the readiness with which they introduced the Dutch and others to their farming. These are some quotations from Thoreau's notes on Adriaen Van der Donck, a Sheriff of New Amsterdam:

"They (the Indians) say that their corn & beans were received from the Southern Indians, who received their seed from a people who resided still farther south."

"It has happened when I have been out with the natives (*Wilden*, for so we name those who are not born of Christian parents) that we have come to a piece of young wood land. When I have told them in conversation, that they would do well to clear off such land, because it would bear good corn, that they said, 'it is but twenty years since we planted corn there, and now it is woods again.'" (5/36)

"Before the arrival of the Netherlanders, the Indians raised beans of various kinds and colors, but generally too coarse to be eaten green, or to be pickled, except the blue sort, which are abundant." Tells how they taught the whites to plant them with corn. "When the Turkish wheat, or, as it is called, *maize*, is half a foot above the ground, they plant the beans around it, and let them grow together. The coarse stalk serves as a bean-prop, and the beans run upon it." (5/40, from *A Description of the New Netherlands*, in *Collections of the New York Historical Society*, sr. 2, vol. I [1841])

From Van der Donck, Peter Kalm, and other writers, Thoreau took further descriptions of cultivating melons and squashes and drying various kinds of berries, for food and dyes. But the most sweeping refutation of the myth that Indians were only hunters came in this excerpt from *A Narrative of the Captivity and Adventures of John Tanner*, edited by Edwin James (1830). Tanner had lived for 30 years with the Ojibways around Lake Superior. James had been on Long's expedition to the Rocky Mountains, and Thoreau respected their authority.

"The very considerable quantities of corn required for the fur trade in the country about Lake Superior were purchased from the Indians, by whom it was raised at a place

called Ketakawwee Seebee, or Garden river, a small stream falling into the strait between Lakes Superior & Huron, about 6 miles below the Sault Ste. Marie."
This within the memory of persons living. Quotes Trumbull's Hist. of Connecticut thus. "The Indians came down to Windsor and Hartford with 50 canoes at one time laden with Indian Corn," which they had sold to the famishing colonists. Ac. to the same the Indians on Block Island "had about 200 acres of corn" which the English destroyed. (8/320)

This information showed that Indian farming was so extensive that it supplied the whites as well as themselves. One could also argue that English destruction of fields forced the people into greater reliance on hunting or scavenging.

Well-established farming made possible a settled village life, as suggested in these descriptions from *Le Grand Voyage du Pays des Hurons* (1632), by Gabriel Sagard, a Recollect missionary. Planting corn, but also surrounded by "a great quantity of wild *froment*, which has the ear like rye and the grain like oats," as well as "wild peas," the Huron were divided into provinces and villages.

There are many provinces in the Huron country which bear dif. names like the provinces in France—commanded by different captains. "In this extent of country [I am not sure whether the whole or one province—(Thoreau's note)] there are about 25 both *villes* and *villages*, of which a part are not closed (clos) nor shut (fermé); & the others are fortified with strong palisades of wood in triple ranks (interlaced one with another) & redoubled within by great thick barks, to the height of 9 or 10 feet. ° ° °
"These 25 ville & villages may be inhabited by 2 or 3,000 *warriors*"—30 or 40,000 souls in all. ° ° °
"In some places they have to change the sites of their towns every 10, 20 or 30 years for want of wood, which they have to carry on their backs with a strap about their foreheads, or in winter on sledges. Also because the soil is exhausted, they not using manure & planting in the old holes.
"Their cabins . . . are made, as I have said, in the form

134

of *tonnelles* or berceaux de jardins, covered with bark of the length of 25 to 30 fathoms (toises) more or less (for they are all equal in length) and six broad, leaving through the midst an alley 10 or 12 feet wide, from one end to the other; on the 2 sides there is a kind of counter 4 or 5 feet high, which stretches from one end of the cabin to the other, where they lie in summer to avoid the importunity of the fleas, . . . & in winter they lie below on mats near the fire, for the sake of warmth." * * *

"They fill with dry wood, to burn in winter all the space below (le dessous) these counters." * * *

"They use only very good wood, caring better to go to seek it very far than to take it green or that which makes smoke." * * *

"In one cabin there are many fires, and at each fire there are 2 families (mesnages) the one on one side the other on the other, & such a cabine will have even to 8, 10, or 12 fires, which make 24 families." No hole but for door & smoke.

"At the 2 ends (bouts) there is à chacun a porch, and these porches serve them principally to put their great cuues or tounes of bark, in which they stow (serrent) their corn of India, after it is well dry and shelled. (9/10–13. Ellipses are Thoreau's omissions, asterisks indicate where I have omitted material.)

I will not try to give a sense of Thoreau's excerpts on marriage, games, child-rearing, burial practices and all the many other customs on which he copied. They are so numerous and varied that they are almost impossible to represent by selections. It is more important to give a sense, next, of his excerpts on warfare and torture, for these were subjects central to the whole debate on savage cruelty.

These are the principal facts which he took from Sagard:

Wars will be got up first by 2 or 3 old or valiant captains. Sometimes by a young man. They excite the people & become the generals but are not always obeyed.

Often feast on their enemies.

"There are properly only surprises & deceptions; for every year anew, & during all the summer, 5 or 600 or more young Hurons go & scatter themselves over an Iroquois country, 5 or 6 in one place, 5 or 6 in another, and as many in another, and lie on their bellies in the fields and forests, and by the side of the highways & paths, and night come they roam everywhere & enter even into the bourgs & villages, to endeavor to catch someone, man, woman or child, and if they take any alive they bring them to their country to make them die by a slow fire, if not after having given them a blow with a club, or slain them with arrows, they bring off the head, but if they were too much burdened with it, they content themselves with bringing off the skin with its hair." In war time these are attached to the end of a long pole on their walls. ° ° °

Prisoners adopted fight against their own nation. Describes treatment of prisoners.

Thinks they wear their finery to war partly that they may delay their pursuers by casting it aside.

"First they draw out their nails and cut off the 3 principal fingers, which serve to draw the bow."

"The Iroquois do not come usually to make war on our Hurons, till the leaves cover the trees, that they may more easily conceal themselves."

Sometimes a prisoner, being tormented, kicking the brands and coals about a cabin, escapes in the darkness & confusion.

Fight not for land but vengeance.

Wars arise from "The little police which lets bad citizens go unpunished . . . for if one among them has offended, killed or wounded another of the same nation, he is quit of it for a present, . . . unless the relations of the wounded or deceased themselves take vengeance for it, which happens rarely. . . . But if the offence is of another nation, then there is undubitably war declared bet. the 2 nations, if that of the guilty man does not purchase peace with great presents." (9/30–34)

In papers collected in *The Documentary History of New York*, Thoreau found a report by the governor of Canada describing an attack on Seneca villages in 1687. He copied a page on the treatment of captives, ending with the burning to death of an old Seneca man. With Spartan courage, the man did not complain. "On the contrary, he exhorted those

136

who tormented him to remember his death, so as to display the same courage when those of his nation would take vengeance on them." Thoreau's penetrating comment on the incident was, "If there was any brutality in the case was it not in the French who permitted him to be burned?" (8/269–70).

Tortures and punishments also differed between nations. Father Vimont, who could be very graphic in his stories of Indian cruelty, happened to tell this story, too.

> "Some savages having learned that in France they put to death malefactors, have often reproached us that we were bad (mechans), that we put our fellow countrymen to death, that we had no wit (d'esprit). They asked if the relations of those whom they condemned to death did not take vengeance for it." (8/208, from *Jesuit Relations* for 1642)

Then Thoreau went on and copied several pages of Vimont's report on what happened to two Algonquin women who, with their children and others, had been captured by the Iroquois.

> "They took our little infants, fastened them to a spit, presented them to the fire & roasted them alive before our eyes. . . . These poor little ones did not yet know fire when they felt the ardor of it. They looked at us, & killed themselves with crying; our hearts were cleft seeing them all baked burning by a slow fire; we endeavored to draw them away but in vain, for our bonds, & these Barbarians prevented us. Heh! Kill them, said we, kill them, miscreants that you are"—but in vain. When they were dead, "They cast them into the kettles, boil them, & eat them in our presence." (8/210)

Between the lines Thoreau wrote, "The women could not have spoken of this if they had not hoped the French would take vengeance for it."

Against these accounts of savage war and cruelty, he balanced other accounts, even about the same people, of eloquence and skill in diplomacy. Traditionally, advocates of

137

the noble savage spoke of one and advocates of the ignoble
savage the other. Thoreau wished to consider both.

> The calm, high-bred dignity of their demeanor, the
> scientific manner in which they progressively construct the
> frame-work of whatever subject they undertake to ex-
> plain . . . and the beautiful wild flowers of eloquence with
> which, as they proceed, they adorn every portion of the
> moral architecture they are constructing, form altogether
> an exhibition of grave interest; and yet, is it not astonishing
> to reflect that the orators in these councils are men whose
> lips and gums are—while they are speaking—black from
> the wild berries on which they have been subsisting—who
> have never heard of education. (5/68. Quoted from Sir
> Francis Head, *The Emigrant* [1847].)

"In the interviews between Indians and whites," Thoreau
commented at another time, "the speeches of the latter [he
means "former"] have the most truth, plain-speaking or di-
rectness, force, poetry" (8/270). And after that he wrote
out part of a Mohawk's speech at the renewing of the chain
of friendship between New York and the 5 Nations.

> "Brother &c. . . . We again desire you to write to the Great
> King, and to get in an answer against the next time the
> trees become green, and that there be no delay. Let it not
> be said to us the canoes are lost under water, or that the
> wind has carried them into another country, or the like
> excuse, but let us have the answer against the trees grown
> green, without fail, for we are in great need of it." (8/270–
> 71. Quotation from E. B. O'Callaghan, *Documentary His-
> tory of New York* [1849–51]. The meeting was at Albany
> in 1696.)

"The words sound real and earnest & I seem to feel the
breath of a man on my cheek," Thoreau wrote below this
speech.

The material on Indian eloquence was also personally
close to him. In the week between December 28, 1854,
when he lectured in Nantucket, and January 4, 1855, when
he lectured in Worcester, he copied 32 pages of extracts

from Cadwallader Colden's *History of the Five Nations* (see 8/470–502). He was not interested in Colden's influential eighteenth-century geopolitical arguments in favor of British-American alliance with the Iroquois; he was interested in the Iroquois speeches at treaties (20 pages of his copying) and what Colden had said about Iroquois justice and government in the introduction. Colden had not lived with Indians for extended periods, but he had attended treaty ceremonies, and Thoreau picked out the information on the eloquence, the deliberations which preceded any formal speech, and the memory-aiding devices: the small sticks a sachem holds while he speaks, passing one to somebody for each point in an agreement, and the wampum belts which symbolized the larger structure of agreements. "Our orators might learn much from the Indians," he had written in his *Journal* a year before, after reading some other speeches. "They are remarkable for their precision; nothing is left at loose ends. They address more senses than one, so as to preclude misunderstanding. A present accompanies each proposition" (January 1, 1854).

An example of these poly-sensual images is in a speech by Canassatego telling the history of his people's relations with the Dutch.

> "It is true, that above one hundred years ago the Dutch came here in a ship, and brought with them several goods; such as awls, knives, hatchets, guns, and many other particulars, which they gave us, and when they had taught us how to use their things, and we saw what sort of people they were, we were so well pleased with them, that we tied their ship to the bushes on the shore; and afterwards, liking them still better the longer they staid with us, and thinking the bushes too slender, we removed the rope, and tied it to the trees; and as the trees were liable to be blown down by high winds, or to decay of themselves, we, from the affection we bore them, again removed the rope, and tied it to a string and a big rock (here the interpreter said, they mean the Oneida country) and not content with this, for its further security we removed the rope to the big mountain (here the interpreter says they mean the Onondaga

country) and there we tied it very fast, and rolled wampum about it." (8/497–98)

There was also conscious wry humor in some of the speeches. This was Canassatego's way of praising Conrad Weiser, the interpreter:

> "When we adopted him, we divided him into 2 equal parts: One we kept for ourselves, and one we left for you. He has had a great deal of trouble with us, wore out his shoes in our messages, and dirtied his clothes by being amongst us, so that he is become as nasty as an Indian." (8/495–96)

The Iroquois were so averse to compelling a person to do what he did not want to do, and also so hospitable, that they refused to return a prisoner and an indentured servant to the British and instead gave them land to farm, protecting the prisoner from the sheriff and paying off the owner of the servant. Thoreau copied this too. It provided precedents for his own protection of fugitive slaves and abolitionists.

His attempts to balance these materials on Indian cruelty and war, justice and eloquence are in various *Journal* entries. Among the Hurons and the Iroquois, he decided,

> everything is done by presents. The murderer and robber are restrained by the very defect of justice, and because the community (his relations or tribe) whips itself for his fault. They must appease the injured with costly presents. They make that he shall involve his friends in ruin along with himself, and if he would injure any one, shall injure them too. By making it impossible for him to do an injury without doing a greater injury than he wishes, they restrain him. (January 6, 1854)

> What an evidence it is, after all, of civilization, or of a capacity for improvement, that savages like our Indians, who in their protracted wars stealthily slay men, women, and children without mercy, with delight, who delight to burn, torture, and devour one another, proving themselves more inhuman in these respects even than beasts,—what a wonderful evidence it is, I say, of their capacity for improvement that even they can enter into the most formal compact

or treaty of peace, burying the hatchet, etc., etc., and treating with each other with as much consideration as the most enlightened states. You would say that they had a genius for diplomacy as well as for war. Consider that Iroquois, torturing his captive, roasting him before a slow fire, biting off the fingers of him alive, and finally eating the heart of him dead, betraying not the slightest evidence of humanity; and now behold him in the council-chamber, where he meets the representatives of the hostile nation to treat of peace, conducting with such perfect dignity and decorum, betraying such a sense of justness. These savages are equal to us civilized men in their treaties, and, I fear, not essentially worse in their wars. (December 30, 1856)

In November 1853, a Concord farmer showed him a pestle which had been plowed up in a field near the river.

It has a rude bird's head, a hawk's or eagle's, the beak and eyes . . . serving for a knob or handle. It is affecting, as a work of art by a people who have left so few traces of themselves, a step beyond the common arrowhead and pestle and axe. Something more fanciful, a step beyond pure utility. . . . It brings the maker still nearer to the races which so ornament their umbrella and cane handles. I have, then, evidence in stone that men lived here who had fancies to be pleased, and in whom the first steps toward a complete culture were taken. . . . Enough of this would have saved him [the Indian] from extermination. (November 29, 1853)

In his reading he found further evidence of "art." As a "bricoleur" himself, he was fascinated by "utility" and did not have great affection, ordinarily, for ornamentation; but this find cut away at a distinction which had implied Indian inferiority.

Other discoveries reaffirmed Indian superiority in knowledge of nature. Birds made nests and Indians could have made fishline, he speculated, from fibers under the bark of milkweed stems.

I hold a piece of the dead weed in my hands, strip off a narrow shred of the bark before my neighbor's eyes and separate ten or twelve fibres as fine as a hair, roll them in

141

my fingers, and offer him the thread to try its strength. He is surprised and mortified to find that he cannot break it. (January 19, 1856)

When he and Daniel Ricketson visited Martha Simons, "the only pure-blooded Indian left about New Bedford," he learned a little about medicine.

> The question she answered with most interest was, "What do you call that plant?" and I reached her the aletris from my hat. She took it, looked at it a moment, and said, "That's husk-root. It's good to put into bitters for a weak stomach." The last year's light-colored and withered leaves surround the present green star like a husk. This must be the origin of the name. Its root is described as intensely bitter. I ought to have had my hat full of plants. (June 26, 1856)

He also gathered some fascinating "Materia medica" from John Dunn Hunter's *Memoirs of a Captivity* (1823), in which many of the names for plants were given according to what they cured.

> Angelica—they smoke it, &c. In Ind. means "agreeable taste."
> Anise—in Ind. "It expels the wind."
> Ashes—or "fire gone out." For sourness in stomach, &c.
> An astringent root—in Ind. "It stops the blood flowing out" —carry it with them.
> "It scares bears away"—plant also is a cathartic, &c.
> "Beavers eat it"—a root carrot-like.
> Black locust—Ind. "it makes sick," an emetic.
> (8/441. These are just the first of Thoreau's copied list.)

A very different testimony to Indian achievement was Hunter's surprising journey, with the Osage and Kansas, up the Arkansas and Platte Rivers, across the Rockies, and down the Columbia to the Pacific Ocean—and back, in "16 moons." If this story was to be believed—and Cass and the anti-Indian experts assuredly did not believe it (Cass attacked it in the January 1826, *North American Review*)— then MacKenzie's Canadian expedition and Lewis and Clark's American one were not the first to cross the West.

Other groups of Indians had very likely made similar journeys for years. A great symbol of white American achievement would fall.

Thoreau's most comprehensive statement on the meaning
of all this intelligence was in the *Journal* entry of February 3, 1859. The entry is four and a half pages long, in print,
and is one of his finest. But it is also one of his most complex, because of another of his intriguing juxtapositions of
material. "Five minutes before 3 p.m.," the entry begins,
"Father died." Thoreau chose the day of his father's death—
on which day he went on to write two and a half pages
of restrained description of the death, thoughts about death;
and a brief chronology of his father's life—as the day on
which to write also an eloquent defense of Indians and a
summary of what he felt about them. The implied identifications and contrasts are profound. It is necessary, therefore, to read what he says about death and his father as
well as the Indians.

> I have touched a body which was flexible and warm, yet
> tenantless,—warmed by what fire? When the spirit that
> animated some matter has left it, who else, what else, can
> animate it?
> How enduring are our bodies, after all! The forms of
> our brothers and sisters, our parents and children and
> wives, lie still in the hills and fields round about us, not to
> mention those of our remoter ancestors, and the matter
> which composed the body of our first human father still
> exists under another name.
> When in sickness the body is emaciated, and the expres-
> sion of the face in various ways is changed, you perceive un-
> expected resemblances to other members of the same family;
> as if within the same family there was a greater general simi-
> larity in the framework of the face than in its filling up and
> clothing.

The next paragraph is on the places John Thoreau had lived
and worked, and includes a period in Bangor, Maine, "selling to Indians (among others)." But by the time of his

143

death, Thoreau continues, he was one of the oldest inhabitants of Concord and "the one perhaps best acquainted with . . . the local, social, and street history of the middle of the town, for the last fifty years." His experience in trade and his affection for gossip in shops and post office made him a major authority. "He belonged in a peculiar sense to the village street."

Then Thoreau wrote an almost equally long memorial to the Indians.

Some have spoken slightingly of the Indians, as a race possessing so little skill and wit, so low in the scale of humanity, and so brutish that they hardly deserved to be remembered, —using only the terms "miserable," "wretched," "pitiful," and the like. In writing their histories of this country they have so hastily disposed of this refuse of humanity (as they might have called it) which littered and defiled the shore and the interior. But even the indigenous animals are inexhaustibly interesting to us. How much more, then, the indigenous man of America! If wild men, so much more like ourselves than they are unlike, have inhabited these shores before us, we wish to know particularly what manner of men they were, how they lived here, their relation to nature, their arts and their customs, their fancies and superstitions. They paddled over these waters, they wandered in these woods, and they had their fancies and beliefs connected with the sea and the forest, which concern us quite as much as the fables of Oriental nations do. It frequently happens that the historian, though he professes more humanity than the trapper, mountain man, or golddigger, who shoots one as a wild beast, really exhibits and practices a similar inhumanity to him, wielding a pen instead of a rifle.

One tells you with more contempt than pity that the Indian had no religion, holding up both hands, and this to all the shallow-brained and bigoted seems to mean something important, but it is commonly a distinction without a difference. Pray, how much more religion has the historian? If Henry Ward Beecher knows so much more about God than another, if he has made some discovery of truth in this

144

direction, I would thank him to publish it in *Silliman's Journal*, with as few flourishes as possible.

It is the spirit of humanity, that which animates both so-called savages and civilized nations, working through a man, and not the man expressing himself, that interests us most. The thought of a so-called savage tribe is generally far more just than that of a single civilized man.

I perceive that we partially die ourselves through sympathy at the death of each of our friends or near relatives. Each such experience is an assault on our vital force. It becomes a source of wonder that they who have lost many friends still live. After long watching around the sick-bed of a friend, we, too, partially give up the ghost with him, and are the less to be identified with this state of things. (February 3, 1859)

The last paragraph is on the subject of writing. "The writer must to some extent inspire himself." The process brings thoughts, and the expressions, in turn, improve with thought. In this case, he surely was inspired, as well as fully conscious of a provocative association.

One association, which he had made many times before, was of Indians with age. Since his earliest writing, they had been associated with sunset, dusk, and antiquity; the white man, "this young and still fair Saxon slip," with dawn. But now he went further and linked Indians with his dead father. The paragraph on "the forms of our brothers and sisters, our parents and children and wives" enduring in the "hills and fields round about us" makes the connection explicit. All go back to and endure with "our first human father" whose matter "still exists under another name." In the next paragraph his thoughts on sickness bringing out family facial resemblances tend, finally, in the same direction. Beneath the "filling up and clothing" are the deeper structures not only of the Thoreaus but the whole human family.

But what other similarities, or differences, did he see between his father and his Indian fathers? The tribute to "Father" for his knowledge of "local, social, and street history" is especially interesting because of Henry's great early difference from him on this point. John Thoreau "belonged in a peculiar sense to the village street." Henry Thoreau fled from the village street. He went off to live like an Indian and belong to the woods. Returning to the village street was, as he wrote in *Walden*, like running the gantlet, being licked by the tribe of John Thoreau till he had given up his gossip. Thus, at that stage of Henry's life, Indians represented a rebellion against his father. They were wild fathers who were preferable to this tame, sociable, civilized one. A young Leatherstocking, Henry went out to find Tahattawan, his Chingachgook. To begin with, he went out with his brother John, also a rebel, who could be thought of as the ideal Indian brother. In brotherly rivalry, conversely, John was also the Indian brother-enemy who was now, like them, extinct.

Yet as Henry came to recognize the amazing social qualities of Indians, both from his reading and his times in Maine, the image of "the Indian" as solitary rebel had to give way. Here Indians and Father looked less and less like opposites and more the same. And in these later years, as the *Journal* shows, Henry asked his father about Concord and family history and became more a part of the village street himself. He enjoyed John's memories of *his* father, a cooper who had become a privateer in the Revolution and who was "a short man, a little taller than my father, stout and very strong for his size" (October 21, 1856). He sought his father's help in listing the owners of the old houses on their street (October 21, 1855). He participated more fully in the affairs of Concord. As Indians had once served his rebellion, they now served his socialization.

The role of Henry's mother is of equal interest, for it was Cynthia Dunbar Thoreau who was the stronger, more voluble, and dominant parent. "Throughout [John Thoreau's] married life," writes Walter Harding, "he lived quietly, peacefully, and contentedly in the shadow of his wife, who towered a full head above him."[3] She ran the house, invited numerous guests and boarders to the family table, worked busily in church, charitable, and anti-slavery societies. It was she who, with some other people, persuaded Emerson to write the open letter to President Van Buren protesting the removal of the Cherokees.[4] Some of Henry's Indian sympathies clearly came from her, and it was also she who was anxious for Henry to leave the family home, "buckle on his knapsack and roam abroad to seek his fortune." Henry cried when she said that, and he was consoled by his sister Helen.[5] Later, when he lived at Walden, the family was, on the other hand, so concerned about him (and he, surely, about them) that "he made a point of stopping off regularly at his parents' house to reassure them all." The somewhat scurrilous Concord rumor, apparently, was that he even took his mother's pies back to the woods.[6] The pattern of maternal ambivalence seems there—telling the children to go away and be independent, but also pulling them back to be dependent. Cynthia Dunbar Thoreau looks as mighty as a Hannah Dustan, the kind of woman who in the seventeenth century could have stood at the gun hole shooting Indians, and equally as protective, one who in the nineteenth century spoke out for the wronged slaves and Indians—and her sons.[7] Living like an Indian was a way for Henry to be wild and independent, but to stay home.

So in defending the Indians and his father at the same time, Thoreau took a position of many ambivalences himself. As a man who had not been a great success in the world, John Thoreau might be disposed of by some Americans as hastily as the historians disposed of the Indians. Yet neither had Henry, in 1859, been a great success to most Americans. He had rebelled against his tame father, then come to see his father's quiet virtues. He had made his white and his Indian fathers opposites; he now came to identify them.

The wider American dilemmas were that both were ancestors, they were rivals to one another, and both were ancestral rivals to the sons. A high estimate of the Indian fathers could nourish and energize filial rebellion against the immediate white father. A low estimate of them, on the other hand, was morally necessary in the national justification of the white fathers' treatment of them. The historians who wielded the pen instead of the rifle knew this well. The white sons and fathers had mythologized them both ways—natural noblemen who were ideals and "as a race possessing so little skill and wit, so low in the scale of humanity, and so brutish that they hardly deserved to be remembered." Thoreau had disproven the latter notion and also come to see that the reality did not quite reach the former either. His reading and his Maine experience had made him aware, perhaps more than anything else, of the variety of Indian life and people. Yet the humanity of "wild men, so much more like ourselves than they are unlike," totally destroyed the historians' and white fathers' justification. How could he pay honor to the Indians and still honor his white fathers? Through which, or against which did he claim inheritance to his mother and the American earth?

Thus the final urgent question in the "Indian Books" is what happened when the red and white fathers met? What were the causes of Indian decline?

Going back to the earliest English settlement in America, the Roanoke Colony, Thoreau copied this from Thomas Harriot's *A Briefe and True Report of the New Found Land of Virginia* (1590).

> There was no town where we had any subtile devise practised against us, we leaving it unpunished or not revenged (because we sought by all means possible to win them by gentleness) but that within a few days after our departure from such town, the people began to die very fast, and many in short space; in some towns about twenty, in some forty, in some sixty, & in one six score, which in truth was very many in respect of their numbers. This happened in no place that we could learn but where we had been, where they used some practice against us, and after such time. The disease also so strange, that they neither knew what it was, nor how to cure it; the like by report of

148

the oldest men in the country never happened before, time out of mind. A thing specially observed by us as also by the natural inhabitants themselves. (10/645–46. I have modernized the spelling.)

Thoreau added of this paragraph, "Indeed, it was as if mere intercourse with the whites caused a mysterious and peculiar disease which swept off the natives. It is pathetic to read—is told more at length–and will be *worth quoting fully.*"

From Thomas Morton's *New English Canaan* (1632), he learned the story of how Massachusetts had been swept by disease a few years before English settlement. A French ship had come to Massachusetts Bay, there had been some provocation, and the natives attacked it.

A short time after, "the hand of God fell heavily upon them, with such a mortal stroke, that they died in heaps as they lay in their houses, and the living that were able to shift for themselves would run away, and let them die, and let their carcasses lie above ground without burial." Sometimes only one of many left alive. "And the bones and skulls upon the several places of their habitations made such a spectacle after my coming into those parts, that as I travelled in that forest, near the Massachusetts, it seemed to me a new found Golgotha." Says that this mortality was not ended when the Pilgrims came. Thinks it was the plague. How like Harriot's account of the Ind. of N. C.!! and the Jesuit ac. of the Hurons!! (10/468)

The "Jesuit ac. of the Hurons" to which Thoreau referred in his note was in Father Hierosme Lalemant's *Relation* for 1639–1640. He had already extracted it:

The malady that now prevailed was the small pox. "They remarked with some kind of foundation that since our arrival in these lands those who had been nearest us were found most ruined by the maladies, and that whole bourgs of those that had received us saw themselves now altogether exterminated." So they resolved to banish the French— believing that they had intelligence with the malady— themselves not being attacked. "I must confess that these

149

poor people are somewhat excusable, for it has happened very often & one has remarked it more than a hundred times, where we were most welcome, where we baptized most people, it was there in fact that they died most; &c." (8/134–35)

In addition to disease, there were, to be sure, the white people's superior technology in war and the treaties and promises broken by the whites. Those causes were summed up in a passage Thoreau quoted from Heckewelder's *History, Manners, and Customs*:

"I have heard them, for instance, compare the English & American Nations to a pair of scissors. . . . By the construction of this instrument, they said, it would appear as if in shutting, these two sharp knives would strike together and destroy each others' edges; but no such thing: they only cut *what comes between them*. And thus the English & Americans do when they go to war against one another. It is not each other that they want to destroy, but us, poor Indians, that are between them. By this means they get our land; when that is obtained the scissors are closed again, and laid by for further use." (9/171)

As Loskiel listed causes in his *History of the Mission of the United Brethren*, there was also rum and intra-Indian war.

"Their decrease is owing to intemperance, drunkenness, poison, irregular marriages, & the many wars they carry on, not only with the Europeans, but with each other, at their instigation." (9/426)

One man, speaking to Father Le Jeune, defended French wine and brandy, giving another explanation:

"No, said he, it is not these drinks that take away our life; but your writings, for since you have described our country, our rivers, our lands (terres) & our woods, we all die, which did not happen before you came here." (7/84)

But disease, the metaphor which Thoreau started to develop, would have covered all of these. Rum, war, treaties which were written and not remembered, even science and writing were the diseases of civilization, before which the wise savage fled. Thoreau further learned that many animals, too, had run from contact with civilized men and women. "The wildest and noblest quadrupeds, even the largest fresh-water fishes, some of the wildest and noblest birds and fairest flowers have actually receded as *we* advanced" (*J.*, March 5, 1858).

Another carrier of the disease was the fur trade.

"The articles necessary for this trade are coarse woolen clothes of different kinds; milled blankets of different sizes; arms and ammunition; twist and carrot tobacco; Manchester goods; linens and coarse sheetings; thread, lines, and twine; common hardware; cutlery and iron mongery of several description; kettles of brass and copper, and sheet iron; silk and cotton handkerchiefs; hats, shoes, and hose; calicoes and printed cottons, etc., etc. Spirituous liquors, etc., are purchased in Canada."

"The produce of the year of which I am speaking (ap. 1798) consisted of the following furs and peltries:

106,000	Beaver skins	6000	Lynx skins
2100	Bear skins	600	Wolverine skins
1500	Fox skins	1650	Fisher skins
4000	Kitt Fox skins	100	Rackoon skins
4600	Otter skins	3800	Wolf skins
17,000	Musquash skins	700	Elk skins
32,000	Marten skins	750	Deer skins
1800	Mink skins	1200	Deer skins dressed"
500	Buffalo robes		

(12/86–87, from Alexander MacKenzie, *Voyages from Montreal . . . to the Frozen and Pacific Oceans . . .* [1802])

Thoreau, impressed by these awful numbers, wondered whether they applied to the whole fur trade of 1798 or just the Northwest Fur Company, in which MacKenzie was a partner. He was disgusted.

What a pitiful business is the fur trade . . . unweariedly pursuing and ferreting out small animals by the aid of all the loafing class tempted by rum and money. . . . The Indian led a more respectable life before he was tempted to debase himself so much by the white man. Think how many musquash and weasel skins the Hudson's Bay Company pile up annually in their warehouses, leaving the bare red carcasses on the banks of the streams throughout all British America,—and this it is, chiefly, which makes it *British* America. It is the place where Great Britain goes a-mousing. (*J.*, April 8, 1859)

Against the disease of civilization, what is the cure? Thoreau's ringing answer is, "Wildness." "In Wildness is the preservation of the World." And wildness is not the West or great forests, it is in every swamp on the fringe of a village, in every wild berry and within each person. In a crucial passage in "Walking," he makes these vital connections.

I enter a swamp as a sacred place, a *sanctum sanctorum*. There is the strength, the marrow, of Nature. The wildwood covers the virgin mould, and the same soil is good for men and for trees. A man's health requires as many acres of meadow to his prospect as his farm does loads of muck. There are the strong meats on which he feeds. A town is saved, not more by the righteous men in it than by the woods and swamps that surround it.[8]

As marrow restores the red corpuscles in the blood, so does a swamp restore fertility and regenerate a town. And Thoreau associated swamps with red men. Both were wild remnants, both restored him (see *Journal*, November 23, 1852).

But the trouble with this cure is that it is mainly for the white man. The white goes to the red to cure himself of his own civilized disease, thereby bringing the small pox and rum, greed and war which are death to the wild and the Indian. The disease is also fiendishly viral, using both the strengths and the weaknesses of the victim as it overcomes him. The fur trade used the Indians' hunting skills and greed for manufactured goods in destroying the animals they had depended on. The Indians who had been most hospitable to white men and Christianity *and* the ones who had stayed and fought white men most heroically were the most likely to be infected. White people may have a self-interest in preventing this and in preserving wildness and Indians, but the Indians would have been better off had the whites never arrived.

The dilemmas of ancestral responsibility, therefore, had no easy solutions. White men bore the disease of civilization, but Indians could not resist it. The process seemed irreversible, and Thoreau continued to believe in the forecasts of Indian extinction. In his *Journal* of December 29, 1853, he saw Indians facing "the end of the world." On January 23, 1858, a year before his father's death, he sounded the same note:

Who can doubt that men are by a certain fate what they are, contending with unseen and unimagined difficulties, or encouraged and aided by equally mysterious auspicious circumstances? Who can doubt this essential and innate difference between man and man, when he considers a whole race, like the Indian, inevitably and resignedly passing away in spite of our efforts to Christianize and educate them? Individuals accept their fate and live according to it, as the Indian does. Everybody notices that the Indian retains his habits wonderfully,—is still the same man that the discoverers found. The fact is, the history of the white man is a history of improvement, that of the red man a history of fixed habits of stagnation. (January 23, 1858)

On the same day, pursuing these winter thoughts, he observed that the white man was to the Indian as the dog to the fox. The bark of the dog has more clarity and music; the fox has a "smothered, ragged, feeble, and unmusical sound," like the dull and mumbled sounds of the Indian. Foxes and Indians are unimproved and frightened of dogs and white men.

Yet such confident approval of improvement was not his usual attitude. Improvement meant something quite different to him from what it meant to other white Americans. Thus, though he pitied Indians for the fate before them, he did not generally pity them for their backwardness or deficiencies and censure them for their refusal to become Christian and educated. Here, too, he was far away from the conventions of savagism. If the fate of the Indians was extinction, then he wished to learn as much as possible while he could. He must supplement his historical study with visits to the Penobscots in Maine.

CHAPTER VI

Maine—The Lessons of
the Forest

The Maine Woods has not been well appreciated or understood. It is nowhere near as famous as *Walden* and "Resistance to Civil Government" nor even as well known as *A Week on the Concord and Merrimack Rivers*. Like *Cape Cod* and *A Yankee in Canada*, it is a travel book, which so far has interested Thoreau scholars and some vacationers, but it has not seemed a book having social import or deserving intense literary study. Its major early sales, according to its modern editor, came during the travel and sporting boom in Maine in the 1880s,[1] and it continues to be a favorite book of climbers of Katahdin, canoeists, campers, and photographers. But it is much more.

From the standpoint of Thoreau's Indian education, it is, unquestionably, his most important book, "the book about Indians" which he *did* write. On the three trips to Maine in 1846, 1853, and 1857, which are the basis of its three parts, "Ktaadn," "Chesuncook," and "The Allegash and East Branch," Thoreau had his longest and closest contacts with real people, as opposed to the savagist Indians he read about and the improved Transcendental or poetic Indians of his imagination. The trips were only of two- or three-week durations, and he had little contact with Indian community life, two disadvantages on which I will have more to say shortly; but the trips were intense, both physically and emotionally, and Thoreau was a master at making the most of such experiences. Moreover, in being spread over a twelve-year period, the trips show a development in his sensitivities which is remarkable. Unlike other nineteenth-century literary visitors to Indian country—Washington Irving, Francis Parkman, and Margaret Fuller, to name

155

three—Thoreau kept going back. And so we can see a growth in both his personal and literary skill which their accounts lack. It is ironic that on the strength of their brief single trips Irving and Parkman were treated as literary experts on Indians and the West. *A Tour on the Prairies,* which established Irving as a man who could write about Western Americana as well as about Europe, led to his two later books on the fur trade. *The Oregon Trail,* still a popular adventure book, laid down Parkman's experiential authority for his histories of the British, French, and Indian wars. Yet he was actually with the Indians a shorter time than was Thoreau. And the extent of Thoreau's "Indian Books" should also lead us to wonder whether Parkman had read any more than he.

The Maine Woods deserves comparison with these better-known and more-popular works because it is Thoreau's "western book." Ever alert to make the most of what was close, he recognized that central Maine in his time was an eastern frontier wilderness. Maine had been a state since 1819, but by the 1840s and 1850s, its population was still confined to its coast. The country he visited, eighty and more miles inland, was too cold and densely forested to attract white settlers. Ktaadn (as he spelled it) had been climbed by only four other parties of white men. The mountains of Maine, by his measurement, were in a region 160 miles long and 60 miles wide, and "the wild or unsettled portion . . . far more extensive." Consequently, "some hours only of travel in this direction will carry the curious to the verge of a primitive forest, more interesting, perhaps, on all accounts, than they would reach by going a thousand miles westward" (p. 4). Thoreau went northeast to go west!

The appeals of this New England west were to him "the Moose, the Pine Tree & the Indian," as he described the subjects of "Chesuncook" when placing it with the *Atlantic* magazine.[2] The moose was the largest animal in northeastern America (the New England buffalo, we might say), and, like the buffalo, was the great source of meat, hide, and other necessities to the Indians. The white pine, perhaps (with the wild apple) Thoreau's favorite tree, was the tallest in the Northeast, and so broad that a yoke of oxen could stand on its stump after one was cut down (p. 229). The Indians of Maine had appealed to him also since a trip he made in May 1838, when looking for a teaching job. As this *Journal* entry shows, they were the daemons of this wilderness.

> The railroad from Bangor to Oldtown is civilization shooting off in a tangent into the forest. I had much conversation with an old Indian at the latter place, who sat dreaming upon a scow at the waterside and striking his deer-skin moccasins against the planks, while his arms hung listlessly by his side. He was the most communicative man I had met. Talked of hunting and fishing, old times and new times. Pointing up the Penobscot, he observed, "Two or three mile up the river one beautiful country!" and then, as if he would come as far to meet me as I had gone to meet him, he exclaimed, "Ugh! one very hard time!" But he had mistaken his man. (May 10, 1838)

The scene here is, in fact, emblematic: the old Indian and the young white man meeting on the river bank, the one having come downstream and the other having come up. It would do for a scene in Conrad's *Heart of Darkness*. The dreaming savage and the dreaming white man. In the old daemon's words is the enigma of the wilderness. " 'One beautiful country!' " But " 'Ugh! one very hard time!' " And, considering the impact of these words on Thoreau, we may doubt whether the Indian had really "mistaken his man." The enigma was the challenge, and a part of the challenge was the implied laziness or inferiority of the speaker. He played the savagist role of being old and listless and barely hinting at what was to be learned. A further challenge of the woods was to learn what such a man knew.

Whether the old Indian was playing listless and inferior or not, it is also important to note that Thoreau almost automatically *thought* of him as inferior. Despite his great curiosity about Indians and admiration of them on some

157

points, face to face the young Thoreau of 1838 found them slightly droll and comical. He did not think that the Indian knew him as well as he knew the Indian. He thought of himself as young and energetic, the Indian as old and sedentary. The Indian was simple, like the one in *Walden* who thought people should buy his baskets just because he had made them. Cynically, it might be said of Thoreau that he thought himself morally and intellectually superior to most men, not alone Indians, but the cause of the Indian's inferiority was racial. Thoreau shared with almost all Anglo-Americans of his time a conscious and unconscious assumption of Anglo-Saxon superiority. Margaret Fuller illustrates the same when she says in her "western book," *A Summer on the Lakes*, that Indians cannot look whites straight in the eye, because they feel their own inferiority! Parkman and Irving certainly manifest this attitude as well. Uncorrupted Indians were, they felt, superior to rabble whites such as infect the frontier. But a drunken or corrupted Indian was beneath even them, and most Indians on the frontier were judged corrupted. The exceptions, to such tourists, were the men they hired as their guides. Irving regarded his guide Pierre Beatte, "a half-breed of French and Osage parentage," as a knight of the prairies, and though he was at first skeptical of Beatte's sullen silence, he came to admire him greatly.[3] Parkman's guide Henry Chatillon, though Indian mainly by marriage to the daughter of a Sioux chief, was a similar ideal figure.

The guides are crucial to the tours. First of all, success and safety depend on them. But they also function as the interpreters and priests who philosophically *guide* the travellers into the secrets of the West, initiate them into mysteries of Indian and wilderness life. Thus they must be the travellers' superiors. But relations between traveller and guide still vary considerably in these books, and the three parts of *The Maine Woods* contain three different ones. We can see the progress of Thoreau's education by studying and comparing these relationships.

"Ktaadn"

Let us begin, then, with Thoreau's story of his and his cousin's engaging Indian guides for their climb of Katahdin in 1846. They had driven up the shore of the Penobscot River by buggy from Bangor, and at Lincoln, forty-five miles north, they went over to an Indian settlement on an island. The small huts were in beautiful, secluded places. Near where Thoreau and Thatcher landed, a young girl was singing on a rock. On the shore was a salmon-spear, which seemed to be of very old design. Like the girl's song, everything was peaceful and "aboriginal." But as they approached the first house, they "were met by a sally of a dozen wolfish-looking dogs." The occupant came out, beat off the dogs with a long pole, then spoke "in his sluggish way." He was a "dull and greasy-looking fellow," and Thoreau clearly did not like him. Yet he and a friend named Louis Neptune, who lived in the next house, were going up river that day themselves. Getting the "same doggish reception," they went to talk to Louis, "a small, wiry man, with puckered and wrinkled face." But he, Thoreau realized, had been up Katahdin in 1837 with the Maine state geologist, and so plans were made. The white men said,

"Well, Louis, suppose you get to the Point . . . to camp, we walk on up the West Branch to-morrow—four of us— and wait for you at the dam, or this side. You overtake us to-morrow or next day, and take us into your canoes. We stop for you, you stop for us. We pay you for your trouble." "Ye!" replied Louis, "may be you carry some provision for all—some pork—some bread—and so pay." He said, "Me sure get some moose;" and when I asked, if he thought Pomola would let us go up, he answered that we must plant one bottle of rum on the top, he had planted good many; and when he looked again, the rum was all gone. He had been up two or three times: he had planted letter—English, German, French, &c. These men were slightly clad in shirt and pantaloons, like laborers with us in warm weather. They did not invite us into their houses,

but met us outside. So we left the Indians, thinking ourselves lucky to have secured such guides and companions.
(Pp. 9–10)

The meeting was obviously tense, and the complacent
last sentence resolves no anxieties. Thoreau simply did not
like these two men as well as he did the "aboriginal" ideals
represented by the girl and the outer surroundings. His own
questions about Pomola also seem slightly condescending—
jovial trifling with what to the others may have been serious beliefs. Pomola is a storm-bird which, according to
Penobscot tradition, lives on Katahdin.[4] In a later passage
Thoreau states his own belief that "the tops of mountains
are among the unfinished parts of the globe, whither it is
a slight insult to the gods to climb and pry into their secrets. . . ." "Simple races, as savages," do not climb them,
he says. "Pomola is always angry with those who climb to
the summit of Ktaadn" (p. 65). He may be wrong in this.
The vast majority of people from "civilized races" don't
climb high mountains either. For those who do, like Thoreau, the experience and challenge are also in some way
sacred. But if he believed this, then his teasing questions
were somewhat perverse. Neptune's tall tale about the
bottle of rum may have been meant to soothe feelings; it
was certainly meant pleasantly. Yet it could not have
pleased Thoreau.

A few pages before, he had given the reader his opinions
about Indians and alcohol. He had seen a "short shabby
washer-woman-looking Indian" beach his canoe by a grocery
store and carry in a bundle of skins to trade for whiskey.
"This picture will do to put before the Indian's history, that
is, the history of his extinction," Thoreau said (p. 6). The
poor effeminate man, who also had "the woe-begone look
of the girl that cried for spilt milk," was selling his birthright for a keg of whiskey. "These were once a powerful
tribe," Thoreau added, after describing their (to him) for-
lorn and cheerless houses and trim Catholic church. "I even

thought that a row of wigwams, with a dance of pow-wows, and a prisoner tortured at the stake, would be more respectable than this" (p. 7). Such clichés and stock responses come, as we have seen, from the most hackneyed commentary on the Indian plight. They seem sympathetic, but there is no understanding. They shift the burden of guilt to the Indians themselves or the French missionaries, and they set up the peculiar logic of savagism and civilization. Drunken or Catholic Indians are bad because they are improperly civilized; dancing or torturing ones are bad because they are too savage. To say that the latter are "more respectable" is idle.

Thoreau and his party then reach the rendezvous point and wait, but the two Indians never show up. As substitute guides they hire two white woodsmen, George McCauslin and Thomas Fowler, and go ahead to climb Katahdin. Days later, as they are again standing on the banks of the Millinocket, they see two canoes coming up stream, and in one are

> Louis Neptune and his companion, now at last on their way up to Chesuncook after moose; but they were so disguised that we hardly knew them. At a little distance, they might have been taken for Quakers, with their broadbrimmed hats, and overcoats with broad capes, the spoils of Bangor, seeking a settlement in this Sylvania,—or, nearer at hand, for fashionable gentlemen, the morning after a spree. Met face to face, these Indians in their native woods looked like the sinister and slouching fellows whom you meet picking up strings and paper in the streets of a city. There is, in fact, a remarkable and unexpected resemblance between the degraded savage and the lowest classes in a great city. The one is no more a child of nature than the other. In the progress of degradation, the distinction of races is soon lost. Neptune at first was only anxious to know what we "kill," seeing some partridges in the hands of one of the party, but we had assumed too much anger to permit of a reply. We thought Indians had some honor before. But—"Me been sick. O, me unwell now. You make

161

bargain, then me go." They had in fact been delayed so long by a drunken frolic at the Five Islands, and they had not yet recovered from its effects. (P. 78)

The entire episode is a kind of miniature of a "broken treaty." In most cases it was the whites who broke the treaties, but frontier whites also had a fixed notion that Indians were deceitful and unreliable, presumably from experiences similar to this. Thoreau and his companions put on their most reproving stares, and it is interesting how he compares them first to Quakers, then to hung-over rakes, and finally to urban beggars. None can stand up beside the accomplished outdoorsmen who have now been to Katahdin on their own. Speculating on the differences between a white man to whom the wilderness is a "new world" and the Indian who lives "three thousand years deep into time, an age not yet described by poets," Thoreau imagines:

> In a bark vessel sewn with the roots of the spruce, with horn-beam paddles he dips his way along. He is but dim and misty to me, obscured by the aeons that lie between the bark canoe and the batteau. He builds no house of logs, but a wigwam of skins. He eats no hot-bread and sweetcake, but musquash and moose-meat and the fat of bears. He glides up the Millinocket and is lost to my sight, as a more distant and misty cloud is seen flitting by behind a nearer, and is lost in space. So he goes about his destiny, the red face of man. (P. 79)

"Red face of man," in this context, surely means drunken and shamed as well as Indian. "Dips his way along" also seems like a pun, referring not only to the Indians' paddling but also to their staggering and tippling. All these debasements being alien to Thoreau, they add to the sense of distance and mist.[5]

We never get the Indians' point of view on the episode. It, too, is lost in the mist. But there seems to be an uncanny connection between Thoreau's prejudgments and their deeds. In telling the story he may have emphasized his prejudgments in order to give greater impact to the final discovery of the "drunken frolic at the Five Islands," but it is still fair for us to say that he got what he expected and that his expectations may have had something to do with the getting. He and his cousin condescended to Neptune and the "greasy-looking fellow" as if they were simple servants. They in turn behaved like unreliable, scoundrel servants, then came up to be reproved. Looking at the episode from another angle, we might consider that the Indians treated the white men to a taste of "Indian time," where schedules are supposedly followed more loosely. But the underlying meaning of "Indian time" is that the Indians set the pace. They did not wish to be servants but guides in the full sense.

Whatever explanation we seek for the "broken treaty," it demonstrates the amazing tension present in the relations between red guides and white travellers. Normally, "western books" don't express or examine these tensions very deeply. Most confident white writer-travellers of the nineteenth century seem not to have felt them. If they criticize their guides, they do so without much self-criticism. Thoreau, on the surface, is no exception. But he reports on his Maine experiences with such candor and detail that we can recognize tensions and rivalries which other travellers don't let us see. Though Thoreau did not publicize his responses and analyses in any overtly confessional manner, he preserved the evidence. As his trips progress he begins to let us see his guides as people who may be as complex as himself. He doesn't take their side, but he sees that it exists and from time to time states it. And thus he makes *The Maine Woods* a psychological as well as geographic journey.

Yet a further consequence of the Indian guides' failure to appear is that Thoreau and his party had a purely "white" experience of Katahdin. They had no natives of the place to tell stories of it and its spirits and mediate between nature and white man. The pioneers McCauslin and Fowler were intelligent, self-reliant, and skillful, synthesizing a foreign worldliness with Indian knowledge of trail-following and batteau-handling, but they provided no mental or spiritual guidance, which helps explain the alienation which Thoreau felt on Katahdin. He was as close as he would ever come to Hannah Dustan's experience of a complete wilderness.

Eager to reach the top, he made his first attempt on it alone, while his companions were making camp after the first day's climb from the base. He went up a waterfall which was like a "giant's stairway," then scrambled over the tops of thick, stunted black spruce trees. Beneath him, he thought, were bears' dens, with the bears "even then at home." Walking on the tops of trees reminded him of Milton's description of Satan crossing the Abyss to the throne of Chaos:

> "——nigh founder'd, on he fares,
> Treading the crude consistence, half on foot,
> Half flying."   (P. 61, from *Paradise Lost*, II, 940–42)

Rocks which he sees later are "gray" and "silent" and look like a herd of goats or sheep "chewing a rocky cud." When a cloud cuts off this dismal scenery, he returns to the desolate campsite.

The next morning, when the party starts up a different trail, Thoreau's emotions are still much the same. The huge rocks and "hostile" clouds make him think of "the creations of the old epic and dramatic poets, of Atlas, Vulcan, the Cyclops, and Prometheus" (p. 64). It is a Nature so remote and inhuman that the climber's spirit escapes, and he imagines Nature asking why he has come and why he hasn't stayed in the valleys where he was meant to be. He answers with another Miltonic excerpt, Satan's address to Chaos:

> "Chaos and ancient Night, I come no spy
> With purpose to explore or to disturb
> The secrets of your realm, but ° ° °
> ° ° ° ° ° ° ° as my way
> Lies through your spacious empire up to light."
> (P. 64, from *P. L.* II, 970–74, Thoreau's ellipses)

It is at this point also that he re-introduces the Indian god Pomola as "always angry with those who climb to the summit of Ktaadn" and speaks of the Indians as not climbing mountains, because the "tops are sacred and mysterious tracts." Mountain-climbing, he is clearly implying, is both a "daring and insolent" civilized pursuit and a deeply rebellious Satanic-Promethean one. He brings these perceptions to their climax during the descent from the mountain itself.

Thoreau and his party were crossing what they called "Burnt Lands," a desolate country ignited by lightning, presumably, years before. It had no sign of human presence— just a "pasture for the moose and deer," with a few patches of blueberries and occasional young trees. It was terrifying for its utter remoteness from man, and yet beautiful in its way, "the fresh and natural surface of the planet Earth." To Thoreau, this land was simply "Matter," not man's "Mother Earth that we have heard of." If men could inhabit it, they would be ancient heathens, "men nearer of kin to the rocks and to wild animals than we." But having produced this fearful estrangement for Thoreau, it finally led to a trembling excitement:

> I stand in awe of my body, this matter to which I am bound has become so strange to me. I fear not spirits, ghosts, of which I am one,—*that* my body might,—but I fear bodies, I tremble to meet them. What is this Titan that has possession of me? Talk of mysteries!—Think of our life in nature,—daily to be shown matter, to come in contact with it,—rocks, trees, wind on our cheeks! the *solid* earth! the *actual* world! the *common sense! Contact! Contact! Who* are we? *where* are we? (Pp. 69–71)

Had Thoreau grown familiar with "men nearer of kin to the rocks and to wild animals" (as he imagined them), he probably could not have written this splendid passage. The "Burnt Lands" gave him a momentary sense of the strangeness of Earth, when perception of it is not mediated

165

by the presence or traditions of human inhabitants. Simultaneously, it gave him sense of the strangeness, the mystery
of his own body. Thoreau is a greater writer and greater
witness to nature, most of his readers today agree, because
his usual familiarity with "Mother Earth" is balanced here
by this sense of terror before "Matter" Earth. Also behind
this experience, in cultural ancestry, is the Puritan association of Indians and the American wilderness with Chaos
and the demonic. Such mystery, to Thoreau, was finally
but greater enticement. "Matter" Earth must become as
well known, whether good or bad, as "Mother Earth."[6] The
Indians, he assumed, must hold the key. They were the
demons or daemons of the place, the kinsmen not of "our
race" but of another race to whom the wild was fair.
"Though the railroad and the telegraph have been established on the shores of Maine," he wrote at the end of this
essay, "the Indian still looks out from her interior mountains over all these to the sea" (p. 82). So return to Maine
he must.

"Chesuncook"

In "Chesuncook," Thoreau's account of his 1853 Maine adventure, we can see substantial progress in his relations
with his guide. Joe Aitteon, whom Thoreau's cousin had
already engaged when Thoreau arrived in Bangor, was the
son of a tribal Governor and had been the guide to two
other white men the year before (p. 85). "We had em-
ployed an Indian mainly that I might have an opportunity
to study his ways," Thoreau says (p. 95), and Joe was selected carefully. He was on time for the beginning of the
trip, he did not drink (so far as we know), and he sub-
mitted willingly to Thoreau's observation and interrogation.
That Thoreau did study him closely is plain.

> He was a good looking Indian, twenty-four years old, ap-
> parently of unmixed blood, short and stout, with a broad
> face and reddish complexion, and eyes, methinks, narrower
> and more turned up at the outer corners than ours, answer-
> ing to the description of his race. Besides his under cloth-

ing he wore a red flannel shirt, woolen pants, and a black Kossuth hat, the ordinary dress of the lumberman, and to a considerable extent, of the Penobscot Indian. When afterward he had occasion to take off his shoes and stockings, I was struck with the smallness of his feet. He had worked a good deal as a lumberman, and appeared to identify himself with that class. (P. 90)

Not even his underclothing and the size of his feet escape notice!

As the lumberman's dress indicates, Joe was himself a synthesis of white and Indian cultures. He knew the Penobscot language and could give the Indian names for birds, animals, and wild flowers, but his English contained expressions like "Sartain," and "By George," and "Yes, Sir-ee." At one point Thoreau was surprised to hear him whistling "O Susanna" as he paddled. He had Indian skills in handling and repairing his canoe, and swore once "about his knife being as dull as a hoe, an accomplishment which he owed to his intercourse with the whites" (p. 95), but he readily admitted to Thoreau that he could not subsist in the woods entirely on the foods of the woods, like his ancestors. That had been all right for them; they were " 'wild fellows, wild as bears,' " but he wouldn't go into the woods without hard bread and pork (p. 107). Thus we get the impression that he was an easy-going man who had made his adjustments between red and white traditions. He was not so conscientious about distinguishing and preserving Indian traditions as Thoreau, and we learn later that Joe and other Indians "knew but little of the history of their race, and could be entertained by stories about their ancestors" (p. 136). At the end of the trip, Thoreau found "some fragments of arrow-heads . . . and one broken stone chisel" on the shore at Oldtown, "which were greater novelties to the Indians than to me" (p. 150). But in most such cases Thoreau seems more pleased that his own knowledge rivals or exceeds Joe's than displeased that Joe and other Indians do not measure up as fully "wild." Thoreau seems inclined to take Joe as he is and to learn, not criticize.

The major exception to this mood comes in the shooting and butchering of moose. In this complex conflict Thoreau is against both Joe Aitteon, to whom the shooting is a common and necessary Indian practice, and also his own cousin, who hunts mainly as a white sportsman.

To begin with, Thoreau's cousin (George Thatcher—he is not named) had never seen moose before and fired at two, a cow and a yearling calf, without properly identifying his targets. Both ran off, and though Joe was extremely keen-eyed in following their trail a part of the way, he gave up sooner than Thoreau thought a good hunter should. It was only by accident that Joe found the cow again a half an hour or so later lying dead in shallow water. Thatcher went once more in pursuit of the calf, which they eventually decided had not been wounded, and Thoreau had to help Joe drag the cow to shore. Thoreau held it by the ears while Joe paddled. Thoreau took time to measure various dimensions of the enormous animal; then the butchering began. "And a tragical business it was; to see that still warm and palpitating body pierced with a knife, to see the warm milk stream from the rent udder, and the ghastly naked red carcass appearing from within its seemly robe, which was made to *hide* it" (pp. 115–16).

Thoreau's objections to this "tragical business" are largely the same as given in "Higher Laws" in *Walden*. Hunting from necessity is acceptable, he says, adding that "I could spend a year in the woods fishing and hunting just enough to sustain myself, with satisfaction. This would be next to living like a philosopher on the fruits of the earth which you had raised, which also attracts me." But hunting for sport, when an animal is so defenseless and the hunter runs no risk, is "like going out by night to some woodside pasture and shooting your neighbor's horses," and shooting moose is like shooting "God's own horses." He further objects to all the hunting he has seen in Maine, however, because it is a coarser use of nature than the philosopher's, artist's, or poet's.

This afternoon's experience suggested to me how base or coarse are the motives which commonly carry men into the wilderness. The explorers, and lumberers generally, are all hirelings, paid so much a day for their labor, and as such, they have no more love for wild nature, than wood-sawyers have for forests. Other white men and Indians who come here are for the most part hunters, whose object is to slay as many moose and other wild animals as possible. But, pray, could not one spend some weeks or years in the solitude of this vast wilderness with other employments than these—employments perfectly sweet and innocent and ennobling? For one that comes with a pencil to sketch or sing, a thousand come with an axe or rifle. What a coarse and imperfect use Indians and hunters make of nature! No wonder that their race is so soon exterminated. I already and for weeks afterward felt my nature the coarser for this part of my woodland experience, and was reminded that our life should be lived as tenderly and daintily as one would pluck a flower. (Pp. 119–20)

Coarse is indeed the key word in this criticism, and he adds a ringing denunciation of other economic exploiters of nature—whalers, ivory-hunters, and even turpentine distillers. "It is the living spirit of the [pine] tree, not its spirit of turpentine, with which I sympathize, and which heals my cuts. It is as immortal as I am, and perchance will go to as high a heaven, there to tower above me still" (p. 122). The coarseness of the exploiters' motives is of a piece with the violence and ugliness of their actions. Indians are lumped together with the exploiters because, by savagist prejudice, they are hunters, *the* hunters, and because in the actualities of frontier economic life Indians and exploiters associate with one another. When Thoreau says "What a coarse and imperfect use Indians and hunters make of nature! No wonder that their race is so soon exterminated," he is in effect wishing the Indians' fate on the hunters also. Both are opposed to the philosophers and poets, whose lives, being refined and spiritual, are prophesied to last longer.

What is confusing is that he comes to these criticisms and prophecies from two sides, one a vaguely Transcendentalist and effete popular ideality, the other a more vigorous

169

Transcendentalist (and Indian) pantheism. The ideality is in the gentle and genteel wish "that our life should be lived as tenderly and daintily as one would pluck a flower" —surely a ridiculous standard when applied to the rough and necessary, albeit tragical, businesses of lumbering and butchering. The pantheism is in the brilliant sentence on the pine: "It is as immortal as I am, and perchance will go to as high a heaven, there to tower above me still." The idea was so pantheistic and anti-Christian to nineteenth-century tastes that Lowell cut it from the *Atlantic*, without Thoreau's permission.[7] The other, apparently, gave Lowell no pause. It was quite suitable. And yet could an Indian have been editing the *Atlantic*, the "daintily as one would pluck a flower" sentence might have seemed laughable and the other heartily endorsed, for that Transcendental vision was, as Thoreau was coming to realize, Indian also. The pine tree, to the Iroquois, was a sacred tree, under which Dekanawida instructed them to bury their weapons in establishing the Great Peace of the Five Nations.[8] Thoreau's criticism of turpentine distillers would have made perfect sense to them, and probably to a Penobscot too.

But in the climax of "Chesuncook" Thoreau was finally able to make a valuable differentiation between Indian and white coarseness. Near the end of the trip, as Aitteon, Thatcher, and he came to the canoe-carry from the Penobscot River to the north shore of Moosehead Lake, they had a choice between stopping for the night at a white men's lumber camp or at the camp of three Indians hunting moose. Thatcher preferred the lumbermen, Thoreau the Indians, and he prevailed. The lumber camp "was close and dirty, and had an ill smell, and I preferred to accept the Indians' offer; . . . for, though they were dirty, too, they were more in the open air, and were much more agreeable, and even refined company" (p. 133).

The choice is the more remarkable because the Indians had been out two months and killed twenty-two moose. They were drying the skins on the ground and smoking the meat on slanting racks exactly like those Thoreau remem-

170

bered from White's illustrations in De Bry's *Collectio Pere-grinationum*, where some of the racks "were frequently shown [with] pieces of human flesh drying along with the rest" (p. 134). It was "about as savage a sight as was ever witnessed, and I was carried back at once three hundred years" (p. 135). After dark, Thatcher and Thoreau, Aitteon and another Indian lay on their backs talking till midnight. At first the Indians chatted in their language, not talking to the whites, but eventually Thoreau told them of the pictures he had seen of human flesh drying on crates, and they began to talk of Mohawks "eating human flesh, what parts they preferred, etc., and also of a battle with the Mohawks near Moosehead, in which many of the latter were killed." Thoreau's historical information was entertaining to them, and though he could not understand a word they said in their language, he still enjoyed it. He preferred roasting, alive, by their campfire, listening to the "purely wild and primitive American sound" of their language, to going out on the cool grass. He consoled himself with memories of what the Jesuit missionaries suffered. When the Abenakis gestured, he tried to guess their meaning, and later he asked them about Indian place names, about hunting stories and laws, and laughed with them about a deer which ran loose through the city of Bangor, "the deer that went a-shopping." Sabattis Solomon, a friend of Aitteon's, advised him on how to cure the ears of the moose which Thoreau had kept from the butchering and how to make them into tobacco-pouches. But it was this long and rambling, easy conversation which was Thoreau's real trophy of the trip, the point where "I stood, or rather lay, as near to the primitive man of America, that night, as any of its discoverers ever did" (pp. 135–42).

This was also the climax of the adventure because the next morning Thoreau, Thatcher, and Aitteon gave up their plan to go further up to the forks of the Penobscot River and turned back south towards the coast. We can see the change in Thoreau's attitudes from some of his different responses to the old bugaboo of cleanliness and coarseness

171

and his more diverse portraits of the Indians met from here on. An Indian at breakfast offends him by licking the platter, but a white logger who gorges himself on the moose that the Indians had shot offends him even more. One of their "bedfellows," who had been out hunting that night, gets up, dresses in a clean white shirt and goes to meet the steamboat, "a true Indian dandy." Two days later, in Oldtown, a "slender old Indian" is "full of mirth and gestures, like a Frenchman." When Thoreau goes to visit Governor Neptune, the eighty-nine-year-old patriarch of Oldtown, he produces a three-page sketch which is mostly free of the clichés of savagism. Neptune is a kind of character simply not to be found in nineteenth-century white literature. Sitting up in bed, his black hair only a little grey, and surrounded by good-humored "squaws," he questions Thoreau and tells stories with gusto and authority. Thoreau clearly likes him. "This was the first time that I ever called on a governor, but, as I did not ask for an office, I can speak of it with the more freedom" (p. 149). He feels comfortable in Indian company and wishes to preserve the wilderness which poets and Indians depend on.

JOE POLIS

Thoreau's last trip to Maine, in late July and early August 1857, was also the longest and most interesting. The account of it, "The Allegash and East Branch," is as long as "Ktaadn" and "Chesuncook" combined, and it is a masterpiece in Thoreau's diaristic form of travel narrative. Joe Polis, the guide, is also the most complex of Thoreau's Indian characters, indeed, the most fully developed person (after the author himself) to appear anywhere in Thoreau's writing. As Jim in *Huckleberry Finn* is the most realistic black portrait by a white writer in nineteenth-century American literature, Joe Polis is the most realistic and attractive native American.

For Thoreau to provide such a portrait is an achievement of several kinds. He was not a novelist and lacked the novelist's skills and methods for presenting character and

172

perhaps also the novelist's basic fascination with character. His famous reticence also seems to have extended to a feeling that it was inappropriate to put his friends in print. In *A Week on the Concord and Merrimack Rivers*, his brother John is neither named nor described and plays no memorable part. In *Walden* there are some affectionate sketches of Alek Therien, Channing, and Alcott, but they are not named, nor are the sketches carried far. The same is true of his other travel books and essays. He journeys with a "companion," usually, but the relationship never grows or changes so as to add unity and variety to the story. Thoreau's interest is primarily in the places and things seen and his own moral reflections, only secondarily in the people. In Irving's *A Tour on the Prairies*, the opposite is true, and the little dramas within the party of travellers and their servants are the most amusing things in the book. In this perspective, the popular misconception of Thoreau as an asocial hermit is hard to refute.

But his factually detailed and plain sequential order of narrative also made it harder for him to create character and drama. He couldn't create either one if it wasn't there to start with. Nor would he do very much for literary effect, like foreshadowing, emphasizing particular themes, or exaggerating particular conflicts. Conflicts between the people on a journey in the forest may make good reading, but good woodsmen avoid them, and in this respect exciting literature and common sense oppose each other. Polis, Thoreau, and the third member of the party, Ed Hoar,[9] who had just returned from the California frontier, were all good woodsmen. This was no tenderfoot's excursion for the magazines, but a very arduous and even dangerous trial, as Thoreau realized in planning it and as he realized still more clearly when it was over.[10]

Once again he selected his guide carefully. Polis was someone Thoreau's cousin in Maine had "known from a boy." Thatcher and Thoreau met him in his yard in Old-town, dressing a deer skin. "His house was a 2-story white one with blinds, the best looking that I noticed there, and as good as an average one on a New England village street. It was surrounded by a garden and fruit trees, single cornstalks standing thinly amid the beans." They asked him if he knew of "any good Indian who would like to go into the woods," and he answered, "out of that strange remoteness in which the Indian ever dwells to the white man, 'Me like to go myself; me want to get some moose'" (pp. 157–58). Pay and schedules were discussed and agreed upon, and that evening Polis came down to Bangor "in the cars." Thoreau met him and led him, with his canoe over his head, through the streets to Thatcher's house. "I tried to enter into conversation with him," Thoreau says, "but as he was puffing under the weight of his canoe, not having the usual apparatus for carrying it, but, above all, was an Indian, I might as well have been thumping on the bottom of his birch the while" (p. 159).

Polis's accomplishments and "strange remoteness" appear further in the stagecoach journey up to Moosehead Lake. His only baggage is his axe and gun, a blanket, his pipe, and tobacco. He scarcely answers the impertinent questions of other people on the coach, and says nothing about the delays and mishaps caused by one passenger's tiresome dog. When a man asks to borrow his pipe, he looks straight at him and lies, "'Me got no pipe.'" Such stolidity hardly bothers Thoreau, however. It is how he thought Indians were and how he often was himself, in imitation of them. But it does not quite square with the information, given by a famous white hunter, that Polis is "said to be worth $6,000." A man who is so rich—probably richer than Thoreau—and so well regarded in the white culture and still so Indian in his silence and hunting prowess is a paradox.

Polis's paradoxes become even more evident once the three men leave the coach, launch the canoe, and are "presented with the freedom of the lakes and the woods" (p. 165). He ceases to be so taciturn and gladly gives Thoreau the Indian names of lichens, birds, and whatever Thoreau asks. "I told him that in this voyage I would tell him all I knew, and he should tell me all he knew, to which he readily agreed" (p. 168). His English is good, though he "could rarely sound the letter r, but used l, as also r for l sometimes; as *load* for road, *pickelel* for pickerel, *Soogle* Island for Sugar Island, *lock* for rock, etc." He also put an *m* after *too*, and added *um* at the end of words—the " 'bow-arrow tang,' " as Thoreau had heard it called (p. 169). In telling a story, Polis, like other Indians in Thoreau's acquaintance, spoke "as if he thought it deserved to have a good deal said about it, only he has not got it to say, and so he makes up for the deficiency by a drawling tone, long-windedness, and a dumb wonder which he hopes will be contagious" (p. 172). But the fact also came out that Polis was buying land and involved in a legal dispute about it on which he wanted Thoreau's and Hoar's advice. On a parcel of fifty acres where he raised grass and potatoes he preferred to hire white men rather than Indians as his laborers, "because 'they keep steady, and know how' " (p. 174). In the evening he sang, in Penobscot, some hymns which had been taught by Catholic missionaries. The next morning he gave the Indian name for the phosphorescent light Thoreau saw that night in rotten "moosewood," " '*Artoosoqu*,' " adding that "his 'folks' sometimes saw fires passing along at various heights, even as high as the trees, and making a noise" (pp. 180–81). Thoreau was enchanted by this discovery, and decided that "one revelation has been made to the Indian, another to the white man. I have much to learn of the Indian, nothing of the missionary" (p. 181).

The trouble was that Polis had come to the opposite conclusion, and in the morning, Saturday, he disclosed it. He wanted to know what Thoreau did on Sundays and whether they would travel the next day! When Thoreau said that at home he usually read in the morning and went for a walk in the afternoon, Polis replied, " 'Er, that is ver bad,' " and that he went to church. He was a Protestant—was Thoreau one too? "I did not at first know what to say, but I thought that I could answer with truth that I was" (p. 182). This opening contretemps over Sabbath observance leads, indirectly, to two other differences on Saturday,

July 25, which become the coincidentally organizing themes of the journey. Both seem minor, at first, but they gain weight. And Thoreau quietly emphasizes them by introducing them in between his general descriptions of the routines of the journey, the procedures at a portage and in making camp.

The first comes out in the midst of a morning conversation about hunting. Polis tells Thoreau and Hoar how as a boy he hunted regularly in the region "up the west branch of the Penobscot, and toward the head of the St. John." He knew it very well, and had made his money hunting "beaver, otter, black cat (or fisher), sable, moose, &c." He survived in the woods on "partridges, ducks, dried moose-meat, hedge-hog," and loons, "only 'bile 'em good.' " This, the reader can see, is a major difference between Polis and the younger guide Joe Aitteon, who could not survive on the foods of the woods. But Polis also told the story of a trip when, as a boy, he and two older men had nearly starved and frozen to death. When Thoreau inquires how he guided himself in the woods, Polis gives a lengthy explanation, ending with another story of how years ago he and a white hunter had chased a moose nearly all day until they were thoroughly turned around. When Polis challenged the white man to show the way back to their camp, he pointed one way; Polis took the lead, and led them straight back—the other way. " 'How do you do that?' " Thoreau asks. " 'O, I can't tell *you*. . . . Great difference between me and white man' " (p. 185).

Yet much as Thoreau clearly respects his guide for this hard-earned wisdom, he is offended by something Polis does at the end of the day. While Thoreau and Hoar are out fishing after supper, Polis fires his gun twice. They learn later that he had fired it "to clean out and dry it after the rain." "This sudden, loud, crashing noise in the still aisles of the forest, affected me," says Thoreau, "like an insult to nature, or ill manners at any rate, as if you were to fire a gun in a hall or temple."

Thus another latent conflict emerges over forest manners,

added to the ones over religion and forest skills. And judging from Thoreau's use of the word "temple," this, to him, is a religious issue too.

The next morning Polis again states his side of the Sabbath controversy:

> "We come here lookum things, look all round; but come Sunday, lock up all that, and then Monday look again." He spoke of an Indian of his acquaintance who had been with some ministers to Ktaadn, and had told him how they conducted. This he described in a low and solemn voice. "They make a long prayer every morning and night, and at every meal. Come Sunday," said he, "they stop 'em, no go at all that day,—keep still,—preach all day,—first one then another, just like church. O, ver good men." "One day," said he, "going along a river, they came to the body of a man in the water, drowned good while, all ready fall to pieces. They go right ashore,—stop there, go no further that day,—they have meeting there, preach and pray just like Sunday. Then they get poles and lift up the body, and they go back and carry the body with them. O, they ver good men." (Pp. 193–94)

Thoreau's private opinion was that these preachers' "every camp was a camp-meeting, and they had mistaken their route." They should have gone to a revival meeting, not Katahdin. We can imagine his amazement. For twenty years he had taken the Indian side against the missionaries, and thought Indians were his allies against the praying Christians. Now he had a praying Indian for a guide! And yet his very historical awareness surely gave him perspective. He now saw first hand how Indians were more oppressed by literal Christianity than whites were.

On his side, Polis was tolerant of his new employers' aberrations. "Plying the paddle all the while," he decided "that if we would go along, he must go with us . . . and he suppose that if he no takum pay for what he do Sunday, then there's no harm." Thoreau told him "that he was stricter than white men"—and noticed that at the end of the trip "he did not forget to reckon in the Sundays." Nevertheless, "he appeared to be a very religious man," says Thoreau, adding that he knelt to pray every morning and evening, "sometimes scrambling up again in haste when he had forgotten" (p. 194). And so was settled the matter of Sundays.

Differences over the religion of wilderness life were more difficult. Thoreau, we know, went to Maine to get away from men and civilization and to renew himself by contact with the wild—old and timeless, vast and inhuman. It was a spiritual quest. Polis, who earned his wealth hunting, was in the woods for food and pay. Thoreau explains later, with some admiration, how Polis would take the stage a hundred miles into the woods, carrying only gun and axe, blanket and a few supplies, get out, go hunting, and return with his furs in a canoe he had made along the way. He availed himself "of the advantages of civilization, without losing any of his woodcraft, but proving himself the more successful hunter for it" (p. 201). Polis's understanding of Thoreau and Hoar, on the other hand, was that they had simply "'come here lookum things.'" He could not understand their avoidance of civilization. In fact, he even liked Boston, New York, and Philadelphia, and would like to live there (p. 197).

The consequence of Thoreau and Hoar's overeager embrace of the wild is a series of blunders and misadventures, and in each case Polis rescues them. On Monday, July 27, at a portage from Umbazookskus Lake to Mud Pond, from which they intend to canoe on to Chamberlain Lake, Thoreau and Hoar take the wrong trail and compound their troubles by getting separated from each other. Polis misses them and goes back to find Hoar and lead him to Thoreau. A blind Canadian and his family who lived in a little hut near the portage advised him that the white men had probably taken the supply road directly to Chamberlain Lake. Now the decision is made for Thoreau and Hoar to head on for the lake, while Polis goes back to complete his carry to the pond and paddle around. Once again, Thoreau gets ahead of Hoar, and the afternoon is getting late. But in time he hears "a noise like the note of an owl," which is Polis, again come to find them.

Polis gently reproves them the next day. They have decided to travel by the East Branch of the Penobscot rather than explore the St. John River because the East Branch is wilder country and less settled. Joe accepts their decision but counsels caution.

> Having observed that we came by the log-huts at Chesuncook, and the blind Canadian's at the Mud Pond carry, without stopping to communicate with the inhabitants, he took occasion now to suggest that the usual way was, when you came near a house, to go to it, and tell the inhabitants what you had seen or heard, and then they tell you what they had seen; but we laughed, and said that we had had enough of houses for the present, and had come here partly to avoid them. (P. 234)

Polis was always curious about the few settlers in the woods. He customarily travelled from hut to hut. He did not make a virtue of isolation. He'd learned this by his own experience and now proved its wisdom to Thoreau and Hoar. But they remained overconfident.

So the initiation continues. On the next day, Wednesday, July 29, they encounter some rapids where it is impossible for all three men to stay in the canoe. Thoreau and Hoar get out and carry some of the baggage down the shore, while Polis guides the canoe down the " 'very strong water' " (p. 253). They wait for each other at bends in the stream or where the water is quiet. Just after one such meeting Polis waved to Thoreau to come back and help him get the canoe over a fall. Hoar had gone fifty or sixty feet ahead of Thoreau and did not see him go back. Thus when he missed the two of them, he thought they were ahead of him; when he ran to catch up, he unknowingly ran away from them. But not aware of what had happened, Thoreau feared that Hoar, who was very nearsighted, might have walked off a cliff. He shouted and searched frantically until night fall, haunted by what he might have to tell Hoar's relatives and by the fact that the nearest camps were twenty or thirty miles away. Polis, meanwhile, remained calm and even "showed some unwillingness to exert himself, complaining that he was very tired, in consequence of his day's work" (p. 259). He rejected Thoreau's suggestions to light a beacon fire and shoot the gun, arguing that Hoar was safer wherever he was than he would be trying to come to them in the dark. He had also seen Hoar's footprints "once or twice along the shore."

> "No use, can't do anything in the dark; come morning, then we find 'em. No harm,—he make 'em camp. No bad animals here, no gristly bears, such as in California, where he's been,—warm night,—he well off as you and I." (P. 260)

The next morning Polis wanted his breakfast before resuming the hunt, but Thoreau "reminded him that my companion had had neither breakfast nor supper." So they set out, made two carries from Webster Stream, where they had been, to the East Branch of the Penobscot, and soon found Hoar "just below the mouth of Webster Stream." He was "smoking his pipe, and said that he had passed a pretty comfortable night, though it was rather cold, on account of the dew." On first seeing Hoar, Thoreau was so relieved and delighted that he shouted and shouted, but "the Indian curtly remarked, 'He hears you,' as if once was enough" (p. 262).

The initiation is so successful that we almost suspect Polis of having orchestrated every event. There is no suspicion from Thoreau that he did, or even an explicit recognition that this has been an initiation, but the results are decisive. Later this day, Thursday, July 30, when Polis shoots a moose, Thoreau does not get so upset as before. While Polis skins it, he discreetly goes fishing. From here on, no one gets lost at portages or while walking down beside rapids. When they are separated at such times, Polis calls to them occasionally but not often, and Thoreau interprets this as an honor. They are doing things the Indian way. That night Polis makes them some checkerberry tea, and they name the campsite "Checkerberry-tea Camp." Polis also amazes them by poking into the woods a little way and finding thirty or forty good steel traps under a log. Thoreau, in his evening wanderings, does not go far from camp. He now recognizes his own limitations.

In the account of Friday, July 31, Thoreau repeats the story of Polis's nearly starving when he was ten.

> He had been hunting far north of this with two grown Indians. The winter came on unexpectedly early, and the ice compelled them to leave their canoe at Grand Lake, and walk down the bank. They shouldered their furs and started for Oldtown. The snow was not deep enough for snowshoes, or to cover the inequalities of the ground. Polis was soon too weak to carry any burden; but he managed to catch one otter. This was the most they all had to eat on this journey, and he remembered how good the yellow-lily roots were, made into a soup with the otter oil. He shared this food equally with the other two, but being so small he suffered much more than they. He waded through the Mattawamkeag at its mouth, when it was freezing cold and came up to his chin, and he, being very weak and emaciated, expected to be swept away. The first house which they reached was at Lincoln, and thereabouts they met a white teamster with supplies, who seeing their condition gave them as much of his load as they could eat. For six months after getting home he was very low, and did not expect to live, and was perhaps always the worse for it. (P. 279)

This, in effect, is Polis's story of his own initiation into wilderness dangers and hardships. Thoreau's and Hoar's has been much less trying, but they seem to respect his the more, having been through their own. Significantly, the Indians' self-sufficiency at that moment failed. They were saved, or relieved, by the "white teamster with supplies." And as if to show that he understands this message of a hunter's dependence on other men, Thoreau ends this day's report with an old story which has the same moral. It comes from the Jesuit Hierosme Lalemant, who, describing the death of another priest who was lost in the woods, dwelt "chiefly on his probable sufferings from the attacks of mosquitoes." Lalemant added that other Frenchmen were sometimes so tormented by mosquitoes that the only thing they could do was keep running and that if one man stopped for a drink, two men had to stop with him and beat the mosquitoes off. The story has extra relevance because of Thoreau and his friends' nightly torment.

In the three days left, Polis changes his relationship to the white men. He is more inclined to accommodate and surprise them with woodcraft skills like making Thoreau a candle from rolled birchbark, leaving notes in trees, and making Hoar a birchbark pipe. More important, he begins to play and tease, and on Saturday, August 1, he suddenly invites Thoreau to race him at a carry around some rapids. He takes the canoe, and Thoreau takes "gun, axe, paddle, kettle, frying-pan, plates, dippers, carpets, &c., &c.," and even Polis's cowhide boots. For once the tension of this whole journey is broken. Thoreau passes the Indian but then drops all the clumsy gear. He gathers it up, "pressing the sooty kettle to my side," and passes Polis again. When the race is over, and they are both "puffing and panting," Polis says, "'O, me love to play sometimes.'" He and his friends, he says, frequently race at carries and portages. On Monday, August 3, Polis and Thoreau get into a similar friendly competition over different techniques of paddling. All through the trip, apparently, Thoreau or Hoar paddled in the bow, Polis in the stern. Now he has them turn around, putting Thoreau in the steering position, and tries to turn the canoe himself from the bow, so that Thoreau has to fight to keep his course. Polis laughs but cannot turn the canoe. Thoreau has earned the name Polis has given him, an Indian name which means "great paddler."

And the tension clearly has been great—not overt but subtle and constant. Thoreau reflects it in his watchful and niggling criticisms of Polis, made to the reader. Polis leaves matches and boots out in the rain. He has a sweet tooth, and they have to stop to obtain more sugar. In his health and daily disposition, he was "subject to taciturn fits, but they were harmless ones" (p. 262). With such an omniscient observer as Thoreau along, any man might easily be nervous, and our sympathies go out to Polis. We wish that Thoreau had not been quite so serious. On Sunday, August 2, Polis comes down with a colic. It troubles him all day, and they cannot travel very far. Thoreau suspects it is from the moosemeat; he is not very tolerant. "It seemed to me that, like the Irish, he made a greater ado about his sickness than a Yankee does, and was more alarmed about himself" (p. 290). But it could also be suspected that the sickness might have had something to do with this being a Sunday, when Polis again was troubled at not going to church or observing a day of rest. In the evening he takes a drink of water and gun powder, and the trouble goes away. Whatever it was, it was a Sunday colic only.

On Monday, August 2, as they are coming back to Oldtown, Thoreau supplies us with his discovery that the Penobscots "seem to be more social, even, than the whites." They do not like to live in pioneer solitude, but within their settlements. Polis also tells Thoreau how much he values education and how he himself contrived to support a Protestant schoolmaster in Oldtown. The community was divided between Catholics and Protestants, and, the former getting aid from the priest and the bishop in Boston, the Protestants were about to give up. To rally them and defend the symbolic liberty pole, which the priest was going to cut down, Polis "got ready fifteen or twenty stout young men, 'stript 'em naked, and painted 'em like old times.'" At the moment the Catholics were about to cut down the pole, Polis's men rushed out, saving it and the school. "We thought," says Thoreau, "that it showed a good deal of tact in him, to seize this occasion and take his stand on it; proving how well he understood those with whom he had to deal" (pp. 293–94).

These observations, and the concluding items of information about Polis's wife and home, prove again what a thoroughly bi-cultural individual Joseph Polis was. They also demonstrate again Thoreau's scrupulous candor in trying to present Polis exactly as he was, without romanticizing him as a savage or playing down his acceptance of civilization. This is as intimate a portrait of another person as Thoreau ever wrote, and it was clearly difficult. As noted already, he would not publish it in the *Atlantic* in 1858, when Lowell asked for it, because if Polis read it, "I could not face him again." He was embarrassed at using someone so exhaustively as a subject of study. In this sensitivity, as also in the amount that Thoreau learned from Polis, he clearly honored him. In his funeral eulogy on Thoreau, Emerson ranked Polis, John Brown, and Walt Whitman as the three people who had had the greatest effect on Thoreau in the last years of his life.[11] Probably no other American personally knew all three men; surely no other chose these original three as influences. We know a man by such a choice of friends; we must imagine Polis's influence by his inclusion in such company.

Yet there is still something puzzling and incomplete in Thoreau's portrait of Polis. In "The Allegash and East Branch," he refers to him, almost everywhere but at the beginning and end, as "the Indian." I have used his last name, Polis, because that is the name by which Thoreau says he and Hoar addressed him during the trip and because I have found "the Indian" awkward—longer to write, confusing in places, stereotypical, and somehow condescending. I think that Thoreau overcame savagism in his recognition of Polis as a person, and as a person who illustrated the depth and diversity of *the Indians*. But Thoreau, it must be considered, wrote of Polis as "the Indian," even after addressing him as "Polis." Thoreau notes this in the following seemingly simple passage, at the end of a paragraph about navigation.

> "I guess you and I go there,—I guess there's room for my canoe there," [Polis says]. This was his common expression instead of saying we. He never addressed us by our names, though curious to know how they were spelled and what

they meant, while we called him Polis. He had already
guessed very accurately at our ages, and said that he was
forty-eight. (P. 167)

Polis, I take this to mean, referred to the three of them as
"you and I," to Hoar and Thoreau as "you," and addressed
each separately as "you," never by name. Convention, at
that time, would have dictated his calling them Mr. Thoreau and Mr. Hoar, and his being called Joe, as Thoreau
and Thatcher apparently addressed Joe Aitteon and as
Thoreau referred to Aitteon in "Chesuncook." It was a mark
of some respect, initially due to his age, probably, that they
addressed him as Polis, for he was eight years older than
Thoreau and about 20 years older than Hoar. But he used a
style in addressing them which was more intimate and less
respectful than convention, while they used one in addressing him which was slightly more respectful.

What is further intriguing is that these brief sentences
on names come at the end of a long paragraph telling of
Thoreau and "the Indian's" puzzlement over distinguishing
an island from the shore, as they paddle up Moosehead
Lake. If the point ahead of them is attached to the shore,
then they must go around it. If it is part of an island, they
can take a shorter course between island and mainland.
The three men have, obviously, the same question before
them in modes of address. Is each a separate person or is
each attached to some mainland of race and culture? (A
similar allegory is suggested in the brief following paragraph when Thoreau describes pouring pork fat into the
water after breakfast and making a "'slick,'" which Polis
sees and calls "'hard paddlum thro!'") Polis's choice, in
saying "you and I," emphasizes separation: "you (two
white men)" and "I (the Indian)." When he chooses not
to use their surnames, he also tends to attach them to their
racial mainland rather than make them insular individuals.
Therefore, if this is Polis's/"the Indian's" way of seeing,
Thoreau may be justified in referring to him the same way.
When with white men, Polis thinks of himself as an Indian.

The disadvantage in this manner of reference is that a certain amount of nineteenth-century racism goes along with it. Thoreau himself frequently seems to condescend to Polis as "the Indian," approving of him as one might approve of a bright inferior, reproving his faults as those of a disappointing inferior. It is hard to realize from Thoreau's narrative that Polis was 48 and clearly his employers' senior by so many years. He is treated as a mature man, but one nevertheless younger than the writer. Secondly, does Thoreau regard Polis/"the Indian" as an island or a point on the mainland? Naming him one way on the trip and the other in the book is strange, to say the least. But the answer, again, may lie in the ingenious image. Coming up the Lake, they saw continuous shore.

> Presently, however, though we had not stirred, the mist lifted somewhat, and revealed a break in the shore northward, showing that the point was a portion of Deer Island, and that our course lay westward of it. Where it had seemed a continuous shore even through a glass, one portion was now seen by the naked eye to be much more distant than the other which overlapped it. (P. 167)

In like manner, Polis was "the Indian" from the distance of first impression and the separation of memory, but "Polis" face to face. Let the mist clear, Thoreau seems to be saying, and you see the individual. Leave the individual, and he fades in the distance; the mist descends again, and you see a continuous culture.

We know from the imperfections in the latter part of *Huckleberry Finn* how difficult it was for both Huck and Mark Twain to see Jim as a person once they were off the raft and once Tom Sawyer had arrived and commenced his "evasion." Jim became property again, a stage property to serve as victim-hero in romantic imaginings. The imperfections in Thoreau's portrait of Polis are not as gross as these, but they may have come from similar misconceptions in European and American imaginations. A journey into the wilderness, with an Indian, was an exploration of the unknown interior-inferior. In the journey, conditions changed; the Indian became the guide, the white men the initiates. But in reporting it, conditions changed again. The memory and the audience saw the Polis-Island as part of the Indian-Main.

Further Lessons

Thoreau's sense of the success of the last Maine trip is described in a letter he wrote to Harrison Blake on August 18, 1857.

Having returned, I flatter myself that the world appears in some respects a little larger, and not, as usual, smaller and shallower, for having extended my range. I have made a short excursion into the new world which the Indian dwells in, or is. He begins where we leave off. It is worth the while to detect new faculties in man,—he is so much the more divine; and anything that fairly excites our admiration expands us. The Indian, who can find his way so wonderfully in the woods, possesses so much intelligence which the white man does not,—and it increases my own capacity, as well as faith, to observe it. I rejoice to find that intelligence flows in other channels than I knew. It redeems for me portions of what seemed brutish before.

It is a great satisfaction to find that your oldest convictions are permanent. With regard to essentials, I have never had occasion to change my mind. The aspect of the world varies from year to year, as the landscape is differently clothed, but I find that the *truth* is still *true*, and I never regret any emphasis which it may have inspired. Ktaadn is there still, but much more surely my old conviction is there, resting with more than mountain breadth and weight on the world, the source still of fertilizing streams, and affording glorious views from its summit, if I can get up to it again. As the mountains still stand on the plain, and far more unchangeable and permanent,—stand still grouped around, farther or nearer to my maturer eye, the ideas which I have entertained,—the everlasting teats from which we draw our nourishment.[12]

187

Such a testimonial could be his answer to those who scorned Indians. Once again he had found value in what other men passed over. He had even been surprised out of his own ideas of savage brutishness. But even more arresting may be the discoveries implied in the image of Katahdin and the mountains as nourishing teats. Eleven years before Katahdin had represented "vast, Titanic, inhuman Nature" (p. 64). Now it is maternal, though still grand, a symbol of his majestic convictions. By so much had his perceptions changed, however changeless the faith. Like his Indian fathers, he now perceived the earth surely as mother. The ambiguities of "matter"/*mater* earth were gone.

The idea that Indian knowledge "begins where we leave off" was one on which he continued to speculate during the winter of 1857–58. As Polis and Aitteon had shown him, that knowledge inhered in the languages, and in February 1858, in the Harvard library, he found Father Sebastien Rasles' "Dictionary of the Abenaki Language," which provided more illustrations. Previously the vocabulary lists which he copied in the "Indian Books" were simply matchings of Indian words with their supposed English equivalents—facts with no meaning. Rasles gave him a much larger vocabulary, with the contexts and nuances of words, and they became revelations. As he wrote in the *Journal* on March 4, 1858:

> Father Rasle's dictionary of the Abenaki language amounts to a very concentrated and trustworthy natural history of that people, though it was not completed. What they have a word for, they have a thing for. A traveller may tell us that he *thinks* they use a *parevent*, or built their cabins in a certain form, or soaked their seed corn in water, or had no beard, etc., etc.; but when one gives us the word for these things, the question is settled,—that is a clincher. Let us know what words they had and how they used them, and we can infer almost all the rest. [I have changed "pavement" in the Torrey and Allen text to the French *parevent* ("windguard"). See the next quotation for the reason.]

188

Father Sebastian Rasles (also spelled Rasle and Ralle) had been a Jesuit missionary at the Indian village of Norridgewock on the Kennebec River. He started his dictionary in 1691, writing "Il y a un an que je suis parme les Sauvages, je commence à mettre en ordre en forme de dictionaire les mots que j'apprens." (It is a year since I came among the savages, and I begin to put the words that I know in order in the form of a dictionary.) In 1724 a raiding party from Massachusetts destroyed the village, killed Father Rasles, and brought the manuscript back as booty, eventually to be lodged at Harvard and published by the philologist John Pickering in 1833 in the *Memoirs of the American Academy of Arts and Sciences*, New Series, vol. I, pp. 370–574. Thoreau borrowed this volume of the *Memoirs* on February 15, 1858,[13] and took notes on the Dictionary in "Indian Book" 11, pp. 74–86. They amply document the generalizations in the *Journal*. (Rasles used "*ȣ*" to signify a gutteral *ou*. Pronunciation should be by French values, and Pickering did not translate the French definitions, as Thoreau sometimes did not either.)

ȣigȣame a cabin—one [word] for a great one—another for a little one—one for a round one of this form **▲** —another for one round above thus: **◖** —another for one en dos d'ane. A word for a kind of pare-vent by the side of the door. Also for the raised bed or for the planks on which it is. (11/76)

Canoe is *agȣiden*. One of wood is *amasȣr*. Roots for one, *ȣadabak*; bark for is *masȣsigȣe, gȣar*. Petits planches de cedre pour faire are *konkskak* (ribs? or lining?) The wood which is at the end is *thin*; which is debout, *ȣnighesȣ*. The wood which one sews au rebours is *ȣssksanraksem*. (P. questions some of the French of the last.) The maitres of the canoe *ȣibodangan, nak*. The bars (barres) *pemitsemen, nak*. The varangues, *ȣanghinannamk*. The lisses (rails?) *anakan, nak* (& 2 other ways or words). The end *ȣsksanr*. The sewing on seam lengthwise (or long) *peporhadangon*. The sewings across on the cuts (corpuses) *nekenanganat*. For it is too much loaded before or behind:

one word for each. For the 1st place in the canoe. The 2nd on each side. (11/77)

When he came to Rasles' lists of fruit trees and "fruits of the earth," Thoreau copied the names of all the species. He also studied the words for magic and playing games. The names of months he copied in translation. It was not always necessary to copy the word itself; the existence of a word "for the bone which is in the middle of the heart of the moose" or "for his left hind leg" was clue enough to the refinement of the cognition. And all this proved to him how much more functional and vital was the Indian's knowledge of nature than the scientist's.

On March 5, having been to hear a lecture in Concord by a Chippeway, who happened to be accompanied by a Penobscot who was Joe Polis's brother, Thoreau wrote more about what he was learning from Indian languages.

> How little I know of that *arbor-vitae* when I have learned only what science can tell me! It is but a word. It is not a *tree* of *life*. But there are twenty words for the tree and its different parts which the Indian gave, which are not in our botanies, which imply a more practical and vital science. He used it every day. He was well acquainted with its wood, and its bark, and its leaves. . . . It was a new light when my guide gave me Indian names for things for which I had only scientific ones before. In proportion as I understood the language, I saw them from a new point of view.
>
> A dictionary of the Indian language reveals another and wholly new life to us. Look at the word "canoe," and see what a story it tells of outdoor life, with the names of all its parts and modes of using it, as our words describing the different parts and seats of a coach; . . . or at the word "wigwam," and see how close it brings you to the ground; or "Indian corn," and see which race was most familiar with it. It reveals to me a life within a life, or rather a life without a life, as it were threading the woods between our towns still, and yet we can never tread in its trail. The Indian's earthly life was as far off from us as heaven is.

190

But despite its remoteness, Thoreau kept pursuing that heaven of Indian "earthly life." *The Journal* shows that on March 16 he was ruminating on Indian words for "mouse-ear leaves, pine-needles, mosses, and lichens, which form the crust of the earth." "The branches of the fir," he had copied from Rasles, "are *sedi*"; and "*sediak*" meant spreading them on the ground for a bed. (11/76. See also *Maine Woods*, p. 190.) Such associations not only implied how things were used, they implied a wholly different way of seeing and thinking.

For years Indian names and stories had enhanced his walks and discoveries. First treating as a foolish superstition the Indian belief that the world was a turtle's back, he had nevertheless gone on to observe turtles more closely and to see the truth. Now Rasles' dictionary held out the promise of a renaming and reconstruction of all that he knew. He seems to have been eager to share his excitement, for there is a record in the journal of John Langdon Sibley, the Librarian at Harvard, of a long conversation with Thoreau in May 1858. "Today [Thoreau] enlarged to me somewhat on the mistake of men of science in not giving more attention to the Indians & their languages & habits. In relation to geology, botany, zoology, &c., they stand between the men of science and the subjects which they study." Thoreau talked of how he was using the insights in the language, as learned from Polis and Rasles' dictionary, and how Polis could hear "a little whistle" made by snakes and imitate the notes and sounds of musquash and other animals. The Indian name for the pout, Thoreau said, was descriptive of the fish's habit of leading its young as a hen does its chickens—something Thoreau had noticed but seen in no books. "Thus men of science might learn best through Indians many of the properties, &c., of the subjects of their studies," Sibley concluded.[14] Thoreau's further objection to the botanists and zoologists of his day, as we know, is that they sought only to classify and anatomize. "We are ready to skin the animals alive to come at them," he wrote in his

191

Journal. Implicit in the Indian languages was information about animal behavior, or ethology, not just anatomy.

With the new enthusiasm, the old pleasures in finding arrowheads and artifacts increased. They were tangible evidence that people speaking these languages had been in Concord. Having become so skillful in finding them, he could judge by their kind and numbers in various places where people had lived, made arrows, and hunted.

> It is remarkable that the spots where I find most arrowheads, etc., being light, dry soil,—as the Great Fields, Clamshell Hill, etc.,—are among the first to be bare of snow, and the frost gets out there first. It is very curiously and particularly true, for the only parts of the northeast section of the Great Fields which are so dry that I do not slump there are those small in area, where perfectly bare patches of sand occur, and there, singularly enough, the arrowheads are particularly common. Indeed, in some cases I find them only on such bare spots a rod or two in extent where a single wigwam might have stood, and not half a dozen rods off in any direction. Yet the difference of level may not be more than a foot,—if there is any. It is as if the Indians had selected precisely the driest spots on the whole plain, with a view to their advantage at this season. (*Journal,* March 13, 1859)

The *Journal* for March 28, 1859, contains a five-page essay on the thoughts and fancies suggested to him by arrowheads. Their durability exceeds that of all other arts, ancient and modern. They may be collected, but time will only redistribute them, to "find themselves at home again in familiar dust, and resume their shining in new springs upon the bared surface of the earth." They are not easy to see ("It is a recommendation that they are so inobvious,— that they occur only to the eye and thought that chances to be directed toward them"), but they are ever and everywhere present. "Some time or other, you would say, it had rained arrowheads, for they lie all over the surface of America," symbols of the spirits of the continent.

As he got into his study of the succession of forest trees

and the larger studies of "Wild Fruits" and "The Dispersion of Seeds," he correlated his findings of arrowheads with his theories of where Indians had cleared land for cultivation. They cleared, he figured, only "level tracts where the soil was light—such as they could turn over with their rude hoes." And that was where relics were most plentiful. Then, "I know of no tree so likely to spread rapidly over such areas when abandoned by the aborigines as the pitch pines —and next birches and white pines" (Nov. 26, 1860).

But, as Walter Harding has said, it was from the outdoor research on tree-growth, particularly on the freezing afternoon of December 3, 1860, that he "contracted a severe cold—the beginning, as it turned out, of his final illness."[15] His health grew worse through the winter of 1861, and in the spring his doctor advised him to travel to a warmer climate for a cure, recommending the West Indies or southern Europe. According to Harding, Thoreau rejected the first as "too muggy" and the second as "too expensive."

> Finally, probably because a distant cousin, Samuel Thatcher, Jr., of Bangor had moved there ten years before because of lung trouble and had found himself improved, Thoreau decided to try the dry air of Minnesota. (Minnesotans had already begun to advertise widely the therapeutic values of their climate.) He had never been west of the Alleghenies and thus could combine the journey for his health with a further study of the American Indian and the flora and fauna of the Middle West.[16]

Today Minnesota may seem like a less than perfect place for someone with bronchitis and tuberculosis, and it would be interesting to know more about this decision. What motive was uppermost? Did Thoreau now so clearly equate wildness and Indians with health and renewal that Minnesota would have been his first choice whatever the doctor advised or economy dictated? Even more tantalizing is the question of what he might have done, then and later, had he regained full health in Minnesota.

CHAPTER VII

On the Sky-Tinted River

In this chapter I want to return to the question of whether Thoreau would have written a "book about Indians," or, as we should say now, *another* one. Hoary old academic question though it may be, it is still instructive.

My method in the preceding chapters has been largely explicative and documentary. I have tried to show what nineteenth-century white attitudes towards Indians were and how Thoreau both used these attitudes as an inspiring and organizing impetus in three books and also broke away from them. Thus the nominal subjects have been whites and Indians and Thoreau's writings, life, and research. But as some readers may already have perceived, he has sometimes been an occasion as well as a subject. I have at times used him as a moral register of the depth of past (and present) white American stereotypes about savages and Indians. Thoreau was once thought to be the one white American in the early nineteenth century who really valued and understood Indians. While Lewis Cass, Andrew Jackson, and others pretended to be their friends, Thoreau was. His sympathy with them and independence from popular American clichés somehow redeemed this whole white "century of dishonor." But as anyone can see, the record is not that simple. He himself held and used a great deal of savage prejudice. Instead of taking Thoreau as a redeemer, people might reflect on how even an independent, critical person like him was affected by these cultural illusions. The illusions were that strong. Nevertheless, rather than feel morally superior to him for the prejudices he used and fought, we should wonder about our own prejudices.

Thus these concluding speculations on what Thoreau's next "book about Indians" might have been are a way of going further in the investigation of nineteenth-century American mythology and ideology and the colonial treatment of American natives. They are not meant as an addition to Thoreauvian apocrypha or pseudobiography. As a person who attempted to synthesize the best of the red and white cultures as he knew them, Thoreau is an extremely interesting kind of witness to both, a center of conscience and consciousness. We can learn from what he saw and felt and from trying to imagine what he might have written. Conversely, we can learn more about his own strengths and limitations, for to try to theorize about what he might have written, we must look again at what kind of writer he was.

Thoreau's health trip to Minnesota, from May 11 to July 9, 1861, is a suitable occasion on which to base this speculation. In a life of so many significant excursions, this was his last. It was also, possibly, the most ambitious. Canada meant the North and the old French and British colonial America. Cape Cod was the beach and the ocean. Maine was the convenient down-east West. But Minnesota was the real West. And hardly any eastern writer of a hundred or a hundred and fifty years ago went to the Mississippi without at least thinking of a book about the trip. Characteristically, Thoreau too made notes or field notes. He also had an extremely talented companion—Horace Mann, Jr., the seventeen-year-old son of the famous educator. Mann would later major in botany at Harvard and become curator of the Harvard Herbarium. From their notes and letters it is possible to trace their route carefully and see in detail what they studied and observed.[1]

They started by rail from Concord to Albany and then Niagara Falls, roughly following, as Thoreau knew, the course of "the great central trail of the Iroquois." In "Indian Book" number 8 he had quoted at length from the description of the trail given by Morgan in *League of the Ho-de-no-sau-nee, or Iroquois*. Though only 12 to 18 inches wide, the trail ran from Albany to Buffalo, and its route, Morgan

195

said, had been "so judiciously selected, that the turnpike was laid out mainly on [its] line" (8/378–79). On May 18 Thoreau and Mann continued by rail across southern Ontario—Huron country—to Detroit, from which they crossed Michigan and Indiana to Chicago. This railroad saved them the long steamboat journey to the Straits of Mackinac and down Lake Michigan. Thoreau was impressed by the predominance of hardwood trees and absence of any evergreens except some white pines. The fences in Canada and Michigan—tools and symbols of an agricultural, animal-raising civilization—were of narrow boards, not posts and rails. Not much native prairie was left, except "small fenny" places which were too wet to farm.

From Chicago, the "cars" took them to Dunleith, Illinois, or what is now East Dubuque, on the Mississippi. Again, Thoreau's eye followed the changing contours of the land —"very level" outside Chicago, then "considerably more undulating" until the northwest corner of Illinois, which was "quite hilly." In the flat stretches "a stack of wheat straw looks like a hill on the horizon 1/4 or 1/2 mile off, it stands out so bold and high" (*MJ*, p. 3). Beside these towering stacks, which surrounded and overshadowed the small houses and barns, the farmers looked like "mice nesting in a wheatstack which is their wealth." It was also quite common to see women working in the fields, and the new small towns laid down on the fields seemed to Thoreau little more than "stations on a railroad" (*MJ*, p. 4). Had he developed these images, they might have become symbols of how the conquest and transformation of this land had occurred. The plow, he had written years before, "is a more fatal weapon" than the rifle. But the plowmen and women were more like industriously gathering and nesting and accumulating mice than like the noble yeomen of the agrarian myth. The opening of the frontier was an invasion of mice. The towns, however patriotically envisioned, were dependent on the railroad, which advanced into the American interior to create the towns and commerce to serve itself.

On the Mississippi he saw more signs of this gnawing and burrowing and cutting kind of advance. Floating down the river were huge rafts of sawn boards and shingles and gigantic log-rafts 60 to 80 feet wide and over 300 feet long. At Cassville, Wisconsin, were "holes in sides of hill . . . where lead dug." At landings where the steamboats stopped twenty men would rapidly load nine or ten cords of wood for a boat's fires, taking only ten minutes. Prairie du Chien, Wisconsin, was "the smartest town on the river," he said, using the promoter's language, and "exports the most wheat of any town bet. St. Paul & St. Louis" (*MJ*, p. 4). Sacks of it and heaps of it lay all over the ground. The farmers seemed to cultivate it alone.

The travellers saw their first Indians "encamped below Wabashaw, Minnesota, with Dacotah shaped wigwams." But there, too, were signs, literal signs of civilization. " 'Storage, Forwarding, & Commission'—one or all these words on the most prominent new buildings close to the waterside." That, in brief, was the commercial process. Such signs on a wharf, with a town behind, were in the lower and more level spaces between the great bluffs of over 200 feet which loomed above the river. The towns were civilization; the bluffs, with their oaks, maples, elms, cottonwood, birch, and white pine, were the wild, still standing in between. The steamboat *"approached"* the bluff, but then tied up, discharged and loaded at the towns, from which men went further up the tributary rivers and gradually took over the bluffs themselves. When the boat was ready to leave, he wrote, it "whistles, then strikes its bell about 6 times funerally & with a pause after the 3rd & you see the whole village making haste to the landing—commonly the raw stony or sandy shore. The postmaster with his bag, the passengers, & almost every dog & pig in the town of commonly one narrow street under the bluff" (*MJ*, p. 5).

Arriving at St. Paul on Sunday, May 26, Thoreau and Mann began a stay of over three weeks there and in the nearby villages of St. Anthony's and Minneapolis. They botanized, and Thoreau's notebook contains long lists of their finds. In fact, botanical material is such a large part of his rough notes that the story of the indigenous plants and animals and their adaptation or extinction might have dominated any later report on this trip. One tree for which Thoreau hunted particularly hard was the wild crab apple. Yet ironically, the one he found had been transplanted and carefully preserved by the nurseryman Jonathan T. Grimes.[2]

In Minneapolis on May 28 Thoreau met and had lunch with Dr. Charles L. Anderson, the state geologist, who advised him about the scientific studies made of the region. "Last bison seen east of the Mississippi in 1832 & last beaver killed in southern part of Wisconsin in 1819," Thoreau copied from the 1852 volume of *Transactions of the Wisconsin State Agricultural Society* (*MJ*, p. 6). From the same volume he took a note on how women tie the stalks of wild rice together in bunches before they harvest it. This keeps the heads from threshing against each other and also from sinking. Then they collect it in canoes, kiln-dry it, and husk it. In the spring they mix it with sugar. When they wish to plant it anew "'in some favorable place, they gather some of it when it is fully ripe, & scatter it in the water, where it grows without any further trouble'" (*MJ*, p. 9). Such was the ingenuity of the old ways, which were neither as easy as romantically pictured nor as hard as the growing of wheat.

Once again, the man-made wilderness of libraries provided glimpses of the old wilderness, and from the *Minnesota Historical Collections* and *Annals of the Minnesota Historical Society* he copied the facts which might someday flower into truth. *Minnesota* in the Dakota language, meant "sky-tinted." *Mankato* meant "blue earth." Waterfalls are called "Ha-ha," he wrote, "never Minnehaha [as Longfellow has it]." *Ha-ha*, pronounced with a strong gutteral *h*, also means to curl (the curling of the waters) and to laugh (the curling of the mouth when laughing) (*MJ*, pp. 11–12). Mankato was also the name of a white town and of a Sioux chief who had been friendly to the whites. A younger Mankato, son of Good Road, would be a leader in the U.S.-Sioux

War of 1862.³ By a further historical irony, the town would be the site of hangings after the war. But the name expressed the earth Thoreau perhaps saw—blue with water, blue with the haze of evening, blue with transcendence. He copied these names because they must have been very suggestive. Indian etymologies were a way of thinking Indian.

But the problem of finding an Indian guide, who could teach him more, was surely even more difficult than in Maine. He had no white friends here who had known Indians from childhood and could introduce him to someone as remarkable as Polis. Minneapolis was a lumber milling town less than fifteen years old, and there was no long-accepted Indian community as near and well known as Oldtown was to Bangor. If a few Indians worked in the mills, Thoreau did not meet them. However, on June 12 he and Mann read a newspaper notice that on June 17 the steamboat *Frank Steele* would start up the Minnesota River carrying passengers and officials to a ceremony near Redwood, where the Sioux would receive their annual payment from the U.S. government. This opportunity was not ideal, but it was at least worth taking. Thoreau and Mann bought tickets.⁴

A letter which Thoreau wrote to F. B. Sanborn on June 25 describes the laborious, grinding progress of the *Frank Steele's* journey some 300 miles up the Sky-Tinted River. "F. Steele in 1837," Thoreau had written in his notebook, was "the first white man that 'flashed his axe in the unbroken wilderness' & commenced improvements in Minnesota" (*MJ*, p. 20). The boat proceeded like an axe, or a sledgehammer. The river was so twisty that it had no straight stretches a mile long. In places its oxbow bends were so extreme that the boat had to go three miles to go around a neck which "you could have thrown a stone across," Thoreau wrote to Sanborn. The boat, 160 feet long and drawing three feet, was too big for it. "In making a short turn," Thoreau wrote, "we repeatedly and designedly ran square into the steep and soft bank, taking a cart-load of earth, this being more effectual than the rudder to fetch us about again." When the channel was close to one shore, "we were obliged to run into & break down at least 50 trees which overhung the water, when we did not cut them off." Sometimes the crew had to go ashore and fasten a line to a tree and then windlass the boat over a shoal. Other times it would completely block the river, bow on one side and stern on the other. "It was one consolation to know that in such a case we were all the while damming the river & so raising it." The sound of the boat rumbling over snags, sunken logs and sand was "the ordinary music."

Yet Thoreau's letter shows little development of this experience as an instance of the coarseness and violence of conquest. Instead, he seems to share in the passengers' frontier humor, their laughter and jokes about the clumsy, tedious journey. There were about 100 passengers, including the governor of Minnesota, the superintendent of Indian Affairs and the newly appointed Indian agent, a half a dozen young Englishmen, and a German band. There was also "a small cannon for salutes, & the money for the Indians (aye and the gamblers, it was said, who were to bring it back in another boat.)"

His account of the village of Redwood—a store and a few houses on the bank of the river, with the great plains all around it—and of the ceremonies themselves was very brief:

> A regular council was held with the Indians, who had come in on their ponies, and speeches were made on both sides thro' an interpreter, quite in the described mode; the Indians, as usual, having the advantage in point of truth and earnestness, and therefore of eloquence. The most prominent chief was named Little Crow. They were quite dissatisfied with the white man's treatment of them & probably have reason to be so. This council was to be continued for 2 or 3 days—the payment to be made on the 2nd day—and another payment to other bands a little higher up on the Yellow Medicine (a tributary of the Minnesota) a few days thereafter.
>
> In the afternoon the half naked Indians performed a

dance, at the request of the Governor, for our amusement & their own benefit & then we took leave of them & of the officials who had come to treat with them.[5]

In his notebook he was more specific about the dance itself and the appearance of the people, not using the phrase "half naked."

Indians, 30 dance, 12 musicians on drums & others strike arrows against bows. The dancers blow some flutes. Keep good time. Move feet & shoulders, one or both. No shirts. 5 bands there.

Pipes, many brought 50 cents or 3 or 4 dollars or much more for fanciful stems &c. Dance a Dream Dance. Fishes leap 40 rods off. See men fishing with lines set. Others as soon as you begin to leave the shore. Pay each chief 100 dollars, each brave 20 . . . Indians hungry, not sleek & round-faced. "Ugh" at the promise of meat and flour. (*MJ*, p. 22)

This was the limit of Thoreau's observation of the Sioux. He saw no more than the ritual of speeches, gifts, and dances that were enacted each summer at dozens of forts and agencies in the West. To the passengers on the *Frank Steele* it was a tourist show. To the gamblers it was an easy mark. To the government agents it was routine. And while Thoreau sympathized with the Indians when he said that their speeches had "the advantage in point of truth and earnestness, and therefore of eloquence" and that they had reason for their dissatisfaction with the white man, he also had a sympathy with the white men among whom he was travelling. His Indian sympathy was moral, but his white sympathy was broader, more spontaneous, and fraternal. It was implicit in the kinship of language and humor, in the jokes about the *Frank Steele* and even in the language used to describe the Indians. Thoreau was not alone in his awareness that the Indians were wronged. Other passengers surely knew that too; but what could be done? The savagists knew what was happening. There was no response but pity, censure, and to relieve the horror, a certain amount

201

of humor. Elsewhere in his letter to Sanborn, Thoreau shows his equal if not greater sympathy with the whole epic of white American expansion. Describing the grandeur of the Mississippi, he says poetically that "it flows from the pine to the palm." He tells Sanborn that "about half the men whom I have spoken with in Minnesota . . . were from Massachusetts." He adds that the Minnesota River "flows through a very fertile country, destined to be famous for its wheat." These are the tones of a patriotic social optimist, not of a primitivist critic. His immediate worries in the letter were over the Civil War and his own health.

Thoreau's letter and notes on this trip to the Sky-Tinted River reveal a lot. He was not totally free of the attitudes of savagism. Moreover, his situation as a mere visitor tightened his connections with the other white men. For him to have given his own independent account of life among the Sioux he would have had to stay much longer and become personally involved. Personal involvement was the essential ingredient of his greatest books and essays. As we look back at *A Week, Walden,* and *The Maine Woods* we can see that his varying kinds of involvement are what make them different from other literary accounts of Indian life and history.

In *A Week on the Concord and Merrimack Rivers* the actual Indians are all historical, indeed, long dead. But that hardly matters because Thoreau's commitment to a true *natural history* of America imaginatively brings them to life. In setting out on their own rediscovery of their homeland, he and his brother John surrendered themselves to reliving a wild native life and rehearing the poetry of the river and grass. We can also speculate, with some assurance that Henry Thoreau conceived of John as his ideal Indian brother and that his involvement with John increased his involvement with the Indians. The older brother, "his brother sachem—Hopeful—of Hopewell," as he addressed him in the mock-Indian letter, had had the wild education, while Henry had gone to Harvard. They had come together again as walkers and ingenious idlers. Then John, like an Indian, had died leaving Henry as the inheritor. So that working out the true Transcendental inheritance and the original poetry of America was a quest which drew upon deep personal resources. The *Week* uses many stereotypes of the savage and the civilized. It is almost a handbook to them. But because the author had "a singular yearning toward all wildness," he was generally on the savage side.

In *Walden* the involvement was equal if not greater, because Thoreau had experimented with Indian life himself. The real Indians are the few gypsylike Penobscots camped near the Concord River and selling baskets, but their insignificance made Thoreau's own imitation all the more possible. He could recreate the wild for himself and out of himself, while using it to regenerate his spirit, with the former wild men as his means and ends. His primitivist attack on civilization was fresh—not a repetition of noble-savage critiques of marriage, education, and so forth—because he attacked still more basic civilized customs, the ways of eating, dressing, and building houses, from the standpoint of his own simpler solutions. Though we can say that he was more involved with the idea of "the Indian" —solitary and self-reliant—than with Indians as people, we cannot dispute the extent of the involvement.

The Maine trips were his adventures with the survivors of the Abenaki or Penobscot life. They were different from the western adventures of Thoreau's contemporaries because, once again, of his saturation in the experience. His desire for a pure saturation and his constant desire for Indian names and tricks must have made him, at moments, a somewhat trying companion; but he was also a close one. He drew more from his weeks with Joe Aitteon and Joe Polis than some anthropologists have learned in years. But unlike modern anthropologists, he was still seeking "the Indian" as a person and example. That Indian life was essentially a social life did not dawn on him until the last trip. Yet the climax of the Chesuncook trip came when, for one evening, he and his white companion slept with Penobscots and St. Francises, outnumbered by them. Listening to their language while moosemeat dried on the racks around the camp was an experience he would never forget.

The questions we must ask in trying to imagine a really good Thoreauvian report on the people of the Sky-Tinted River are several. Could he have become engaged in the life there? What was it? How would his literary methods and forms have had to change in order to write about it? These are, admittedly, all conditional questions. His health, which he described to Sanborn as "considerably better than when I left home, but still far from well," clearly did not permit any stay at the Lower Sioux Agency. Nor did the other circumstances around the agency. But these are the circumstances we are now more interested in. What was happening on the Sky-Tinted River in the summer of 1861?

One source of information is the report of Thomas J. Galbraith, the United States agent, to his superiors at the Department of the Interior. Galbraith, who may have been the new agent travelling on the *Frank Steele*, was carrying out the government policy at that time of "separating . . . each family from the tribes or bands and settling them upon a separate farm." With farming came such other civilized traits as "the dress of white men," "habits of industry," thrift, and "a desire for literary education." This policy with the Sioux had begun in 1858, and by 1861 only 125 families out of nearly 14,000 people had been so separated, yet Galbraith's short, factual report clearly indicates that it was both his major interest and the major controversy among the people. The report reads today like an old letter from a misionary.

> Five new root-houses are in progress, and a good plain picket fence has been erected around the agency buildings and garden, and nearly four thousand bushels of charcoal have been burned. A school-house, dwelling, and a blacksmith's house and shop have been erected at Lac qui Parle, and are nearly ready for occupation. A stone warehouse for the Lower Sioux is in progress, and will be completed very soon. It promises to be one of the most substantial buildings

in this valley. It is 43 by 23 feet, 20 feet in height, with a good substantial cellar, 8 feet deep. The cellar walls are 3 feet, the first story wall 2 feet, and the second story walls 18 inches thick. This building was commenced from necessity and at the urgent request of the Lower Sioux, and will, when completed, afford a permanent and *safe* place to store the goods, provisions, grain, and general supplies of the Lower Sioux. A great portion of the labor and nearly all the hauling connected with this building has been and is being done by the farmer Indians. The Indians are now busily engaged in securing their crops and preparing for winter. The upper saw-mill has cut the whole stock of logs on hand, and will close in a few days. The grist or corn mills are being put in order to grind the corn, which will begin to come in in a few days. The carpenters have been kept busy in repairing wagons, ploughs, and doing other work belonging to their department.[6]

Like many a conscientious, ambitious administrator, Galbraith wanted more staff and funds. He wished more schools, teachers, and services for the "still wild or 'blanket Indians' " who had not yet been reached. Some of these were directly hostile to "the civilization process," but others were bitter that nothing had been done for them. Both groups, therefore, tended to abuse the "farmer Indians." They criticized them for working on agency projects without pay, a system Galbraith found necesary in order to stretch his budget but which was also criticized, he implied, by various white outsiders who wanted the Indians to be paid cash so that they could get it from them. This rivalry, perhaps, lay behind constructing the warehouse with such massive walls. It was to protect the farmer Indians' grain and provisions, and, in emergency, themselves. The government policy was working, but because of lack of time and money it had so far affected only a favored few. This, in turn, had increased resentments between the farmer Indians and "wild" Indians.

Also implicit in Mr. Galbraith's report were his savagist prejudice against all these thousands of " 'blanket Indians' " and his gentle, fatherly good will towards the others, his eager pupils. He was genuinely an *agent*, agent of a civilization he unquestionably believed in. He accepted the presence of Christian missionaries on the agency, but wished that they would be more helpful with practical matters and less sectarian. Civilization was *his* religion: in the form of plain picket fences, schools, granaries, and the white man's dress and thrift. If he feared the people he had not reached and tended to be fatherly towards those whom he had, how could he be otherwise? The latter liked and benefited from his work; the former would like it when it reached them.

To balance Galbraith's report, we must also read an Indian's reminiscences of the same time and place. The only one that I know of, however, confirms in most ways Galbraith's description of the agency conflicts. It is the reminiscence of Big Eagle, a leader in the "Sioux Outbreak of 1862." His account of the conditions leading up to the war is as follows:

> There was great dissatisfaction among the Indians over many things the whites did. The whites would not let them go to war against their enemies. This was right, but the Indians did not then know it. Then the whites were always trying to make the Indians give up their life and live like white men—go to farming, work hard and do as they did— and the Indians did not know how to do that, and did not want to anyway. It seemed too sudden to make such a change. If the Indians had tried to make the whites live like them, the whites would have resisted, and it was the same way with many Indians. [They wished to go on selling furs to the traders, he continued, but they also felt the traders had cheated them.]
>
> Then many of the white men often abused the Indians and treated them unkindly. Perhaps they had excuse, but the Indians did not think so. Many of the whites always seemed to say by their manner when they saw an Indian, 'I am much better than you,' and the Indians did not like this. There was excuse for this, but the Dakotas did not believe there were better men in the world than they. Then some of the white men abused the Indian women

in a certain way and disgraced them, and surely there was
no excuse for that.

. . . Then a little while before the outbreak there was
trouble among the Indians themselves. Some of the Indians
took a sensible course and began to live like white men.
The government built them houses, furnished them tools,
seed, etc., and taught them to farm. At the two agencies,
Yellow Medicine and Redwood, there were several hundred acres of land in cultivation that summer. Others staid
in their tepees. There was a white man's party and an
Indian party.[7]

Big Eagle further explains that Little Crow (whom Thoreau
heard talk) was considered the "principal chief" by the
whites but was not. He and others, including Big Eagle,
who had been to Washington in connection with the treaty
of 1858, were blamed for selling land on the north shore
of the Minnesota River which had belonged to two other
bands.

Perhaps because of his role in the 1862 war, for which
he was later imprisoned three years in Davenport, Iowa,
Big Eagle was very conciliatory in this dictated history.
He wished to correct his errors, to show how he had
changed, and to meet white men more than half way. There
must have been an enormous change between the energetic
tribal leader of age 34 or 35 and the pardoned prisoner of
67. But the groups which Galbraith called the "blanket Indians" and the "farmer Indians" correspond to the ones he
called the "Indian party" and the "white man's party." He
saw through Galbraith's and other white men's dislike of
the one and nurture of the other. Both attitudes meant " 'I
am much better than you.' " The people resented this, as
they also resented the favor shown the farmer Indians. Big
Eagle knew that the U.S. agents, by not paying the people
in cash but in goods, were trying to protect them from the
fur traders, and he knew the fur traders cheated them. But
he also knew that some people needed cash in order to pay
their debts. The rapes and abuse of women which Big

207

Eagle mentions were not mentioned by Galbraith, but surely did occur.

From opposite sides we get corroborative accounts of the tensions among the people on the Sky-Tinted River. They had been far more affected by white civilization than appeared to the visitors watching the rhythmical "Dream Dance." Little Crow, who eloquently pled their complaints, was nevertheless suspected by the majority of having sold out (though he later was a leader in the 1862 war). The Sioux were divided; and the whites were divided into the sincere (if patronizing) government agents like Galbraith; the traders and gamblers who wanted Indian money; the missionaries who wanted their souls; and the encroaching settlers who wanted their land. This was the tense situation which Thoreau would have encountered had he stopped on the Sky-Tinted River.

Describing this situation would have required a literary form much different from what Thoreau was used to. It would take much more extensive development of character than he had usually done. The kinds of brilliant sketches or portraits which enliven parts of *The Maine Woods* and the latter volumes of his *Journal* would certainly be valuable, but he would have to go beyond them to full treatment of the conflicts in human relationships. As part of such a dramatic method, he would have to subdue some of his fine sense of moral urgency in order to give each character or point of view a fair hearing.

For example, how would a writer like Thoreau handle the conflict between the "Indian party" and the "white man's party"? He might side with the first because of their maintenance of their old hunting skills, but could he approve of their collaboration in the wasteful killing done in the fur trade? What would he say about their going to war against other Indians? In treating the "white man's party" he would have to give up some of his own aversions to farming. He would have to dramatize their peculiar position as the envy of many of the other party and yet still show how they themselves resented being separated from their clans and bristled under the condescension of Galbraith and the missionaries. The fact that Galbraith's names for these two sides—"still wild or 'blanket Indians'" and "farmer Indians"—differed from Big Eagle's would make another sign of the tension between red and white. Thus a further difficulty would be in finding how to present the white men, who were the initial cause of the conflict. The Indians might have been happy with a return to their old economy of hunting, wild rice, fish, and wild fruits; but the Swedes and Germans downriver were no more likely to permit the Sioux to hunt on their land than the Puritans had permitted Philip's people to continue hunting on theirs two hundred years before. We can imagine Thoreau as responsive in some measure to each of these positions, but having to present all of them clashing would have demanded an extremely difficult book.

The advantage of savagism, as a literary convention, is that it focused on "the Indian," to the exclusion of numbers and variety—society. One or more white men alone in the forest with "the Indian" was a situation which writers had learned how to handle. Whether malicious or good, a Magua or an Uncas, this solitary figure represented the white author's idea of the Indian nature, which came down to meaning American nature, the wilderness. The uninitiated white men and the towns, the eastern seaboard behind represented civilization. Then one white man, experienced in the wilderness, mediated between the sides to produce a character like Leatherstocking or Thoreau himself. These writers (and mediators) did not have to deal with much of the reality or complexity of Indian life. Occasionally, a scene (perhaps borrowed from Catlin) would describe some ceremony or ball game or drunken riot, but that was simply savage behavior. The mediators and white men could ignore that and concentrate on the useful or admirable traits of Indian character which they sought to imitate. Those traits, repeatedly, were in "the Indian."

Thus this singular figure had both a lofty romantic stature

and a convenient artistic economy. He embodied half the world of the American imagination, and to many Americans the better half. He was vigorous, generous, clear-eyed and self-controlled, and marvelously self-sufficient and resourceful. It is not hard to see how a manly and passionate person like Thoreau would identify with him intensely. Nor is it surprising that in the early twentieth century several nationwide youth movements—the Boy Scouts, Ernest Thompson Seton's Woodcraft Indians, the Campfire Girls, and Julia Low's Girl Scouts—would enshrine this good Indian and the fawnlike Indian maid.

But savagism was also extremely distorted and oversimplified. For dealing with a difficult political, economic, and military situation such as existed in Minnesota in 1861 and 1862 it was utterly inadequate. Yet no other structure of ideas then existed. For Thoreau, or any artist, to enter such a situation and suddenly invent the new forms of truth necessary to portray all the elements and characters in it would have been impossible.

A few thoughts about the later history of the sciences of ethnography and anthropology may reveal how much more had to be done. Gradually, the post-Civil War ethnographers, building upon the work of Lewis Henry Morgan, abandoned the myth of "the Indian." Their emphasis on kinship patterns, tribal governments, and social structure necessitated a broader view. They also tried to record more exactly everything about a tribe which they could learn. Their voluminous reports on myth, language, tools, ceremonies, and so on now bend library shelves. This immense labor not only took several generations, it also required the abandonment of the traveller's point of view (in which the Indians were seen from the outside) and the adoption of a professed scientific point of view by which Indians were seen from above or all around. The traveller, we can somewhat reductively say, went to the limits of his known world and looked across the boundary. He could only compare the savagery he saw, and perhaps briefly flirted with and imitated, to the civilization he had come from and to which he returned. The ethnographers, profiting from the conquest of savagery, were able to encircle their subjects. Then little by little (the professional debates over changes in name are significant) the *ethnologists* tried to enter savage life and see it in its own terms. The change in name to *anthropology* dates from still later theories of cultural relativity and the fact that Indians and non-European peoples are no longer the only subjects. "Savage" was dropped or put in quotes.

One of the reasons so many people have found the idea of a book about Indians by Thoreau so very appealing, I think, is that such a book is imagined without the bloodless detachment, impersonal viewpoints, and professional jargon of scientific investigation. The "I" of *Walden* and *The Maine Woods* is supposed as still there—along with the brevity, the wit, and the depth of moral insight. Thoreau was less ill at ease with the terms "savage" and "civilized" and not afraid to speak boldly about the superiority or inferiority of each. He made his standards of judgment known and so made known his private thoughts and values. He did not attempt to be "value-free." Moreover, he did not confine himself to very narrow and isolated inquiries. Although his major literary subjects were nature and life and Concord, as he responded to them, he was also, in the Enlightened-eighteenth-century sense, a world traveller. He did not feel that he had *seen* anything until he had developed its widest contexts.

Still another reason for the appeal of this imaginary book is Thoreau's underlying sense of human equality. The anthropological investigator and his subject did not stand on the same ground. Science, in this respect, was socially regressive. Thoreau, when he wrote on the same day of the traditions of the American Indians and the death of his father, was tracing both back to "our first human father." "It is the spirit of humanity, that which animates both so-called savages and civilized nations, working through a man, and not the man expressing himself, that interests us most." This was an extraordinary sentence for a nineteenth-century American. It was also, some people may think, an

211

extraordinary sentence for Thoreau the legendary dissenter
and individualist. It subordinates the individualist value of
"man expressing himself" to the higher value of "the spirit
of humanity . . . working through a man." A transcendental
reverence for tradition is in this statement which is not
usually associated with Transcendentalism as a New England radical movement. Thoreau's next sentence, "The
thought of a so-called savage tribe is generally far more
just than that of a single civilized man," may seem somewhat illogical or even condescending unless this reverence
is borne in mind. The tribe is generally more just because
it embodies the spirit of humanity. Thus the position of
one civilized man placing himself above a whole tribe, in
order to catalogue its quaint customs rather than to learn
modestly from them, might have seemed almost ridiculous
to him.

We see another instance of Thoreau's humanity in the
brilliant passage in *The Maine Woods*, when he is subtly
comparing names and race with islands and shore. It evokes
the line in John Donne's "Meditation XVII," "No man is
an *Iland*, intire of it selfe; every man is a peece of the
Continent, a part of the *maine*." His involvement with Indians was a part of his involvement with mankind, and
their cruelly forecast extinction meant the extinction of
something in himself. Likewise, he considered Polis as good
a man as himself, and one of the virtues of his savagism
may have been that it encouraged this friendship, in his
sense, more than have our current liberal notions of racial
equality. Neither man gave up being who he was; they were
friends.

So Thoreau was not an anthropologist, a point worth
making because of the assumption, sometimes, that his
"Indian books" were a kind of anthropological research.
If he was, he might in some ways have been better informed; but for the reasons just mentioned it is a blessing
that he wasn't. He was a poet and traveller.

While Thoreau saw, on his Minnesota trip, portents of how
frontier American society was moving, he could not have

written a book which would have done very much to change it or to protect the old integrity of Indian life. Given the power of savagism and the other forces and ideas to which it was related, no one in the 1860s could have. Further, if we believe Big Eagle, a great many Sioux wanted to give up the old ways, though they bitterly resented being forced and humiliated into doing so.

Initially, for Thoreau "the Indian" served as a point of view about nature and the past. That emblematic figure stood on the shore of the new world, like the Caribes in Columbus's time, with lights in the darkness. The figure illuminated an unknown continent, guiding the traveller up the rivers, showing the berries, the animals, the ways to live. It personified the land as the daemon of the place.

For just as long, "the Indian" had been a point from which to criticize white American culture, the joyless sabbaths and resignations to joyless work and expensive comforts. "The Indian" meant leisure and health. A synthesis of civilized and savage life could bring renewal. If the ignorant and backward savage was doomed, the reborn white savage or Transcendental Indian could incorporate his virtues, metaphysically eating him as the Indian warrior ate the heart of his enemy.

Thoreau's adoption of this point of view meant that he himself became, in part, the figure he had imitated. For the synthesis to continue, he needed contact with more original figures, the living Indians of Maine and the passed-over and unassimilated reports from early explorers' experience. The wilderness of Maine and the swampy bogs of libraries were, for this purpose, almost the same. Both were places where much original or aboriginal material had been forgotten and left behind. But in visiting these valuable reserves of the wild, he came upon people like Aitteon and Polis who were not "the Indian" of savagism. They bore out the stereotype in some ways, but contradicted it, too. History further disproved the savagist myths of ignorant and wasteful hunters and of philosophically ideal figures who had never existed.

When Thoreau went to Minnesota in 1861, he was intellectually beyond savagism but not yet established in any new view. He was also still very much a member, on a day-to-day level, of the white culture. Indeed, he was more sociable with it than he had been fifteen years earlier. His intellectual independence had not been sacrificed, but the challenges of finding, now, who the Indians were and what literary forms would express them were enormous. Such forms might have to be radically different from the personal narratives which were Thoreau's well-practiced method. While it was invigorating to synthesize himself with "the Indian," how was he to synthesize himself with a complex multitude of unknown people? *An* Indian point of view was no longer possible. Now he saw *points* of view. The strength and confusion, custom and novelty of life itself were there in no smaller and simpler measure than anywhere else.

Nevertheless, it was his declining health which controlled his later personal and literary decisions. He spent the winter and spring of 1862 working over his earlier manuscripts, publishing some and revising others to leave to his family. "You know it's respectable to leave an estate to one's friends," he said to a visitor.

He died, William Ellery Channing said, with "moose" and "Indians" his last audible words. The legend has lent a certain other-worldly authority to other legends that he was the "Friend of the Indian" who died before he could complete his "broken task." But in the months before his death friends at his bedside heard various near-to-last words which were equally telling. When an antislavery orator said to him, "You seem so near the brink of the dark river, that I almost wonder how the opposite shore may appear to you," Thoreau answered, "One world at a time." On another day his Aunt Louisa asked him if he had made his peace with his Maker. Thoreau answered, "I did not know we had ever quarrelled, Aunt."[8] There is another story, inscribed in a copy of *A Week on the Concord and Merrimack Rivers.* His sister Sophia had been reading aloud to him from the *Week*, and as they came to a bend in the Merrimack, Thoreau said, "Now comes good sailing." That, according to Sophia, was his last spoken sentence.[9]

"The *apothegmata morientum* of a great man have, for some," as Austin Warren has written, "a special significance."[10] And the survival of so many of Thoreau's words testify not only to his irrepressible, clear spirit but also to the affection that family and friends had for him. They loved him both as a person and as a home-grown oracle. They knew his greatness. From the same recognition, people today continue speculating on what more he might have done had tuberculosis not killed him so early. And, since he was nineteenth-century America's most qualified, dedicated student of his red fathers and of his and their mother, it is natural that people have been curious about his possibly greater potential. If we still wonder at this, we need only look afresh at the 3,000 pages of the "Indian Books" and the outstanding works he did write.

On the Name and Number of the "Indian Books"

THOREAU's "Indian Books" have, over the years, been given various names and systems of numbering. In the Pierpont Morgan Library, New York, they are catalogued as "Indian Notebook" numbers 1–11 and assigned the call numbers MA 596 through MA 606. (The book of readings on Canada, which may or may not belong with them, is catalogued as "Canadian Notebook" and given the call number MA 595.) On their covers, however, they are labeled "Extracts relating to the Indians" numbers 2–12, in the same sequence. "Indian Notebook" 1, MA 596, is the same as "Extracts . . ." 2, and so on. MA 595 is labeled "Canada, etc." Previous scholarship has referred to them by all these names and numbers, though the name "Indian Notebooks" and the 1–11 numbering have been used most often. The apparent authority for this is a note written in the first by George S. Hellman, the book dealer who purchased them in 1904 from E. Harlow Russell (who had acquired them from Harrison Blake, Thoreau's friend).

> This volume, which has been numbered "2" by either Blake or Russell, is Vol. 1 of Thoreau's Note Books (11) on Indians. Its No. "2" is accounted for by the fact that these eleven Indian journals were together with one book on "Canada, etc.," this latter being looked upon as No. 1 of this series of 12. G. S. H.

Since our idea of Thoreau's methods and intentions in compiling these books is dictated, in large measure, by the name used for them, we should try to find out what he himself called them. An author's *notebook*, today, usually suggests notes made in preparation for another book or article.

It contains facts, quotations, and the author's first thoughts. A book of *extracts* could be made for the same purpose, but it would be more like a scrapbook. It would have no original thoughts.

But Thoreau used neither of these names. When he referred to them by name, he called them the "Indian books." He numbered them 1–12, beginning with "Canada, etc." as No. 1—or possibly with another which has not been located. The evidence is in one *Journal* passage and two passages in "Indian Book" No. 9.

In his *Journal* for June 25, 1853, is a long paragraph on the extraordinary abundance of amelanchier berries around Concord that summer. "These are the 'service-berries' which the Indians of the north and the Canadians use. *La poire* of the latter (vide Indian books, No. 6, p. 13)." On page 13 of book 6 by Hellman's numbering (1–11) is a passage from the *Jesuit Relations* for 1634 with no connection to service-berries. But on page 13 of book 6 by the 2–12 numbering (No. 5 to Hellman) is a paragraph from Sir John Richardson's *Arctic Searching Expedition* with the words ". . . service berry, is La Poire of the voyagers, the Misass-ku-lu-mina of the Crees, and the Tchè-ki-ch of the Dog-ribs."

In "Indian Book" No. 9 (No. 8, Hellman), page 160, Thoreau wrote, referring to Heckewelder's account of the Indian tradition regarding the Dutch arrival, "*For this see the Interlineations in No. 5.*" On pages 25–35 of No. 5 (No. 4, Hellman) is Heckewelder's account as Thoreau copied it from *The Collections of the New York Historical Society*, with Thoreau's interlineations quoting the slight differences in the story as Heckewelder gave it in his *History, Manners, and Customs*. Book 5 by Hellman's renumbering has nothing relevant.

In "Indian Book" No. 9, page 319, at the beginning of material from Charles Thomson's *An Inquiry into the Causes of the Alienation of the Delawares and Shawnese from the British Interests* is another cross-reference, "V. also Barton's mention of Thomson in Ind. book no. 10." Once again, this fails to make sense if we use Hellman's numbers. But if we use the 2–12 numbering, we arrive at a quotation from Benjamin Smith Barton's *New Views of the Origins of the Tribes and Nations of America* on 10/134, " 'Mr. Charles Thomson, the respectable secretary of the first American Congress, speaks of the Mohickanders & Mahiccon as 2 distinct tribes.' "

These cross-references in the "Indian Books" are in Thoreau's handwriting and show no signs of having been corrected or tampered with. Nor can the variations in number be explained by one or two books' being out of order. The numbers 2–12 were assigned according to the order in which they were filled, and as I show in chapter four, the years and months when they were kept can be established. Books 2–12 are in chronological sequence.

The question remains whether Thoreau counted the Canada book as No. 1 or whether there was another Indian book which has been lost. The entries in it were made between September and December 1850. Chronologically, therefore, it belongs between "Indian Books" 3 and 4, except that it was apparently started before No. 3 was finished and No. 4 started before the Canadian book was finished. The three were, for a while that fall, all used at once. Its contents bear mainly on white Canadian history, while the Indian books' contents bear on Indians and the Indians of Canada. There are a few other overlaps in the early books. The explanation probably is that Thoreau did not number any of these early books until about 1851, when he had filled five or six of them and numbers became necessary. Then, for convenience, he placed Canada first. There is also the possibility that there was an earlier Indian book which contained more of the material used in *A Week* and *Walden*. It may have been lost; or it may have been torn up and incorporated in drafts of them and what is now undated pages of "Journal" material.

The name "Indian Books" does not answer entirely the question of Thoreau's methods and intentions. But it does give a better idea of his more general use of them. They are *both* notebooks *and* extract books, a combination. As I say in chapter four, they supported his other writing and interests at all times; at particular periods, especially between 1853 and 1857, they were an aid in what he called—to answer the Association for the Advancement of Science —his scientific interests. But "Indian Books" was Thoreau's name for them, and "fact books" the most accurate way in which we can today describe them.

For a further history of their ownership and a precise bibliographic description of their size and format, the reader should consult William L. Howarth's *The Literary Manuscripts of Henry David Thoreau* (Columbus, Ohio, 1974), pp. xxii–xxviii and 294–301. Howarth uses the 1–11 numbering, however, so in order to arrive at Thoreau's number for each book the reader should add 1.

Notes

NOTES TO PREFACE

1. Ralph Waldo Emerson, "Thoreau," in *The Complete Works* . . . (Boston, 1903–1904), x, 451–485; Nathaniel Hawthorne, *The American Notebooks* . . . , ed. Randall Stewart (New Haven, 1932), pp. 166–67; William Ellery Channing, *Thoreau: The Poet Naturalist* (1902; rpt. New York, 1966).

2. Franklin Sanborn, *The Life of Henry David Thoreau* (New York & Boston, 1917), p. 509; Henry S. Salt, *Life of Henry David Thoreau* (1890; rpt. New York, 1968), p. 135. For source of Sanborn quotation, see note 1 to chapter four, below.

3. Albert Keiser, "Thoreau's Manuscripts on the Indians," *Journal of English and Germanic Philology*, 27 (1928), 183–99; and *The Indian in American Literature* (New York, 1932), pp. 209–32.

4. The major speculations on Thoreau's unwritten book are in the essays by Lawrence Willson, "From Thoreau's Indian Manuscripts," *Emerson Society Quarterly*, 11 (1958), 52–55; and "Thoreau and the Natural Diet," *South Atlantic Quarterly*, 57 (1958), 86–103; and Edwin Fussell, "The Red Face of Man," in *Thoreau: A Collection of Critical Essays*, ed. Sherman Paul (Englewood Cliffs, N. J., 1962), pp. 142–160, rpt. in Fussell's *Frontier: American Literature and the American West* (Princeton, 1965). Among more general commentaries on Thoreau's interests in Indians are: Reginald L. Cook, *Passage to Walden* (Boston, 1949); Sherman Paul, *The Shores of America* (Urbana, 1958); Walter Harding and Milton Meltzer, *A Thoreau Profile* (New York, 1962); Walter Harding, *The Days of Henry Thoreau* (New York, 1970); and John Seelye, "Some Green Thoughts on a Green Theme," *TriQuarterly*, Nos. 23–24 (Winter/Spring 1972), pp. 606–37. *The Indians of Thoreau: Selections from the Indian Notebooks*, edited by Richard F. Fleck (Albuquerque, N. M., 1974) contains 65 pages of excerpts from the "Indian Books" illustrating the variety of Thoreau's interests. All of these works, however, use the incorrect name and numbering. This, in turn, has often led to errors regarding the history and purpose of Thoreau's study. (See Appendix, "On the Name and Number of the 'Indian Books.'")

5. Roy Harvey Pearce, *The Savages of America: A Study of*

the Idea of Civilization (Baltimore, 1953). Despite some defects, this book is extremely valuable as a guide to the literature of savagism.

6. See, for example, Ethel Seybold, *Thoreau: The Quest and the Classics* (New Haven, 1951); Arthur Christy, *The Orient in American Transcendentalism* (New York, 1932); F. O. Matthiessen, *American Renaissance* (New York, 1941), pp. 110–25; and John Christie, *Thoreau as World Traveller* (New York, 1965).

NOTES TO CHAPTER I

1. Roy Harvey Pearce, *Savagism and Civilization* (Baltimore, 1965), p. 74 (first published, 1953, as *The Savages of America: A Study of the Idea of Civilization*).

2. Between 1829 and 1849 thirty-five plays were produced having the "noble savage" as their theme or major character, according to Richard Moody, ed., *Dramas from the American Theatre, 1762–1909* (Cleveland, 1966) in his introduction to the most popular of these plays, *Metamora, or, the Last of the Wampanoags*, pp. 199–204. John Augustus Stone wrote the play for a competition held in 1828 by the flamboyant actor Edwin Forrest for "the best tragedy, in five acts, of which the hero, or principal character, shall be an aboriginal of this country." Based loosely on the life of Metacomet or King Philip, the play broke attendance records in city after city and was one of Forrest's favorite roles. Stone, coincidentally, was born in Concord, Massachusetts.

3. John Collier, *Indians of America* (New York: Mentor, 1948), pp. 18–19.

4. Barbara Graymont, *The Iroquois in the American Revolution* (Syracuse, 1972), pp. 213, 215, 340n.

5. Dale Van Every, *Disinherited: The Lost Birthright of the American Indian* (New York: Avon, 1967), p. 53.

6. *The Complete Works of Montaigne*, trans. Donald M. Frame (Stanford, 1957), p. 693, in the essay "Of Coaches."

7. Wilcomb E. Washburn, *The Indian and the White Man* (New York, 1964), p. 415.

8. Washington Irving, *The Sketch-Book*, ed. Elmer E. Wentworth (Boston, 1948), pp. 321–30, 539n.

9. George Catlin, *North American Indians, Being Letters and Notes on their Manners, Customs, and Conditions . . . 1832–*

1839, 2 vols. (Edinburgh, 1926), ɪ, 4. First published as *Letters and Notes on the Manners, Customs, and Conditions of the North American Indians* (New York, 1841).

10. "Parkman on Cooper's Indians," in Washburn, pp. 439–41, quoted from Parkman's unsigned review of Cooper in *North American Review*, vol. 74 (January 1852), 150–52.

11. Sources of this description of communal life are Peter Farb, *Man's Rise to Civilization* (New York, 1968) chaps. 7, 10; Charles Eastman, *Indian Boyhood* (New York, 1902); John Dunn Hunter, *Memoirs of a Captivity among the Indians of North America* (1824; rpt. New York, 1973); and Gabriel Sagard, *Le Grand Voyage du Pays des Hurons* (1632), as excerpted in Thoreau's "Indian Book" number 9, pp. 10–13.

12. John G. Neihardt, *Black Elk Speaks* . . . (Lincoln, Nebraska, 1961), p. 1.

13. Chief [Luther] Standing Bear, *Land of the Spotted Eagle* (Boston, 1933), p. 1.

14. See Walter O'Meara, *Daughters of the Country: The Women of the Fur Traders and Mountain Men* (New York, 1968).

15. Richard Drinnon, *White Savage: The Case of John Dunn Hunter* (New York, 1972), pp. 61–94.

16. Lewis Cass's attack was in "Heckewelder on the American Indians," *North American Review*, vol. 26 (April 1828), 357–403.

17. John Adams to Benjamin Waterhouse, February 26, 1817, in *Statesman and Friend: Correspondence of John Adams with Benjamin Waterhouse, 1784–1823*, ed. W. C. Ford (Boston, 1927), p. 123; qtd. in Pearce, p. 151.

18. Washburn, "The Animals, Vulgarly Called Indians," in *Indian and White Man*, pp. 111–117. Qtd. from Brackenridge, *Indian Atrocities: Narratives of the Perils and Sufferings of Dr. Knight and John Slover* (Cincinnati, 1867), pp. 62–72.

19. Washington Irving, *A Tour on the Prairies*, ed. John Francis McDermott (Norman, Oklahoma, 1956), p. 74.

20. These are chapter titles in Albert Keiser, *The Indian in American Literature* (New York, 1932); and in Walter Harding and Milton Meltzer, *A Thoreau Profile* (New York, 1962).

21. Edwin S. Fussell, "The Red Face of Man," in *Thoreau: A Collection of Critical Essays*, ed. Sherman Paul (Englewood Cliffs, N. J., 1962), p. 148.

22. Henry D. Thoreau, *Early Essays and Miscellanies*, ed. Joseph J. Moldenhauer and Edwin Moser, with Alexander Kern (Princeton, 1975), pp. 108–11.

23. Ralph Waldo Emerson, "Letter to President Van Buren," *Complete Works* (Boston, 1903–1904), XI, 92, 94.

24. Henry D. Thoreau, "Resistance to Civil Government," in *Reform Papers*, ed. Wendell Glick (Princeton, 1973), p. 76.

25. On missionary philanthropy to Indians and resistance to Indian removal, see Francis Paul Prucha, *American Indian Policy in the Formative Years: The Indian Trade and Intercourse Acts, 1790–1834* (Cambridge, Mass., 1962).

26. A stimulating study of these familiar archetypes in white-Indian relations appears in Michael Paul Rogin's new biography *Fathers and Children: Andrew Jackson and the Subjugation of the American Indian* (New York, 1975).

27. D. H. Lawrence, "Fenimore Cooper's White Novels," in *Studies in Classic American Literature* (1923; republished New York, 1964), pp. 33–34.

28. Lewis Henry Morgan, *League of the Iroquois* (Secaucus, N. J., 1972), p. 457.

Notes to Chapter II

1. James Russell Lowell, *Massachusetts Quarterly Review*, III (1849), 47.

2. Henry Seidel Canby, *Thoreau* (Boston, 1939), p. 272.

3. Lawrence Buell, *Literary Transcendentalism: Style and Vision in the American Renaissance* (Ithaca, N. Y., 1973), pp. 203–38.

4. Henry David Thoreau, *A Week on the Concord and Merrimack Rivers*, in *The Writings of . . .* (Boston, 1906), I, 3. Future references will be given in parentheses. I am also grateful to my research assistant Carol Krob for locating early uses of the expression "as long as grass grows and water runs." The earliest which she has found is in a letter from Augus, a Tuscarora chief, read at a council in Lancaster, Pennsylvania, August 11, 1762, ". . . a Peace that shall be lasting and undisturbed, while Waters run, and the Grass grows." See Carl Van Doren and Julian P. Boyd, eds., *Indian Treaties Printed by Benjamin Franklin, 1736–1762* (Philadelphia, 1938), p. 266. See also pp. 115–16, 159, 238, 254, 276, 283 for similar expressions like "so long as the Sun shall shine, and the Waters run."

5. Melville's uses of the phrase are in *Typee* (Ch. 27), and *Pierre* (Bk. I, Ch. 3). Carol Krob located these, too. Thoreau used it earlier in an 1837 Harvard essay. See *Early Essays and Miscellanies*, ed. Joseph J. Moldenhauer, et al. (Princeton, 1975), p. 102.

6. For an easily available modern history of King Philip's War, see the chapter on Philip in Alvin M. Josephy, Jr., *The Patriot Chiefs* (New York, 1961). The magnitude and influence of the war were immense, as can be learned from Josephy and also Richard Slotkin, *Regeneration Through Violence: The Mythology of the American Frontier, 1600–1860* (Middletown, Conn., 1973). Further, in 1675–1763 frontier New England was engaged in six wars with Indians which lasted forty of these eighty-eight years:

1675–1676 King Philip's War
1688–1697 King William's War/ also called 1st Intercolonial War
1702–1713 War of Spanish Succession/ Queen Anne's/ 2nd Intercolonial
1722–1726 Three Years' War/ Father Rasles'/ Lovewell's
1744–1748 War of Austrian Succession/ 3rd Intercolonial/ Old French & Indian
1755–1763 Seven Years' War/ 4th Intercolonial/ Last French & Indian

(This list from Emma Lewis Coleman, *New England Captives Carried to Canada Between 1677 and 1760* [Portland, Maine, 1925], pp. 2–6.) In Thoreau's time, as we can tell from his references to these fights and the ballads about them, every New England schoolboy and schoolgirl was familiar with this history.

7. Henry's story is in *The Adventures of Alexander Henry*, ed. James Bain (1901; rpt. Rutland, Vt., 1969), p. 100.

8. Walter Harding, *The Days of Henry Thoreau* (New York, 1970), p. 135.

9. *The Correspondence of Henry David Thoreau*, ed. Walter Harding and Carl Bode (New York, 1958), pp. 16–19.

10. See Leslie Fiedler, *The Return of the Vanishing American* (New York, 1968), pp. 107–8; and Richard Slotkin, *Regeneration*, p. 523.

11. Evidence for climbing "the mountain" is in *Journal* for September 10, 1839. The Indian name Agiocochook was apparently reasonably well known. Emerson uses it in his "Ode" to Channing.

12. Leslie Fiedler gives a brief history of treatments of the

Hannah Dustan (also Dustin, Duston) myth in *The Return of the Vanishing American*, pp. 100–102. Cotton Mather's version of it is in Book VII, Article XXV of the *Magnalia Christi Americana*, "A Notable Exploit . . ." Hawthorne's "The Duston Family," first published in *The American Magazine of Useful and Entertaining Knowledge* (May 1836), is reprinted in *Hawthorne as Editor*, ed. Arlin Turner (Baton Rouge, La., 1941), pp. 131–37.

13. Thoreau's continuing interest in Hannah and her exploits appears in a visit to the site of her house, *Journal*, May 12, 1850 —he found the apple tree gone—and another visit to the pond in Haverhill near where "the Indians are said to have taken their way with Hannah Dustin and her nurse in 1697 toward the Merrimack. I walked along it and thought how they might have been ambuscaded" (*J.*, April 24, 1853).

14. Thoreau's first notes on Schoolcraft's *The Red Face of America* (New York, 1844), are in "Indian Book" No. 4, pp. 91–96. He probably made these notes—on the Duck-Man Shingebiss—during the first half of 1851.

Notes to Chapter III

1. John G. Neihardt, *Black Elk Speaks* . . . (Lincoln, Nebraska, 1961), p. 198.

2. Henry D. Thoreau, *Walden*, ed. J. Lyndon Shanley (Princeton, 1971), p. 19. Further references will be given in parentheses.

3. Thoreau mentions "the last Indian" of Nantucket in *Journal* for December 28, 1854, and a visit to a small settlement at "Betty's Neck," near New Bedford, on October 2, 1855. On June 26, 1856, he talked to Martha Simons, "the only pure-blooded Indian left about New Bedford." In *Walden*, pp. 257–65, is the record of the old Negroes who formerly lived near the Pond.

4. Natahniel Hawthorne, *The American Notebooks*, ed. Randall Stewart (New Haven, 1932), pp. 166–67. The entry is dated Thursday, Sept. 1 (1842).

5. Claude Lévi-Strauss, *Tristes Tropiques* (New York, 1974), pp. 39–40.

6. An early American study of the vision quest is Ruth Benedict's *The Concept of the Guardian Spirit in North America*, in Memoirs of the American Anthropological Association, No. 29 (Menasha, Wisc., 1923).

7. John Filson, *The Discovery, Settlement, and Present State of Kentucky* . . . (New York, 1793), pp. 47–48.

8. For this summary of Indian symbolism, I am indebted to Hyemeyohsts Storm and his book *Seven Arrows* (New York, 1972), pp. 4–7.

9. Sherman Paul, "The Wise Silence: Sound as an Agency of Correspondence in Thoreau," *New England Quarterly* 22 (1949), 511–27.

10. The most comprehensive study of trickster tales is Paul Radin's *The Trickster: A Study in American Indian Mythology* (New York, 1956).

11. On derivation of "amock," see *American Heritage Dictionary of the English Language* (New York, 1969).

12. Arthur Parker, *Constitution of the Five Nations*, in *Parker on the Iroquois*, ed. William N. Fenton (Syracuse, N. Y., 1968), bk. iii, pp. 24–25.

13. John (Fire) Lame Deer and Richard Erdoes, *Lame Deer, Seeker of Visions* (New York, 1972), p. 50.

14. Luther Standing Bear, *Land of the Spotted Eagle* (Boston, 1933), p. 38.

15. Storm's discussion of "medicines" in *Seven Arrows* (especially pp. 7–10) is most informative.

16. Charles Eastman, *From the Deep Woods to Civilization* (Boston, 1916), p. 35.

17. Charles Eastman, *Indian Scout Craft and Lore* (New York, 1974), pp. 42–43. (Reprint of *Indian Scout Talks*, 1914.)

18. Charles Eastman, *Indian Boyhood* (New York, 1971), p. 62.

19. Eastman, *From the Deep Woods*, p. 176.

20. Cláude Lévi-Strauss, *The Savage Mind* (Chicago, 1966), pp. 16–19.

21. Edward Waldo Emerson, *Henry Thoreau as Remembered by a Young Friend* (Boston and New York, 1917), pp. 32–39.

22. Kenneth Walter Cameron, "Books Thoreau Borrowed from Harvard College Library," in *Emerson the Essayist* (Raleigh, N. C., 1945), ii, 191–208.

23. In J. Lyndon Shanley, *The Making of Walden* (Chicago, 1957), p. 204.

24. Thoreau, *Walden*, ed. Shanley, p. 366.

25. For Kiowa birth, see Scott Momaday, *The Way to Rainy Mountain* (Albuquerque, N. M., 1969).

Notes to Chapter IV

1. "Literary Review . . . *The Maine Woods*. By Henry D Thoreau," *The Commonwealth* (June 10, 1864), p. 1. *The Commonwealth* was a Boston reform paper. The evidence indicating that this review and the one next mentioned are by Franklin B. Sanborn is a clipping pasted in Bronson Alcott's Journal (in the Houghton Library, Harvard), with Sanborn's name written in, and Sanborn's saying, years later when he was working for the *Springfield Republican*, that he wrote hundreds of reviews for the *Commonwealth*. I am indebted to Thomas Blanding for telling me about these reviews and giving me the attribution.

2. "Literary Review: *Cape Cod*. By Henry David Thoreau," *The Commonwealth* (March 25, 1865), p. 1.

3. Henry S. Salt, *Life of Henry David Thoreau* (1890; rpt. New York, 1968), p. 135.

4. William Ellery Channing, *Thoreau: Poet Naturalist*, ed. F. B. Sanborn (New York, 1966), p. 10.

5. Channing, p. 19.

6. Edward Waldo Emerson, *Henry Thoreau as Remembered by a Young Friend* (Boston, 1917), pp. 109–10.

7. Walter Harding and Carl Bode, eds., *The Correspondence of Henry David Thoreau* (New York, 1958), p. 239.

8. *Correspondence*, p. 310.

9. Richard F. Fleck, "Thoreau's 'Indian Notebooks' and the Composition of *Walden*," *The Concord Saunterer*, 7 (June 1972), no page nos.

10. Kenneth Walter Cameron, "Books Thoreau Borrowed from Harvard College Library," in *Emerson the Essayist* (Raleigh, N. C., 1945), II, 191–208.

11. William L. Howarth, *The Literary Manuscripts of Henry David Thoreau* (Columbus, Ohio, 1974), p. 294. Howarth thinks that "In his own mind that project [the "Indian Books"] may have become, like the *Journal*, a task of intrinsic merit. Apparently he thought of them as physical parallels, for between 1853 and 1860 the *Journal* volumes and the Indian notebooks are identical in paper and format."

12. *The Correspondence of Henry David Thoreau*, p. 504.

13. According to Thomas Blanding, who is reconstructing Thoreau's hundreds of pages of first draft manuscripts of "Wild Fruits" and "The Dispersion of Seeds," this would have been

a substantial volume. It, rather than a book on Indians, was the task on which Thoreau was most actively engaged in the late 1850s and early 1860s.

NOTES TO CHAPTER V

1. Walter Harding, *Thoreau's Library* (Charlottesville, Va., 1957), pp. 92–95.

2. Leslie A. White, ed., *Lewis Henry Morgan: The Western Journals* (Ann Arbor, Mich., 1959), pp. 7f.

3. Walter Harding, *The Days of Henry Thoreau* (New York, 1965), pp. 8f.

4. Harding, *Days*, p. 74.

5. Harding, *Days* p. 55.

6. Harding, *Days*, p. 190, and Edward Waldo Emerson, *Henry Thoreau as Remembered by a Young Friend* (Boston, 1917), p. 61.

7. There is great need for further psychoanalytic study of Thoreau's life, combining the approaches of Raymond D. Gozzi's *Tropes and Figures: A Psychological Study of Henry D. Thoreau* (Ann Arbor, Mich.: University Microfilms, 1957) and Michael Rogin's study of Andrew Jackson's Indian policy, *Fathers and Children*.

8. Quotations are from "Walking" in *Thoreau: The Major Essays*, ed. Jeffrey L. Duncan (New York, 1972), pp. 209, 212.

NOTES TO CHAPTER VI

1. Joseph J. Moldenhauer, "Textual Introduction" to Henry D. Thoreau, *The Maine Woods* (Princeton, 1972), p. 369. References to Thoreau's text will, as usual, be given in parentheses.

2. Walter Harding and Carl Bode, *The Correspondence of Henry David Thoreau* (New York, 1958), p. 504.

3. Washington Irving, *A Tour on the Prairies*, ed. John Francis McDermott (Norman, Okla., 1956), p. 24.

4. Marion Whitney Smith, *Katahdin Fantasies* (Millinocket, Maine, 1953), p. 11.

5. A different, and to my mind less complete, reading of this image may be found in Edwin S. Fussell, "The Red Face of Man," in *Thoreau, A Collection of Critical Essays*, ed. Sherman Paul (Englewood Cliffs, N. J., 1962), p. 146.

6. For another reading of this important *"Contact! Contact!"*

passage, see James McIntosh, *Thoreau as Romantic Naturalist* (Ithaca, N. Y., 1974), pp. 198–210.

7. Moldenhauer, pp. 362–63.

8. Arthur C. Parker, *The Constitution of the Five Nations*, in *Parker on the Iroquois*, ed. William N. Fenton (Syracuse: 1968), bk. 3, p. 9. Thoreau was, of course, aware of the custom of "burying the hatchet" and also of burying chiefs under spruce and fir trees. See *Journal*, July 12, 1858.

9. Walter Harding, *The Days of Henry Thoreau* (New York, 1970), p. 385.

10. Harding & Bode, *Correspondence*, pp. 490–92.

11. Harding, *Days*, p. 376, the source being F. B. Sanborn, "Emerson and His Friends in Concord," *New England Magazine*, 3 (1890), 430–31.

12. Harding & Bode, *Correspondence*, pp. 491–92.

13. Kenneth Cameron, *Emerson the Essayist* (Raleigh, N. C., 1945), p. 197.

14. Harding, *Days*, pp. 391–92, quoting from Kenneth Cameron, *The Transcendentalists and Minerva* (Hartford, 1958), II, 485–86.

15. Harding, *Days*, p. 441.

16. Harding, *Days*, p. 445.

Notes to Chapter VII

1. Walter Harding, ed., *Thoreau's Minnesota Journey: Two Documents—Thoreau's Notes on the Journey West and The Letters of Horace Mann, Jr.*, Thoreau Society Booklet No. 16 (Geneseo, N. Y., 1962). Quotations from this *Minnesota Journey* will be cited in the text as *MJ*, with the page number.

2. Walter Harding, *The Days of Henry Thoreau* (New York, 1970), p. 448.

3. Robert I. Holcombe, ed., "A Sioux Story of the War: Chief Big Eagle's Story of the Sioux Outbreak of 1862," *Minnesota Historical Society Collections*, 6 (1894), p. 392.

4. Harding, *Days*, pp. 448–49.

5. Walter Harding and Carl Bode, eds., *The Correspondence of Henry David Thoreau* (New York, 1958), pp. 618–22.

6. Thomas J. Galbraith, "Sioux Agency, Yellow Medicine, October 1, 1861," Section No. 30 of "Report of the Secretary of the Interior," in *Message of the President of the United States to*

the Two Houses of Congress, 37th Congress, 2nd Sess. (Washington, 1861), Executive Document I, pp. 701–2.

7. Holcombe, ed., "A Sioux Story of the War," pp. 384–86.

8. These versions of Thoreau's last words may all be found, with their printed sources, in Harding, *Days*, pp. 461, 464–65, and 466.

9. Authority for this last sentence is in Sophia Thoreau's copy of *A Week* (1849 ed.) in the Robert H. Taylor Collection, Firestone Library, Princeton, N. J. It was shown to me by Thomas Blanding.

10. Austin Warren, *The New England Conscience* (Ann Arbor, 1966), p. 116.

Index

Abenakis, 171, 203
Adair, James, 120, 128
Adams, John, 16, 223n
Africans, 22
Agiocochook (Mt. Washington),
    49, 58, 225n
Aitteon, Joe, frontispiece, xiii,
    166–172, 176, 188, 203, 213
Alcott, Bronson, 193, 228n
Allen, Francis H., xix, 101
Anacreon, 43
Anderson, Dr. Charles L., 198
animals, ix, 71, 144; as subject of
    Walden, 81–88
anthropology, 210–12
apple tree, 50, 52, 56, 226n;
    also see wild apple trees
apple-tree wood, 100
arrowheads and relics, ix, 35, 40,
    45, 61, 75, 89, 115, 117,
    141, 167, 192–93
art (as subject of *A Week*),
    47–55
Association for the Advancement
    of Science, 104, 118, 125, 220
Aztecs, xii

Barber, John Warner, 100
Barton, Benjamin Smith, 129
Bartram, William, 68
Benedict, Ruth, 226n
Big Eagle (Sioux chief), 206–7,
    213, 230n
Black Elk (Sioux chief), ix, 14,
    59, 62
Blake, Harrison, 101, 187, 217
Blanding, Thomas, xviii, 228n,
    231n
blanket Indians (Sioux faction),
    205, 207, 209
Bode, Carl, 225n, 229n, 230n

Boone, Daniel, 14, 39, 66
Brackenridge, Hugh Henry, 16
Bradford, William, 124
Brebeuf, Father, 113
bricolage, 88, 90, 141
Brown, John, 26, 184
Buell, Lawrence, 28, 224n
Burder, George, 129
burning of forests, 111
busk, 68

Calumet, 131
Cameron, Kenneth Walter, 109,
    227n, 228n, 230n
Canada, 129, 195; *also see*
    Thoreau, "An Excursion to . . ."
    and "Canada, &c."
Canassatego, 139–40
Canby, Henry Seidel, 224n
captivity narratives, 12, 121
Cartier, Jacques, 112
Carver, Jonathan, 98, 126
Cass, Lewis, 15, 16, 18, 127, 194,
    223n
Castaneda, Carlos, 86
Catlin, George, 12, 14, 209, 222n
Champlain, Samuel, 112, 122
Channing, William Ellery, ix,
    101, 103, 193, 214, 221n, 228n
Charlevoix, 111, 114
Chateaubriand, Vicomte François
    René de, 9
Chaucer, Geoffrey, 57
Cherokees, 7, 22–24, 128, 147
Chippewas (Ojibways), 75, 133,
    190
Christianity, 25, 38, 43; coming
    of, 32; HDT's attack on, 34
Christie, John, 222n
Christy, Arthur, xvii, 222n
Church, Benjamin, 39

233

civilization, 22, 33, 43, 67, 102, 115, 151, 152, 205–6, 210; as opposite of savage life, 3–5; civilized improvements, 116–17; HDT's primitivist attack on, 63–69
Clark, William, 15, 142
classicism, 35
Clemens, Samuel L.; *Huckleberry Finn*, 28, 172, 186; *Life on the Mississippi*, 28
Colden, Cadwallader, 139
Coleman, Emma Lewis, 225n
Collections of the Massachusetts Historical Society, 111
Collections of the New York Historical Society, 112
Collier, John, 222n
commerce, HDT's opinion of, 40–43
Confucius, 70, 106
Cook, Reginald L., 221n
Cooper, James Fenimore, 13, 15, 26, 74, 105, 209, 224n; Natty Bumppo, 44
Corn Planter, Chief, 12
Crantz, David, 129
Creek Indians, 68
Cromwell (fur trader), 41
Crusoe, Robinson, 46
Cusick, David, 128

Dakotas, 197, 198, 206; *also see* Sioux
de Bry, Theodor, 171
Dekanawida, 170
de la Hontan, Baron, 98, 114, 126
Delaware (Leni-Lenape Indians), 16, 130
de Vries, David Pieterszoon, 132
Diderot, Denis, 9, 64
disease, 123, 149, 150–52
Documentary History of New York, 136
Donne, John, 212

Drake, Samuel Gardner, 11, 121
Drinnon, Richard, xiv, 15, 223n
Duncan, Jeffrey L., 229n
Dustan, Hannah, 47, 48, 50–52, 54, 56, 83, 124, 131, 147, 164, 226n
Dutch, 130, 133, 139

East Indian religion & philosophy, xii, 38, 40, 91, 106
East Indians, 32, 62, 69
Eastman, Charles, 83, 85, 223n, 227n
Eliot, John, 34
Emerson, Edward Waldo, 88, 227n, 228n
Emerson, Ralph Waldo, ix, 23, 29, 55, 87, 101, 104, 147, 184, 221n, 224n; *Nature*, 29
Erdoes, Richard, 227n
Ethiopians, 115
Every, Dale Van, 222n

Farb, Peter, 223n
farmer Indians (Sioux faction), 205, 207, 209
farmers, 56, 62, 80; Indians as, 6, 7, 22; HDT's opinion of, xiv, 32, 41
farming, 113, 133, 204, 206; HDT's attitude to, 208; *also see* hunters & hunting
Farwell (Indian-fighter), 39, 40, 43, 124
Fiedler, Leslie, 47, 48, 225n
Filson, John, 66, 227n
fish, 31
fish weirs, 89, 111
Fleck, Richard F., 108, 221n, 228n
Forrest, Edwin, 222n
Fowler, Thomas, 161
Franklin, Benjamin, 9
Freneau, Philip, 9
friendship, 43–46, 138

frontier, 102, 196, 212
Fuller, Margaret, xiii, 155, 158
fur trade, 40, 114, 151, 152, 156, 206, 208
Fussell, Edwin S., 221n, 223n, 229n

Galbraith, Thomas J., 204–5, 207, 209, 230n
Garland, Hamlin, xiv
Goethe, 47, 54
Gookin, Daniel, 34, 46, 67, 108
Gozzi, Raymond D., 229n
Graymont, Barbara, 222n

Halkett, John, 127
Hall, James, 12, 121
Harding, Walter, 45, 146, 193, 221n, 223n, 225n, 229n, 230n
Harriot, Thomas, 148
Hawthorne, Nathaniel, ix, 52, 60, 71, 104, 123, 221n, 226n
Head, Sir Francis, 138
Heckewelder, John, 16, 126, 130, 150, 223n
Hellman, George S., 217
Henry, Alexander, 15, 42–45, 124, 225n
historians, HDT's opinions of, 144, 147–48
history, HDT's kind of, 37, 131
Hoar, Ed, 173, 175–81
Hogkins, John, 43
Homer, 31, 36, 43, 56
Horace, 43
Howarth, William L., xviii, 220, 228n
Howe, E. W., xiv
humor, 17, 140, 182; frontier humor, 200; also see tricksters
Hunter, John Dunn, xiv, 15, 16, 127, 142, 223n
hunters, 35, 56, 72, 86, 133, 178, 181, 213; ethics of, 79; HDT's opinions of, 21, 168–69;

Indians as, 14, 22, 23, 43, 55, 61, 64, 84; in savagism, 4–6; Polis as, 178
hunting, 113, 176, 208
Hurons, 113, 135, 149, 196; villages, 134
Hutchings, Thomas, 39

imitation, 124; as subject in A Week, 47–55
Incas, xii
Indians, and alcohol, 130, 160, 162; capacity for "improvement," 4–5, 33, 140, 153; causes of decline, 148–50; daemons of America, 157, 166, 192, 213; diplomacy & eloquence, 137, 139–41; dwellings, 66–68, 111, 134, 189; extinction, 5–6, 8, 55, 141, 153, 160, 212; farming, 6, 7, 22, 133–34; foods, 64; guides, 11, 158–61, 163, 166, 173, 176, 187, 199 (also see Aitteon, Joe, and Polis, Joe); hunter's ritual, 80 (also see hunters); languages, 188–90; origins of, 128–30; poetry, 34, 55, 124; religions, 31–37; sociability, 183; and tragedy, 6, 23; warfare, 135, 137, 140–41
Iroquois, 7, 77, 113, 128, 135, 137, 139, 140, 141, 170, 195, 224n
Irving, Washington, xiii, 10–11, 18, 105, 155–56, 158, 173, 222n, 223n, 229n; A Tour on the Prairies, 16–17; "Traits of Indian Character," 10–11, 16

Jackson, Andrew, 18, 194, 224n
James, Edwin, 133
Jesuit Relations, 93, 112, 113, 122, 137
Jesuits, 93, 111, 113, 149, 171

Joseph, Chief, ix
Josephy, Alvin M., Jr., 225n

Kalm, Peter, 133
Kansas Indians, 15, 142
Katahdin, xiii, 177, 187–88;
    also see Thoreau, Maine
    Woods
Keiser, Albert, x, 221n, 223n
King Philip (Metacomet), 209,
    222n, 225n; King Philip's War,
    36, 37, 39, 46, 225n
Kiowa, 99, 227n
Kip, Rev. William, 111

Laing, Samuel, 116
Lalemant, Father Hierosme, 149,
    181
Lame Deer, John (Fire), 227n
La Salle, Sieur de, 122
Lawrence, D. H., 26, 224n
Le Jeune, Father, 21, 25, 58, 150
Lévi-Strauss, Claude, 61, 88, 89,
    226n, 227n
Lewis, Meriwether, 15, 142
Little Crow, 200, 207–8
Locke, John, 9
Logan, Chief, 9
Longfellow, Henry Wadsworth,
    55, 198
Loskiel, George Henry, 120, 150
Lovewell, John, 51; Lovewell's
    Fight, 37, 39–40
Lowell, James Russell, 28, 119,
    170, 224n

McCauslin, George, 161
McIntosh, James, 230n
McKenney, Thomas, 12, 121
MacKenzie, Alexander, 142, 151
Mankato, 198
Mann, Horace, Jr., 195, 199
Marquette, Jacques, 122, 131
Massasoit, 74, 108
Mather, Cotton, 52, 124, 226n

Matthieson, F. O., 222n
medicines, 82
meditation (in Walden), 69–75
Meltzer, Milton, 221n, 223n
Melville, Herman, 17, 18, 30,
    42, 105, 225n; Queequeg and
    Ishmael, 44
Metacomet, 222n; also see
    King Philip
Mexico, 116–17
Middle West, xiv; HDT's
    impressions of, 196
Milton, John, 52; Paradise Lost,
    164
missionaries, 35, 56, 69, 80,
    175, 177, 206, 208, 209,
    224n; HDT's opinion of, 25
Mississippi River, 197
Mohawks, 138, 171
Moldenhauer, Joseph J., 229n
Momaday, Scott, 227n
Montaigne, Michel Eyquem de,
    8–9
Moody, Richard, 222n
moons (months), 98–99
moose, 156, 165, 168, 170–74,
    180, 214
Morgan, Lewis Henry, 27, 130,
    195, 210, 224n
Morton, Samuel George, 112, 115
Morton, Thomas, 149

natural history, 35, 109, 122, 202
Neihardt, John G., 14, 62, 223n,
    226n
Neptune, Governor, 172
Neptune, Louis, 159, 161, 163
noble savage, 9, 203; also see
    primitivism

O'Callaghan, E. B., 138
Ojibways, see Chippewas
Olson, Charles, xiii
O'Meara, Walter, 223n

originality, as subject of
A Week, 55–58
Osage, 15, 142
Ossian, 36, 56

Parker, Arthur C., 227n, 230n
Parkman, Francis, xiii, 13, 105, 155–56, 158
Pasaconaway, 46, 108
Paul, Sherman, xviii, 72, 221n, 227n
Paxton Boys, 7
Pearce, Roy Harvey, x, xiv, 4, 6, 221n, 222n
Penobscots, 154, 203
Peru, 116–17
Pickering, John, 189
Pocahontas, 44
Polis, Joe, xiii, 119, 121, 172–87, 188, 190–91, 199, 203, 212, 213
Pomola (Katahdin storm-bird), 159, 160, 165
Pontiac, Chief, 12
primitivism, 63–69, 203
Prucha, Francis Paul, 224n
Puans, 114
Purchas's Pilgrims, 126

Radin, Paul, 227n
Raleigh, Sir Walter, 36
Rasles, Father Sebastien, 122; Dictionary of the Abenaki Language, 188–91
Red Jacket, 9
Rice (hill farmer), 41
Richardson, Sir John, 112
Ricketson, Daniel, 142
Robertson, William, 20
Roberval, Jean François de la Roque, 112
Rogers, Major Robert, 39
Rogin, Michael Paul, xiv, 224n, 229n
Rousseau, Jean-Jacques, 9, 16, 64
Russell, E. Harlow, 217

Sagard, Gabriel, 134, 223n
St. Francis Indians, 204
Salt, Henry S., ix, 102, 221n, 228n
Samoset, 74
Sanborn, Franklin B.; theory of HDT's book about Indians, ix, xii, 102, 103, 199, 202, 204, 221n, 228n; HDT's letter to, 199–202
satire, 49, 53, 86
Sauk Indians, 98
savage, etymology of, 8
savage life, synthesis with civilized, 26–27, 68, 115, 145, 211, 213
savagism, x-xiv, 3, 26, 64, 66, 127, 161, 202, 205, 209–10, 212–14, 222n; definition of, 4–6; inaccuracies of, 6–9; influence on HDT, 3, 18, 19–27, 29–30, 61–63; HDT's use of, 30, 35, 80, 194; HDT's overcoming, 123–54, 188, 208–14
scalping, 47, 49, 54, 124, 129
Schoolcraft, Henry Rowe, 15–16, 18, 55, 113, 120
Seattle, Chief, ix
Seelye, John, 221n
Seybold, Ethel, 222n
shamans, 78, 81, 86, 87, 113–14
Shanley, J. Lyndon, 99, 227n
Shea, John Gilmaury, 132
Sibley, John Langdon, 191
Simons, Martha, 226n
Sioux, 199, 201–2, 204–5, 208
Sioux Outbreak of 1862, 206, 230n
slavery, 26, 78
Slotkin, Richard, xiv, 39, 47, 225n
Smith, Col. James, 14, 39
Smith, John, 44
Smith, Marion Whitney, 229n
Solomon, Sabattis, 171

Squanto, 44
Squier, E. G., 93, 95–96
Standing Bear, Chief, 223n, 227n
Stone, John Augustus, 222n
Storm, Hyemeyohsts, 227n
Sullivan's Expedition, 7
Sumner, Sen. Charles, 125

Tahattawan, xiv, 146
Tanner, John, 133
Tecumseh, Chief, 12
Thatcher, Benjamin, 12, 98, 121
Thatcher, George, 168, 170, 173
Thatcher, Samuel, 193
Therien, Alek (woodcutter),
  65, 75
Thomson, Charles, 218
Thoreau, Cynthia Dunbar
  (HDT's mother), 146–47
Thoreau, Helen (HDT's sister),
  147
Thoreau, Henry David; influence
  of savagism on, 3, 18, 19–27,
  29–30, 35, 123–54, 202;
  attitude towards blacks &
  Indians, 24–26; resemblances
  to an Indian, 60–61; theory of
  a book about Indians, ix,
  18, 101–22, 155, 194, 211;
  travel writing, 155–56, 158,
  172–73, 202, 208–10; trips
  to Maine, xii, 119, 155–88, 195,
  199; trip to Minnesota, xiii–
  xiv, 193, 195–214; health,
  101, 193, 204; death, 101,
  214–15
Thoreau, H. D.; published works:
  "Barbarities of civilized States,"
  18–20, 68; Cape Cod, xiv, 102,
  122, 155; An Excursion to
  Canada (A Yankee in Canada),
  xiv, 155; Journal, xiv, xix, 19,
  30, 45, 59, 95–96, 101, 104,
  108–9, 118, 122, 125, 127,
  132, 139, 146, 152, 208;
  quoted, 140–41, 143–44, 152,
  157, 188, 190–92, 218, 226n;
  The Maine Woods, xiii, xiv, 8,
  102, 119, 155–87, 202, 208,
  212; Minnesota Journey, 195–
  201, 230n; "Natural History of
  Massachusetts," 71, 86;
  "Resistance to Civil Government" ("Civil Disobedience"),
  24, 155; Walden, xi, xiv, 40,
  59–100, 101, 108, 111, 119,
  123, 155, 168, 202, 203;
  "Walking," 152; A Week on
  the Concord and Merrimack
  Rivers, xi, xiv, 28–58, 66, 101,
  108, 111, 123–24, 128, 155,
  173, 202, 203
Thoreau, H. D.; unpublished
  works: "Canada, &c.," 111;
  Commonplace books and fact
  books, 106–9; "Indian Books,"
  xii, 86, 105, 107–8, 118, 120–
  21, 156, 188, 212, 217–20;
  quoted, 93–94, 98, 114–16,
  120, 126–40, 142, 148–51,
  189–90, 195–96, 218–19;
  "Wild Fruits" and "The Dispersion of Seeds," 193, 228n
Thoreau, John (HDT's brother),
  45–47, 56, 146, 173, 202–3
Thoreau, John (HDT's father);
  death of, 143–47, 211
Thoreau, Sophia (HDT's sister),
  101, 104, 231n
Torrey, Bradford, 101
tortures, 113, 116, 135, 136,
  137–40
travel books, 155–56, 195; also
  see Thoreau, H. D., travel
  writing
traveller's point of view, 210
treaty ceremonies, 139, 199–201
tricksters, 75–76

Tuscarora, 128
Tyng, Jonathan, 36, 43, 56–57, 124

Van Buren, Martin, 23, 147, 224n
Van der Donck, Adriaen, 133
Vikings, 116
Vimont, Father, 113, 137
Virgil, 31, 35, 36
vision quest, 61–63, 69–70, 100
Voltaire, 130

Walton, Izaak, 31
Wannalancet, 34, 57, 124
Warren, Austin, 215, 231n
Wars, White-Indian, 47; as subject of A Week, 37–40; also see Indians, warfare

Washburn, Wilcomb E., 222n, 223n
Washington, Gen. George, 49, 54
Wawatam, 14, 43, 44, 45, 124
Webster, Noah, x, 3, 19
Weiser, Conrad, 140
Welch, James, 123
White, John, 171
White, Leslie A., 229n
white pine, 157, 197
Whitman, Walt, 184
wild apple trees, 43, 58, 157, 198
wilderness, 51, 53, 152
Willson, Lawrence, 221n
Winnebago, 75
Winslow, Edward, 74, 108
Winthrop, John, 124

Yankees, 33, 38–39

Library of Congress Cataloging in Publication Data

Sayre, Robert F.
  Thoreau and the American Indians.

  Includes bibliographical references and index.
  1. Thoreau, Henry David, 1817–1862—Criticism
and interpretation.   2.   Indians of North America
in literature.   I.   Title.
PS3057.I5S2   818'.3'09   76–45910
ISBN 0–691–06330–3